W9-BWN-527

The Cooperative Classroom: Empowering Learning

Lynda A. Baloche
West Chester University

Prentice Hall

Upper Saddle River, New Jersey   Columbus, Ohio

Library of Congress Cataloging-in-Publication Data

Baloche, Lynda A.
   The cooperative classroom: empowering learning / Lynda A.
Baloche.
      p.   cm.
   Includes bibliographical references and index.
   ISBN 0-13-360090-4
   1. Group work in education—United States. 2. Cooperation—Study and teaching—United States. 3. Multicultural education—United States. 4. Classroom management—United States. 5. Learning.
   I. Title.
LB1032.B284   1998   97-31563
371.39'5—dc21   CIP

Cover art/photo: © Christie's Images/Superstock
Editor: Debra A. Stollenwerk
Production Editor: Alexandrina Benedicto Wolf
Photo Editor: Anthony Magnacca
Cover Design Coordinator: Karrie M. Converse
Text Design and Production Coordination: Custom Editorial Productions, Inc.
Cover Designer: Brian Deep
Production Manager: Patricia A. Tonneman
Director of Marketing: Kevin Flanagan
Marketing Manager: Suzanne Stanton
Advertising/Marketing Coordinator: Julie Shough

This book was set in Souvenir and Frutiger by Custom Editorial Productions, Inc., and was printed and bound by Quebecor Printing Book Press, Inc. The cover was printed by Phoenix Color Corp.

 © 1998 by Prentice-Hall, Inc.
Simon & Schuster/A Viacom Company
Upper Saddle River, New Jersey 07458

All rights reserved. No part of this book may be reproduced, in any form or by any means, without permission in writing from the publisher.

Photo credits: pp. xiv, 38, and 114 by Scott Cunningham/Merrill; pp. 16, 144, 174, 188, and 240 by Anthony Magnacca/Merrill; p. 66 by Todd Yarrington/Merrill; p. 90 by Barbara Schwartz/Merrill; and p. 208 by Anne Vega/Merrill.

Printed in the United States of America

10 9 8 7 6 5 4 3 2 1

ISBN   0-13-360090-4

Prentice-Hall International (UK) Limited, *London*
Prentice-Hall of Australia Pty. Limited, *Sydney*
Prentice-Hall of Canada, Inc., *Toronto*
Prentice-Hall Hispanoamericana, S. A., *Mexico*
Prentice-Hall of India Private Limited, *New Delhi*
Prentice-Hall of Japan, Inc., *Tokyo*
Simon & Schuster Asia Pte. Ltd., *Singapore*
Editora Prentice-Hall do Brasil, Ltda., *Rio de Janeiro*

PREFACE

The Cooperative Classroom: Empowering Learning has been written to guide teachers and prospective teachers as they develop a vision and learn the needed skills to create classrooms where cooperation is a way of being that helps to empower their students and themselves as learners. I define empowered learners as learners who are capable of—and committed to—high levels of meaningful cooperative inquiry, high levels of independent thought, and active and productive participation in a diverse, democratic society. I believe that cooperation and empowerment are not "zero-sum," "win-lose" games. (Cooperation and empowerment are not like poker where the total that is won must equal the total that is lost.) When any of us becomes empowered to participate constructively and creatively in society, everyone gains; when any of us feels unempowered and unable to participate, everyone loses.

We have entered an age when we realize that we are interdependent with the planet, and we are coming to realize that we are interdependent with each other. Whether this interdependence will be positive or negative may well depend on whether we are able to build commitment to work together and move towards learning and living that is genuinely empowering for all. Anything less may be too little.

🌿 ABOUT THIS BOOK 🌿

I have worked for about twenty-five years as a teacher—in public schools, in university teacher-preparation programs, and as a consultant and staff-development specialist in school districts. During this time I have continually worked to learn about the power of cooperation—for teaching and learning, for working, and for living. One part of that work has been to listen to the questions teachers ask about cooperative learning. These are the questions I have heard most often:

- "Why should I use cooperation?"
- "Where should I start?"
- "When, how, and how much should I use cooperation?"
- "What about the kid, or class, who just won't cooperate?"
- "What happens if my students argue?" and
- "It's too hard to do it alone—how can I get other teachers interested?"

As I have worked to find ways to help teachers answer these questions, I have also pondered why they have asked them so frequently. This book is an attempt to respond to these questions and also to explore the issues behind the questions. This book is also a celebration of the answers some wonderful teachers have discovered through their own study and reflection, their own classroom implementation, and their commitment to teaching and learning.

Intended Audience

The Cooperative Classroom: Empowering Learning is appropriate for teachers and those preparing to be teachers; it will also be useful to school counselors, psychologists, and administrators. It can be used in general methods courses and as a supplement in educational psychology courses and courses in school counseling. The material is appropriate for teachers who work with students in special populations and with students at elementary, middle, and high-school levels. In addition to its use as a course text, it can be appropriately used—and has been successfully field tested—in school-based staff development seminars and teacher study groups.

Organization

The Cooperative Classroom: Empowering Learning begins with a brief introductory chapter that examines "Why Cooperation"—in schools, in the workplace, and in society. The purpose of this chapter is to provide a context for the power of cooperation that extends past a lesson. Following this introduction the book is divided into two main parts.

Part I: "Developing the Classroom as a Learning Community" includes three chapters and is designed to provide a "big-picture" view of classrooms—a view that I think is frequently lacking in books about cooperative learning and often underemphasized in teacher-preparation programs. The first chapter in this section, Chapter 2, examines basic theories in group structure and development and includes classroom-relevant applications; it also provides procedures and sample instruments to encourage teacher research. The purpose of Chapter 3 is to contextualize diversity issues and multicultural education within a framework of group dynamics and classroom cooperation. Again, teacher research is encouraged, and procedures, tools, and sample data are included. The focus of Chapter 4 is learning communities and parent involvement. This chapter uses group development theory and diversity issues to frame the discussion; classroom scenarios and examples are used throughout to help bring the basic framework to life.

Part II: "Building Small-Group Cooperation" includes six chapters. These chapters encourage teachers to build a vision of how cooperative learning might be used to empower students as learners; they provide a wealth of practical "how-tos" for building high-quality cooperation throughout the school day and week and for meeting the needs of diverse learners through inclusion in meaningful small-group work.

Part III: "Developing Commitment to an Exciting Profession" consists of one brief chapter and has been written to reflect current thinking about educational change processes. The purpose of this chapter is to encourage teachers to focus on themselves and to understand the importance of building an exciting profession through community, commitment, life-long learning, and vision.

Significant Features

The Cooperative Classroom: Empowering Learning has several important features that make it both instructor and student friendly.

Each chapter is introduced with a series of open-ended **conceptual questions** that have been designed to help focus but not narrow the readers' attention. Additional questions have been included throughout each chapter to help readers reflect on what they are learning and apply this learning to their own experiences. These questions have been set apart from the main text to facilitate their use.

Chapters 4 through 10 include fairly extensive **scenarios** that are intended to contextualize chapter content and integrate conceptual and structural approaches to cooperative learning. These scenarios describe highly-skilled teachers and classes from Kindergarten through Grade Twelve, multi-age groups, a variety of subject areas, and integrative thematic units. During field testing, both preservice and inservice teachers have commented repeatedly on the helpfulness of these scenarios.

Because reading about cooperative learning is just a beginning to learning how to build an empowering classroom through the effective use of cooperation, each chapter ends with a section called "**Working with Peers**." The activities in these sections have been extensively field-tested with a variety of preservice and inservice teacher populations and are designed to help participants (a) review chapter concepts, (b) begin to build a sense of community through significant interaction with peers, and (c) experience a working model of cooperation. These sections can also be analyzed as sample lessons.

🍂 ACKNOWLEDGMENTS 🍂

Every book is a cooperative effort, and many people have influenced me in the writing of this book. First, I must thank David and Roger Johnson. It was their work that first showed me just how important cooperation is; it was their work that got me started; it has been their personal support that has helped me to keep going for many years. They have made it possible for me to network with many wonderful people who are committed to the use of cooperation to empower learning. Thank you, Edye, Karl, Laurie, Susan, Susan, Linda, Vicki, Diane, and Janet. Special thanks to Carol Donaho, a genuine colleague and friend, who is always available—by long-distance phone and with outrageous good humor—for problem solving and honest reflection.

I have been incredibly fortunate to study with Spencer Kagan, Yael Sharan, Carol Cooper, Robert Slavin, and staff developers at the Child Development Project and equally fortunate to work with Liana Forest, former Executive Director of the International Association for the Study of Cooperation in Education. Thanks to each of them for their dedication, insight, and inspiration.

I am very lucky to work at West Chester University—a university where teaching is valued and where I have many colleagues who like to talk about teaching and learning. Their friendship and conversation remind me just how important it is to have genuine collegial support. Special thanks to Jim Egan, John Hynes, Cynthia Haggard, Debbie Mahlstedt, LeeAnn Srogi, Sharon Kletzien, Lesley Welsh, Mary Ann Maggitti, and to my "Cool-operative Learning" colleagues.

Thanks to the school administrators who have been most generous in their willingness to share their districts, their time, and their insights. Special thanks to Barry Ersek, Terri Freed, Joe Serico, Barbara Michalsky, Donald Dearborn, Loris Grunow, Marie Condo, and Joan Jackson.

Thanks to editor Debbie Stollenwerk for her enthusiasm, good humor, and willingness to be a real human being, and to copyeditor Marianne Newman for her thoughtful work. Thanks to the following reviewers for their feedback on drafts of this manuscript: Beatrice S. Fennimore, Indiana University of Pennsylvania; Janet Handler, Mount Mercy College; Cynthia G. Kruger, University of Massachusetts-Dartmouth; Robert B. Lowe, Angelo State University; Charleen D. Peryon, University of Dubuque; Betty Jo Simmons, Longwood College; Norma J. Strickland, Rust College; and James E. Watson, Trinity Evangelical Divinity School.

Most of all, thanks to my students, student teachers, and all the teachers and their students who have shared their classroom communities with me, have asked me hard questions, and have inspired me with their honesty, dedication, and insight. You will meet many of them in the chapter scenarios. Special thanks to Joe, Kathleen, Jean, Terry, Marilyn, Betty, Janet, Joyce, Linda, Julie, Dana, Tara, Jane, Stacey, Brenda, Colleen, Meg, Tom, Mary, Val, Gail, Angela, Kristen, Lynnette, Eileen, and Patrick.

CONTENTS

Chapter 1

Introduction: Why Work Together   xii

     Why Work Together in the Classroom   3

     Why Work Together on the Job   8

     Why Work Together in Society   9

     Working with Peers   11

PART I: Developing the Classroom as a Learning Community   15

Chapter 2

Building an Understanding of the Classroom as a Group   16

     Group Structure   18

     Group Development   22

     Recurring Themes in Group Structure and Development   25

     A Practical Theory: Using Theory As a Framework for Learning to Look at Classrooms   26

     Working with Peers   33

Chapter 3

Building an Understanding of the Power of Diversity in Groups   38

     Multicultural Education and the Construction of Knowledge   41

     Multicultural Education and the Reduction of Prejudice   43

     Multicultural Education and Equity Pedagogy   48

     Multicultural Education and an Empowering School Culture and Social Structure   53

A Practical Theory: Using Theory as a Framework for
Learning to Look at Classrooms   59

Working with Peers   63

Chapter 4

Building an Understanding of the Learning Community   66

The Significance of Inclusion in the Building
of a Classroom Learning Community   68

The Significance of Control and Influence in the
Building of a Classroom Learning Community   72

The Significance of Affection, Appreciation, and Caring
in the Building of a Classroom Learning Community   81

Working with Peers   86

PART II: Developing Small-Group Cooperation   89

Chapter 5

Base Groups and Informal Groups: Building Stability and Variety Into Small-Group Cooperation   90

Building an Understanding of Cooperation as a Discipline   92

Base Groups: A Home away from Home   93

A View from the Classroom: Using Base Groups   98

Informal Groups: Casual and Effective   99

A View from the Classroom: Using Informal Groups   108

Working with Peers   111

Chapter 6

Formal Learning Groups: Building Positive Interdependence   114

Formal Groups: Careful Designs for Learning   116

Positive Interdependence—The Heart of the Matter   116

A View From the Classroom: Building Positive Interdependence into Learning   135

Working with Peers   141

Chapter 7

Interpersonal and Small-Group Learning Skills:
Teaching the Basics   144

The Essential Skills of Cooperation   146

Teaching the Skills of Cooperation   149

Challenges   160

A View From the Classroom: Teaching Interpersonal and
Small-Group Learning Skills   168

Working with Peers   172

Chapter 8

Reflection and Planning: Examining Interpersonal
and Small-Group Learning Skills By Looking Back
and Planning Ahead   174

The Essential Aspects of Reflection and Planning   176

Designing Reflection and Planning   177

Challenges   181

Working with Peers   185

Chapter 9

Individual Responsibility and Assessment: Checking
for Understanding   188

Using Monitoring, Roles, and Structures to Build Individual
Responsibility and to Check for Understanding   191

Using Reflection and Planning to Build Individual Responsibility
and to Check for Understanding   192

Using Tests, Journals, and Portfolios to Build Individual
Responsibility and Positive Interdependence   195

Challenges   201

A View From the Classroom: Checking for Understanding   202

Working with Peers   204

Chapter 10

The Role of the Teacher: Guiding Learning in the
Cooperative Classroom   206

Arranging the Physical Environment for Cooperation   208

Planning Group Size and Composition for Cooperation   212

Planning Lessons for Cooperation   215

Planning Units for Cooperation   224

Getting Started with Cooperative Learning in the
Classroom   230

Working with Peers   235

Part III: Developing Commitment to an Exciting Profession   237

Chapter 11

Becoming an Excited—and Exciting—Professional   238

Meaningful Learning in an Exciting Profession   240

Working with Peers   246

Books with More Information   250

References   252

Name Index   258

Subject Index   259

CHAPTER 1

Introduction:
Why Work Together

As you read, you might want to ask yourself:

Why might cooperation affect achievement and motivation?

How is cooperation related to the goals of a democracy?

How does cooperation relate to job satisfaction and success?

Why do some work teams perform better than others?

What are the characteristics of a psychologically healthy person?

How might I begin to establish a sense of cooperative inquiry with my peers?

I love teaching, but it has not always been that way. When I first became a teacher more than twenty years ago, it took only about three days for me to realize that my students were fascinating people who were much more interested in each other than in me or in learning what I wanted them to learn. Within a week I realized I was but an annoying intervening variable in my students' day. Within a month I was contemplating graduate school in a field other than education. But I persevered. After all, I was young. I was energetic. I would try anything—stand-up comedy, Big Bird imitations, cool clothes, bribes. I even tried groups. I thought, "Why not 'let' the students talk to each other?" Some days groups worked and I wished my principal had been observing. I drove home from work smiling. Other days groups were a disaster. Within five minutes I was closing the classroom door to keep the noise from spilling into surrounding rooms. Within ten minutes I was saying, "OK, everybody sit down in their own seats" and thinking, "Forget it, it's not worth it, I'll never do this again." I did not smile on these days; I did try to compare these disasters to days when things seem to go well and to ask myself what I had done differently. Often I had no idea.

I began to read about teaching, and while I was reading, I discovered the cooperative learning literature—especially the work of David and Roger Johnson. I discovered that cooperative learning was what I had been trying to do; I discovered that there were basic principles that I could apply in my own teaching. I was excited. I was hooked. I was sure I could master it in about six weeks.

It has been a long time. I am still hooked. I have studied with many experts, I have guided many teachers in a discovery of ways they might use cooperation in their own classrooms, and I have used cooperative learning to teach a variety of academic subjects. I have thought a great deal about the power of a cooperative context and how working individually and working competitively might fit into this context. I know now that I will never master cooperative learning or fully understand the power of cooperation, and that is OK, because I now know that learning to teach, like learning to live, is an ongoing process—not a point of mastery.

The purpose of this book is to provide a vision for how cooperation and cooperative learning might be integrated into classroom life to empower learning and learners. To me, empowering students as learners means helping them to become capable of—and committed to—high levels of meaningful cooperative inquiry, high levels of independent thought, and active and productive participation in a diverse, democratic society. To accomplish its purpose, the book includes explanations of different theories, models, and strategies that can be used to inform teacher decision making that is aimed towards building cooperation; it also includes many scenarios from cooperative classrooms. I particularly enjoy the scenarios because they represent teachers and students for whom I have a great deal of respect and admiration and because they celebrate the many hours that I have had the honor to spend with them in their classroom communities.

I hope you will find this vision of cooperation interesting and, more importantly, that it will encourage you to develop your own vision and your own passion about the power of working together. We begin, in this introductory chapter, with a brief examination of the question, "Why work together?".

In the classroom, in the workplace, and in life, there are basically three ways we can work towards our goals: cooperatively, competitively, or individualistically. When we work cooperatively, our efforts towards a goal help others and their efforts help us. When we work competitively, our efforts towards a goal make it less likely that another person will achieve the same goal. When we work individualistically, our own efforts to achieve a goal are unrelated to the efforts of others. All three goal structures are useful. Sometimes it is satisfying and important to work by oneself to achieve a desired goal. Sometimes it is fun to compete. Oftentimes working together is key.

Think of a time when competing was fun. Think of a time when you enjoyed working alone. Think of a time when you enjoyed working cooperatively with others. What made each of these experiences positive?

🐜 WHY WORK TOGETHER IN 🐜 THE CLASSROOM

Achievement and Motivation

When well structured, learning goals that are designed to emphasize cooperation tend to promote higher achievement than learning goals that are designed to emphasize either individualism or competition. This is true in every subject, at all grade levels, and particularly when higher-level thinking skills are required (D. Johnson, Maruyama, R. Johnson, Nelson, & Skon, 1981). Cooperative efforts result in better performance in problem solving than competitive efforts do. This is true at all grade levels, for both linguistic and nonlinguistic problems, and regardless of whether a problem has a clearly defined operation and solution or operations and solutions that are less clear or are ill defined (Qin, D. Johnson, & R. Johnson, 1995). Learning that is structured cooperatively tends to increase achievement for all students, and achievement results are particularly potent for some groups who are more cooperative in their cultural and social orientations (Kagan, 1980, 1992).

Think about a time a peer helped you learn. What did the peer do?

Why Do Cooperatively Structured Learning Goals Tend to Promote High Achievement?   The *constructivist-developmental theories* of Vygotsky and Piaget are good starting points for reflecting on this question. Piaget believed that maturation, active experience, social transmission, and self-regulation were fundamental factors in cognitive development (Ripple & Rockcastle, 1964). Social transmission, of course, implies that a child understands the information being transmitted, and because children often seem to be able to describe things to each other in ways that adults cannot, interaction with peers is important in social transmission. Piaget (1965) himself believed that peer interaction was important.

> It is idle . . . to try and transform the child's mind from outside, when his own taste for active research and his desire for cooperation suffice to ensure a normal intellectual development. The adult must therefore be a collaborator and not a master. . . . All moral and all logical norms are the result of cooperation. Let us therefore try to create in the school a place where individual experimentation and reflection carried out in common come to each other's aid and balance one another. (p. 404)

Like Piaget, Vygotsky (1978) understood the essential link between social transmission and cognitive development, stating that "human learning presupposes a specific social nature and a process by which children grow into the intellectual life of those around them" (p. 88). His idea of a *zone of proximal development*—the distance between the actual level of development and the potential development that can be reached with adult guidance or in collaboration with peers—is central to his notions of the social construction of knowledge and to an understanding of how working with peers can be academically beneficial. When high-school students discuss their own experiences with cooperative learning, they sometimes describe Vygotsky's basic principles quite well; their explanations are much simpler—and probably much closer to our own levels of proximal development—than Vygotsky's. For instance, in a chemistry class, a student described the nature of proximal development: "Sometimes, coming from the teacher it is a lot more technical. I know they try to bring it down to your level, but when you do it with your friends, you can just say 'Well, I don't understand' and they can rephrase it and they can help you." In their English classes, two students described the idea of the transfer from group to individual understanding: "I don't know really what I think till I try to tell somebody" and "[Sometimes] you have no idea what a line [of poetry] means and somebody else says something and then it like just clicks to you."

Information processing is a second theoretical perspective that can be used to help explain why cooperative learning tends to promote high achievement. From this perspective, the development of memory and problem-solving capabilities are due, in part, to *strategies* used to transfer information into memory, to *world knowledge,* and to *planfulness* (Heterington & Parke, 1986). *Memory strategies* that are likely to be enhanced by the use of cooperative learning include *oral rehearsal*—the repetition of the information that needs to be remembered, *semantic organization*—the reorganization and reconstruction of information in ways to make it more meaningful, and *elaboration*—the creation of a context into which different and perhaps seemingly unrelated ideas fit together. *World knowledge*—what children know about the world from past experience—influences what they understand about the present and can recall later. When children have the opportunity to share experiences within the cooperative context, they frequently help each other expand their capacity for understanding. *Planfulness*—the development of systematic strategies for gathering and sifting information—is potentially enhanced when children work together to solve problems. A child working alone can dive into a problem without a well-thought-out plan, but "planning" becomes increasingly important to successful completion of the task when several children work together. Planning, in the words of fourth graders, meant "You have to take the time and figure out how to split it up so all of you can do or be a part of something instead of just one person."

Peer discussion is essential both to the constructivist-developmental perspectives of Piaget and Vygotsky and to information processing theory. Discussion is important for several reasons. First, discussion—described by one student as "a spontaneous explosion of ideas with nothing held back"—has the potential to positively affect achievement because it encourages frequent repetition of information and explanations. "I enjoy seeing someone's face light up when I explain an idea he or she never considered" is how one student described this experience. Second, discussion brings conflicting ideas face to face in a way that increases retention, understanding, and integration of different points of view. High-school students seem genuinely to appreciate the integrative nature of discussion: "Being in a group helps because there are facts which one person could never think of, and by working together and switching opinions, more understanding can be achieved." "When they started talking, . . . it made me start thinking on another track. . . . Through groups, students can learn new angles or approaches that might escape them if they were working independently." Third, discussion can provide considerable opportunity for peer feedback, support, and encouragement. Students notice that in cooperative discussion "people learn to listen to what others have to say. People learn to probe out more from others." Or, in the words of a fourth grader: "If you make a mistake there is someone to help you."

Although constructivist and information processing theories are helpful, it is also important to consider *motivation* when examining why high levels of achievement are often associated with cooperative learning. Motivation—which is sometimes described as a combination of the perceived likelihood of and incentive for success (D. Johnson & R. Johnson, 1994) or as the difference between what a person can do and will do (Amabile, 1983)—is key to learning. Cooperative settings generate a feeling of connectedness that produces considerable positive energy and high levels of motivation. When students describe their experiences with cooperative discussion, they tend to be quite animated.

Competition has the potential to *undermine* motivation for learning—especially intrinsic motivation (Amabile, 1983; Kohn, 1992a; Nicholls, 1989). Competition tends to create more interest in how one's performance compares to others' than interest in the task itself (Nicholls). When learning is highly competitive, high-achieving students tend to be considered "nerdish," and they often have low social status (Slavin, DeVries, & Hulton, 1975). In addition to competition, other factors influence motivation as well. The best predictor of burnout, for instance, may not be too much work, too little time, or too little reward, but rather powerlessness—a perceived lack of control over what one is doing (Kohn, 1993). Feelings of power—of self-determination—affect many aspects of life including general well-being, responsible behavior and prosocial values, and academic achievement. The thoughtful use of cooperative learning can help provide students with opportunities to make challenging and relevant choices and to feel empowered in their learning. In reflecting on his own experiences with cooperative learning, one student said: "When a teacher hands over the power of teaching to us, we learn more, we are more interested and motivated. My experiences with cooperative learning are good ones."

Providing a Model for Democracy

Congress Hall [where the original U.S. Constitutional Convention was held in Philadelphia] is a room designed for conversation. The acoustics are exceptional. One hundred and fifty people can carry on a conversation as if they were seated in a living room. . . . Participants are very aware of the larger natural world outside the building, yet still focused on the conversation at hand. The chairs are set in a semicircle so everyone can see everyone else. Clearly, the designers of that room understood that conversation and self-governance are inextricably intertwined. If we lose our ability to talk with one another, we lose our ability to govern ourselves. (Senge, 1990, p. xiv)

Collaborative work is at the center of John Dewey's notions of education for democracy. Dewey (1915/1956) believed that if children are to learn to live in a democracy, they must experience the process of democracy in classroom life—a process which includes substantive opportunities to make meaningful choices and build productive relationships based on genuine interpersonal respect and empathy. Herbert Thelen (1981), like Dewey, was interested in the creation of democratic social and learning environments where power is "handed over" or shared with students. He described "becoming educated" as a process by which individuals develop increasingly successful styles for coping with "more and more complex, challenging and socially significant situations" (p. 137). These ideas suggest the development of an active voice that "utilizes dialogue, and makes knowledge meaningful, critical, and ultimately emancipatory" (Aronowitz & Giroux, 1985, p. 37) and provide sharp contrast to Goodlad's (1983) contemporary description of America's schools as places where students have few opportunities to develop "products and satisfying relations with others based on respect, trust, cooperation, and caring" (p. 240). One suspects that Dewey and Thelen would be excited by how two high-school students describe their experiences in classrooms with well-designed opportunities for cooperative interaction: "We could discuss with our friends how we felt about moral issues" and "The exchange of ideas and quick thinking lead to discussion and 'deep thought' outside the classroom."

Positive Relationships with Peers and Improved Attitudes towards School

Constructive peer relationships—described by one fourth grader as simply "We learned to like each other"—are critical to the development and socialization of children and adolescents. Children with poor peer relationships are at greater risk for dropping out of school and for criminality (Parker & Asher, 1987).

Why are positive peer relationships so critical? Children and adolescents learn through interaction with peers many things they are unlikely to learn readily from adults. Peers provide models for appropriate social behavior. Peers help one another to gain in impulse control—described by one fourth grader as "I took the time to wait for other people in my group." Peers tend to permit one another to experiment with a variety of social roles that help integrate a "sense of self." Through constructive peer relationships, children and adolescents tend to gain a sense of self-worth and self-acceptance. And, perhaps most importantly, through interaction with peers, both children and adolescents develop the ability to create and sustain cooperative relationships (D. Johnson & R. Johnson, 1983; D. Johnson, R. Johnson & Holubec, 1993).

When children and adolescents experience the kinds of constructive peer relationships that are facilitated by well-designed cooperative learning environments, they tend to develop positive attitudes. They see their teachers as supportive, both academically and personally. They are more positive about the subject matter—they check more books out of the library and are more likely to take related, advanced-level courses. They seem to value school more—attendance increases and vandalism decreases. A tenth-grade boy described his experience in a class that has been structured cooperatively this way:

> [The teacher] is such a good teacher—we interact every single day. [The teacher] thinks you need to gain something . . . and you really do. And that is one of the supporting things and why we know each other so well. I feel like I could call every single person in that class if I had a problem because they are all so down to earth. . . . We have become really good friends. . . . Some of the activities have just really brought us together.

✿ WHY WORK TOGETHER ON THE JOB ✿

Job Success and Satisfaction

> In 80 percent of airline crashes, pilots make mistakes that could have been prevented, particularly if the crew worked together more harmoniously. Teamwork, open lines of communication, cooperation, listening, and speaking one's mind—rudiments of social intelligence—are now emphasized in training pilots, along with technical prowess. (Goleman, 1995, p. 148)

Think of people you know who enjoy working with others on the job. How do they talk about their work?

A recent survey found that 68% of Fortune 1000 companies use self-managed or high-performance teams (*"CEO Briefing"* 1994), partly because teams have the potential to help businesses and organizations be more productive, flexible, innovative, and creative. At Federal Express, for instance, 1,000 clerical workers were organized into teams of five to ten people and were given the training and authority to manage themselves. Ideas generated by one team's problem solving saved the company $2.1 million in one year (Dumaine, 1990). At Levi Strauss & Company, they have changed the way they make blue jeans. Workers are no longer responsible for making just one part of a pair of blue jeans. They now sit together and, as a team, work on jeans from start to finish. When one part of the process slows down, the team figures out how to solve the problem. Teams set their own work schedules; compensation and incentives are tied to team goals. Since this approach has been implemented, quality is up and injuries and absenteeism are down (*"Levi's Lessons"* 1992). When a team of seven managers at Burlington Northern Railroad teamed up, they created a fundamentally new concept of transportation within the railroad industry that, over an eighteen-month period, broke all records in the industry (Katzenbach & Smith, 1993).

What Are the Characteristics of Work Teams That Tend to Promote Job Success and Satisfaction?   Most of us know that merely being told to "work as a team" does not insure high-quality work—either in the classroom or on the job. On the job, certain characteristics tend to describe "teams that work" or "high-performance teams." First, high-performance teams tend to be small. Second, during the course of their work together, members develop complementary skills—including technical skills, problem-solving and decision-making skills, and interpersonal skills. Third, the team members share a meaningful sense of purpose that inspires both pride and responsibility. Fourth, the team shares a compelling set of goals that are directly related to the purpose. Fifth, team members invest time in developing an understanding of how they will work together to accomplish their purpose and goals and how they will promote the high levels of mutual trust and constructive conflict necessary for success. Sixth, the team has enough commitment and trust to hold itself accountable as a team (Katzenbach & Smith, 1993).

What Kinds of Interpersonal Skills are Needed for Productive Work in Teams?   Time and time again, when asked how it feels to be a member of a high-performance team, members indicate that they genuinely respect the members of their team and enjoy working with them. Respect, enjoyment, and high productivity do not just happen. They require many well-developed interpersonal skills—interpersonal skills such as "risk taking, helpful criticism, objectivity, active listening, giving the benefit of the doubt, support, and recognizing the interest and achievements of others" (Katzenbach & Smith, 1993, p. 48).

A recent study at the scientific think tank Bell Labs illustrates just how important the ability to work with others is to job success. The work at Bell Labs is complex; because one person cannot complete a project alone, people work in teams. The most successful engineers and scientists in this organization are the ones who are able to work in their formal teams and also to build several strong, reliable, informal networks as well—networks for technical expertise, networks for communication, and networks for trust. When difficulties arise, informal "ad-hoc" teams are often crucial to success, and the people who are best at building these informal networks tend to be the star performers. In general, these "network stars" are good at promoting cooperation, coordinating efforts in a team, building consensus, understanding the perspectives of others, taking initiative, and managing themselves (Kelley & Caplan, 1993; Krackhardt & Hanson, 1993).

Poor interpersonal relationships and social inappropriateness account for over 80% of job terminations (D. Johnson & R. Johnson, 1984), and nearly two-thirds of Nobel prizes have been named for work done collaboratively (Zuckerman, 1977). At all levels of the world of work—from clerical and assembly-line workers to Nobel laureates—working together is key. It is hard to overemphasize the importance of good interpersonal skills.

❧ WHY WORK TOGETHER IN SOCIETY ❧

Physical Health

People who feel isolated—people who feel they have no one with whom they can share their private thoughts and feelings—get sick more often and die sooner than people with well-established support networks. In studies of heart attack patients and bone-marrow transplant patients, those who reported two or more people on whom they could rely for emotional support were more than twice as likely to survive than patients who reported a lack of interpersonal support. Similarly, women with advanced breast cancer live longer when they participate in support groups. Although high stress is often correlated to increased death rates, this does not appear to be true of men who report dependable support networks (Goleman, 1995).

Think about a time a friend helped you through a rough time. What did your friend do?

Psychological Health

Having a good support system may positively influence not just physical health but also psychological health. Positive attitudes towards cooperation have been shown to relate positively to a variety of measures of psychological health; competitive attitudes relate positively to few indices of psychological health; and individualistic attitudes relate positively to numerous indices of psychological pathology (D. Johnson & Norem-Hebeisen, 1981; D. Johnson & R. Johnson, 1983).

Psychologist Abraham Maslow (1962, 1970, 1976) greatly influenced modern psychological thought by studying psychologically healthy people. His ideas can be used to help us build an understanding of why it is important to learn to work with others, not only in the classroom and on the job but in the larger society as well. Maslow developed a classification of basic needs that motivate human behavior. He grouped these needs into five broad categories: (a) physiological needs, (b) safety needs, (c) belongingness and love needs, (d) esteem needs, and (e) self-actualization needs. Maslow believed that these needs are somewhat hierarchical and that physiological needs are the most basic and self-actualization needs are the most complex or "advanced."

Physiological needs include hunger and thirst. Safety needs include security, protection, and a sense of well-being. Maslow suggested that *perception* is influenced by safety needs and that the world can be perceived in two basic ways—as a rich and unique myriad of possibilities or in terms of preestablished categories. Maslow believed that the need to filter reality and perceive familiar categories at the expense of rich and fresh perceptions is strongest when safety needs dominate. As safety needs become increasingly met, the needs for belongingness and love emerge—the needs to give and receive love, belong to a group, and find an appropriate place within the group. Maslow divided esteem needs into two categories: mastery needs and prestige needs. Mastery needs relate to how we see ourselves—our feelings of adequacy, power, independence, freedom, and self-esteem. Prestige needs relate to how other people see us—their feelings of respect and esteem. When esteem needs are largely met, people tend to feel self-confident, worthy, strong, and capable. When esteem needs are not met, people tend to feel inferior, weak, and helpless. As physiological, safety, love, and esteem needs become increasingly satisfied, self-actualization needs become more important. Maslow found it difficult to define self-actualization, but through his studies of psychologically healthy individuals, he began to develop a portrait of self-actualized people. Maslow described psychologically healthy people as possessing (a) an accurate perception of reality, (b) an acceptance of themselves and others, (c) spontaneity and simplicity, (d) vision and the ability to focus on problems outside of themselves, (e) a good sense of humor, (f) an internal locus of evaluation, and (g) affection and compassion for others. It is hard to overemphasize the importance of characteristics such as these.

Social Perspective Taking— Developing an Ecological View

The images of Conestoga wagon trains, quilting bees, and barn raisings are symbolic of a kind of basic interdependence that has often been associated, perhaps somewhat romantically, with the Agricultural Age. By contrast, the Industrial Age has been associated with expansion, competition, individualism, and isolation. The Information Age has provided us with diverse images from all over the planet and beyond. The idea of a representative, global village is one way to conceptualize this image. If we were to create a global village of exactly 1,000 people and we kept all existing racial and ethnic ratios the same, the village would contain 564 Asians and Oceanians, 210 Europeans, 86 Africans, 80 South Americans, and 60 North Americans; there would be 820 people of color and 180 white people. And the diversity would not end there. In this global village, for example, a mere 60 people would hold 50% of the village's wealth, while 700 people would be illiterate, 500 people would suffer from the effects of malnutrition, and 600 would live in substandard housing (J. Gibbs, 1994). It is hard to imagine how a village such as this might thrive.

We are at the transition to an Ecological Age; we are at a time when we are slowly becoming aware that we are interdependent with the planet and with each other. To navigate this transition and build this awareness requires the abilities to take the perspectives of others, share and conserve resources, realize that more is not always better, resolve conflicts through negotiation, and build community through an emphasis on inclusiveness, respect, and caring. In the school, in the workplace, and in a global society, success requires the ability to perceive genuine interdependence and to understand that interdependence is essential.

🐜 WORKING WITH PEERS 🐜

Reading about cooperative learning is just a beginning to learning how to build an empowering classroom through the effective use of cooperative learning. Another step in learning about cooperative learning is to participate in a variety of cooperative groups. Each chapter in this book concludes with a section called "Working with Peers." These sections contain ideas for activities that are designed to (a) help you work with peers to review the ideas presented in the chapter, (b) begin to build a sense of community through significant interaction with peers, (c) experience many formal and informal cooperative learning "structures" that are discussed in later chapters, and (d) experience working models of cooperation. As you read and participate in these and other cooperative activities, you will, of course, be paying attention to academic content, your peers, and your own participation. Try also to ask yourself these questions: "What are the goals of this activity?" and "How does the design of this activity help it to achieve these goals?" Even if you are reading this book outside of the context of a course structure and do not have the opportunity to work with peers as part of your learning, it will still be useful to read these sections and ask yourself these questions.

Using *Graffiti* (Bennett, Rolheiser, & Stevahn, 1991) and Cooperation to Review Chapter Content

1. Three large pieces of paper are placed around the room. Papers are headed:
   - "Why cooperation is important in school."
   - "Why cooperation is important on the job."
   - "Why cooperation is important in society."
2. Students mill around the room freely. They stop at each paper, read what has been written by class-mates, and add one idea about why cooperation is important.
3. Papers can be used to focus further discussion.

Using a *Three-Step Interview* (Kagan, 1992) and *Simultaneous Roundtable* (Kagan, 1992) to Get Acquainted

1. Using a *Three-Step Interview,* random pairs, and things they have worn or objects they have brought to class with them, students each take three minutes to introduce themselves—through their objects—to their partners. (For instance, I might say: "My name is Lynda, and when I looked at myself and what I brought to class today, I decided to introduce myself through two things. I am wearing running shoes. I wear running shoes a lot because I speed walk, almost every day, for five miles. It takes only a few months before my shoes lose their cushion and don't feel good anymore. When that happens, I buy new ones for exercise, but I keep the old ones to wear around. When I looked in my wallet, I saw a membership card for my local public radio station. I enjoy public radio and listen a lot, so I feel good about being a member. This card also gets me discounts at several local stores. My favorite place to get a discount is at the CD store. I buy mostly classical. I used to be a classical pianist.") While students each introduce themselves, partners listen and ask clarifying questions but do not tell their own stories.

2. Each pair joins with another pair. Without revealing the nature of the objects, students each take one minute to introduce their partners by sharing their own impressions of the person. (For instance, Lynda's partner might say: "My partner is Lynda. Lynda likes to exercise and listen to classical music. I think she likes bargains and doesn't like to waste things.")

3. In their groups of four, students each receive a 4x6 index card and, if possible, they are given felt-tip markers of different colors. Students each write their first names on their own cards. In a *Simultaneous Roundtable,* students pass their cards around their group, and each student writes a positive adjective about each group member on that student's card. When students receive their own cards back they have, ready to wear, colorful name tags with positive, descriptive words supplied by their peers.

4 Reflection and Planning:
   Group:
   - Students are asked to discuss what kinds of interpersonal skills they needed to use in their small groups?

Using a *Treasure Hunt* to Get Acquainted

1. Each student receives a copy of a Treasure Hunt. (See Figure 1.1 for an example of a Treasure Hunt that might be used.) Students mill around and collect data about each other.

2. When it seems students have had enough time to talk and gather information, everyone stands or sits in a circle and information is shared. (For instance, the facilitator might start by saying, "Who learned something about Maria? What else did people learn about Maria?" and proceed around the circle until everyone has been talked about? The facilitator might also start by saying, "Who found someone in this class who has lived in a different country? Who was it? Where did that person live? Who else has lived in a different country?" If information is shared in this way, it is important that each person is talked about. Make it a point, after all the questions have been discussed, to say, "Who haven't we talked about? Who learned something about that person during the *Treasure Hunt?*")

TREASURE HUNT

FIND SOMEONE IN THIS CLASS WHO . . .

1. has traveled to an interesting place. Why was it interesting? Record the person's name and important details.
2. shares a hobby or a part-time interest with you. Record the person's name and important details.
3. has accomplished something this year that she has wanted to do for a long time. Why was it important? Record the person's name and important details.
4. grew up living with an older relative who was not a parent. What did the person learn from that experience? Record the person's name and important details.
5. has a parent who came from another country. What is one tradition the parent brought to this country? Record the person's name and important details.
6. has a family member with a disability. What is one thing the person has learned from interactions with that person? Record the person's name and important details.
7. has a joke that isn't racist or sexist and doesn't put down any ethnic group. Write the person's name and remember the joke.

Figure 1.1
Sample *Treasure Hunt* that can be used to help students gather information about each other.

Using a *One-Minute Paper* and *Mix-Freeze-Pair* (Kagan, 1992) to Reflect on How to Build Cooperation Together

QUESTION: *What is one thing you think you can do in this class to foster a sense of cooperation among class participants?*

1. Each student writes a response.
2. Everyone mills and *mixes* around the room. When the facilitator says *"freeze,"* everyone stops, points to the closest person, *pairs,* and shares ideas.
3. Students repeat *Mix-Freeze-Pair* several times.

PART I

Developing the Classroom as a Learning Community

CHAPTER 2
Building an Understanding of the Classroom as a Group

CHAPTER 3
Building an Understanding of the Power of Diversity in Groups

CHAPTER 4
Building an Understanding of the Learning Community

CHAPTER 2

Building an Understanding of the Classroom as a Group

As you read, you might want to ask yourself:

Why do teachers in empowering classrooms view their classes as groups?

How do values, norms, and roles affect classrooms? How do we determine what they are in a classroom? What can teachers do to establish shared values and norms and roles that will help students become empowered learners?

Why are feelings of inclusion and trust essential in an empowering classroom?

Why is conflict normal in groups?

How might we observe ourselves and others to learn how people work together?

Working with others—in classrooms, at work, and in families and communities—is a challenge. Sometimes working together is frustrating and unproductive. Other times, working together seems easy, exciting, and productive. It is often as difficult to describe and replicate "good" group work as it is to determine why working together is frustrating. Group dynamics is the study of how groups work. The field of group dynamics was not developed specifically to explain life in classrooms, but classrooms are groups and, therefore, an understanding of basic principles and theoretical frameworks in group dynamics can be used to help us understand and describe what happens in classrooms. In this chapter we will examine two basic principles of group dynamics: first, the principle that *all* groups share some basic structures; second, the principle that groups change and develop over time.

Some people believe that the study of group dynamics began formally with the work of Kurt Lewin; he realized that group life was complicated, interesting, and worth studying. Lewin fled Nazi Germany in the 1930s and lived through World War II. Perhaps because of this, he believed that something was worth studying if it could help restructure social relationships and make them more productive and satisfying. He also believed that a better world would not be created without scientific insight into the nature of group life (D. Johnson & F. Johnson, 1994; Marrow, 1969) Lewin developed the concepts of action research and force-field analysis; we will examine these briefly in Chapter 11. One of Lewin's students, Morton Deutsch, defined the three goal structures—competitive, cooperative, and individualistic—that were described in Chapter 1.

🌸 GROUP STRUCTURE 🌸

Think of two class-room situations— one that you enjoyed participating in and one that you did not enjoy. Keep these examples in mind as we learn some basic concepts about groups that we can use to understand class-room life more fully.

Groups have structures that are more basic than their unique features. This means that even though you are a member of many groups, and even though all these groups are different—with different people, settings, sizes, purposes—these groups have some structures in common. To help us build an understanding of the classroom as a group, we will explore three of these structures: values, norms, and roles. Because this is a book about classroom life and we will focus our discussion on groups in classrooms, I will often use the word *classroom* instead of *group*.

Values: What Are They and How Do They Affect Classroom Life?

Values are, in the simplest of terms, beliefs that are considered important and that tend to elicit emotional responses. Our values are formed as we interact with others in important groups such as our families. Later as we interact in other groups—such as school, social, religious, and work groups—

our values are reinforced or altered. When students and teachers come together in classrooms, they bring their values with them and, therefore, values are a part of every classroom. When class members come from similar backgrounds, their values tend to be similar. When class members come from dissimilar backgrounds, their values tend to be more dissimilar. Similar values are important determinants of interpersonal attraction. Value differences make interpersonal attraction more difficult and the formation of shared values more challenging. Value differences are often seen as threatening (Wheelan, 1994). Conflict, which is inevitable in all groups, tends to be greater when people with dissimilar values come together. Building shared values is important and leads to increased interpersonal attraction and the successful resolution of conflict. In a classroom it is easier to build shared values if the class is characterized by (a) cooperative goal structures (Aronson, Blaney, Stephan, Sikes, & Snapp, 1978; D. Johnson & R. Johnson, 1989; Slavin, 1985); (b) supportive teacher behaviors (Cohen, 1984); (c) the perception of equal status among class members (Cohen, 1984); (d) communication among students and between students and teachers that is personal in nature (Slavin, 1985); (e) frequent behavior by class members that disconfirms stereotypic expectations for their behavior (Rothbert & John, 1985); and (g) genuine success (Cook, 1984).

All groups that work together need to establish *some* shared values, both to achieve their goals and to keep members committed. In classrooms—where the stakes for both cognitive and affective learning goals are high, and where the effects of a lack of commitment to learning, to other students, and to school can be long term and devastating—it is essential to work continually to build shared values. Throughout this book we will learn how to build shared values by learning to build supportive, cooperative class interactions that encourage communication, reflection, and success.

What is one value that you share with your family? How about that classroom you enjoyed? What is one value that you shared with other members of that class?

Norms: What Are They and How Do They Affect Classroom Life?

Norms are the implicit and explicit "rules" that are established by the group to help individuals know what is expected of them and what they can reasonably expect from others. Norms are found at all levels of organizations. Institutional norms tend to be fairly uniform and last for long periods of time. In schools, extended summer vacations and discreet subject "periods" are examples of institutional norms that are based on the assumptions of agrarian and industrial society. So are the use of standardized tests, grades, and class ranks to sort the relative worth of individual students. Institutional norms help to keep schools fairly stable and predictable organizations; when left unexamined, they can become barriers to innovation. As educators have agreed to question the basic usefulness of some institutional norms in a modern, post-industrial society, experimentation with different models for year-around schooling, block scheduling, thematic teaching, performance assessment, and "restructuring" has begun to change the nature of some norms. Because everyone in the society is affected, either directly or indirectly, by changes in the institutional norms for schooling, changes in these norms are often slow and controversial.

In additional to norms that tend to affect schools as social institutions, there are many norms—typically in the form of rules and routines—that govern daily behavior in individual schools. Schools often have rules about tardiness, cheating, safety, and behavior in hallways; classrooms have rules about courtesy, quiet voices, and "traffic flow" to the pencil sharpener and drinking fountain. How students enter the classroom, where they sit, and how work is done are examples of norms that are generally established through daily procedures and routine. Norms that are formalized as rules and those that are established through procedure and routine help to create a kind of predictability and orderliness and can contribute substantially to feelings of safety, belongingness, and esteem. They also help to influence the perception of what is important. The challenge is to keep these norms dynamic—to keep them responsive to the situations and genuine needs of students, teachers, and learning.

How about that classroom you enjoyed? What were the norms? Were there "rules"? What kinds of routines were established? How were they established? How was that classroom influenced by the norms of the school?

Interpersonal norms influence the behaviors of teachers with colleagues, of teachers with students, and of students with each other. Interpersonal norms are more likely to be helpful when individuals share values. Throughout this book we will learn how to establish teacher-student and student-student norms that encourage all students to become learners capable of high levels of meaningful cooperative inquiry and independent thought. In Chapter 11 we will examine why positive norms for collegiality and inquiry are important and how these norms can help to sustain teaching as an exciting profession.

Roles: What Are They and How Do They Affect Classroom Life?

In addition to values and norms, which help give groups unity and identity, there are also roles that individual group members assume. Roles vary for different group members; roles help members differentiate their rights and responsibilities, help define expectations and behaviors for self and others, and, optimally, help groups communicate and accomplish their tasks. Sometimes roles are formally assigned. In schools, for instance, the roles of principal, teacher, and student are different and interrelated. Sometimes roles are not formally assigned. In a meeting with a superintendent, for instance, two principals each contribute an idea for solving a problem and are acknowledged quite differently; two teachers assume very different roles with colleagues in a faculty meeting and behave quite differently in their classrooms; two students assume very different classroom roles, and these roles define their behavior, rights, and the expectations of others. In each of these instances, behavior and communication patterns—patterns that dictate who talks to whom, about what, and for how long—are determined more by informal roles than by formal roles. These behaviors, patterns, and roles form quickly but change slowly (Mills, 1967). Sometimes informal roles are based on skills and interests; sometimes other factors influence the roles that people assume in groups.

In Chapter 3, we will examine how the informal roles that students assume can be affected by race, gender, class, and status. In later chapters, we will explore how to use assigned roles to help establish new communication patterns, structure cohesive groups, and teach important interpersonal skills. Now we will turn to two frameworks that we can use to help us understand how roles tend to influence communication patterns in classrooms.

How about that classroom you enjoyed? What roles did you assume? What roles were available to other members of the class? How would you describe the teacher's role?

Interaction-Process Analysis: How Do We Get the Job Done and Feel Good About It?
In an analysis of verbal communication in small groups, Bales (1950, 1970) described two main types of verbal statements. *Task statements* help groups get the job done. When people make task statements, for instance, they may give information or suggestions, ask for information or suggestions, summarize, help clarify the task or directions, or help energize the group. *Maintenance statements* are related to the social and emotional life of the group. Positive maintenance statements help the group build and maintain the relationships among members. When people make positive maintenance statements, they may encourage others to participate, support or praise others, relieve tension, or help solve interpersonal problems. Negative maintenance statements—those that discourage participation or criticize people—harm group cohesiveness. In "good groups," members are committed both to the completion of their tasks and to the maintenance of their interpersonal relationships. Too much or too little of either ultimately lowers both productivity and group morale. In classrooms, teachers face a constant challenge to build a positive atmosphere and simultaneously to accomplish cognitive learning objectives; part of this challenge is teaching every student to use both task and maintenance skills appropriately. We will examine how to teach these skills in Chapters 6 and 7.

Think about a time you were in a group that had a task to accomplish and, although everyone had a great time, the group did not get its job done. How about a group that got the job done but left you feeling annoyed or less than committed to the results? And how about a group where you got the job done and felt good about the results, yourself, and the other members?

The Verbal Interaction Category System: Who Talks in Classrooms? What Do They Say? How Do They Say It?
Amidon and Hough (1967) developed The Verbal Interaction Category System to describe both teacher and student talk in classrooms. We can use these categories to help us reflect on the roles that both teachers and students might assume in classrooms and to help us understand why some classrooms seem more comfortable, productive, and "open" than others. The VICS categories are

How about that classroom you enjoyed? How would you describe the balance of task and maintenance?

Teacher-Initiated Talk
1. gives information or opinions
2. gives directions

Think about a class-room you have been in where the teacher claimed to value an open exchange of ideas but seemed to act in ways that dis-couraged student discussion. What did the teacher do? How about a class where students felt free to initiate conversation? How did that happen?

3. asks narrow questions
4. asks broad questions

Teacher Response

5. accepts
    (a) ideas
    (b) behaviors
    (c) feelings
6. rejects
    (a) ideas
    (b) behaviors
    (c) feelings

Student Response

7. responds to teacher
    (a) predictably
    (b) unpredictably
8. responds to another

Student-Initiated Talk

9. initiates talking to teacher
10. initiates talking to another student

Other

11. silence
12. confusion

How about your two classroom situations? Try to describe them using terms from the Verbal Interaction Category System.

Teachers tend to talk a lot. In fact, about 65% of classroom talk is teacher talk. When one group of researchers (Hertz-Lazarowitz & Shachar, 1990) used an observation system like VICS, they discovered that when teachers used whole-class instruction, about 70% of teacher talk was related to categories 1, 2, 3, and 6. When teachers used small-group, cooperative instruction, about 75% of teacher talk was related to categories 4 and 5. It seems that small-group, cooperative instruction helped provide these teachers, and hopefully students, with opportunities to develop different roles and communication patterns in their classrooms.

🐾 GROUP DEVELOPMENT 🐾

Humans develop over time. Studying human development helps teachers to understand how individual students develop and change and to design "developmentally appropriate" learning opportunities. Groups develop, too. Classes are different at the end of the school year than at the beginning. Some of these differences arise because individual students develop. Some of these differences arise because the class itself—the class as a group— develops. The study of group development can help us understand how classes develop and change. It can help us design learning opportunities that are developmentally appropriate, not only for individual students but for whole classes as well. There are many theories of group development. We will explore just a few that can help us build active, cooperative classrooms.

Inclusion, Control, and Affection: Do I Belong or Am I An Outsider? Can I Keep Up or Will I Be Put Down? Will I Be Liked or Not?

According to Schutz (1966), individuals express three basic interpersonal needs: inclusion, control, and affection. Jeanne Gibbs (1994) uses the terms inclusion, influence, and community to describe similar needs. In general, these needs are hierarchical and are expressed in different phases of the development of a group. At the beginning of the school year, for instance, as students anxiously enter the room, they might ask themselves *inclusion* questions such as "Who will notice me?" "Whom will I accept?" "What do I have to do to fit in?" and "Do I want to fit in?" These questions can be answered only as students get to know each other and the teacher. When students are focused on these kinds of questions, academic learning may seem comparatively unimportant. If students are given opportunities to get to know more about each other and their teacher, and if a class is able to begin to build shared values, anxiety will decrease and students will begin to feel a sense of belongingness or inclusion. When this happens, the focus on academic learning tends to increase.

As students feel more included, classes begin to struggle with issues of *control and influence*—they begin to develop behavioral and decision-making norms, and they decide how responsibility will be shared, or not shared, among members and between the students and teacher. Through interaction with learning tasks and each other, students concern themselves with questions such as "Am I competent?" "Will my voice be heard?" and "What role can I play?" Conflict is inevitable and necessary as students test the teacher and each other in an attempt to establish comfortable levels of influence. In general, students who become more influential have both valuable task skills—they are good at doing things—and valued personal and interpersonal characteristics such as strength, good looks, and friendliness (R. Schmuck & P. Schmuck, 1996). As students feel more powerful and influential, they tend to become more curious and effective learners.

As levels of influence become established and the struggle for influence becomes less important, students begin to examine issues of *community, caring, and interpersonal affection and appreciation.* At this stage, students wonder "Who will like me?" and "Whom will I feel close to?" In some classrooms the bonds of interpersonal appreciation are narrow; when students are

How about that classroom you enjoyed? Did you fit in? Did you feel competent? Did you like other members of the class? Try to describe both of your classroom situations using the concepts of inclusion, control or influence, and affection.

asked to name classmates they like, only a few students are mentioned. In other classrooms, however, expressions of interpersonal attraction are more widespread and evenly distributed; when students are asked to name classmates they like, more students are mentioned and it is less common for a few students to receive a disproportionately high number of "votes." The influences of both personal characteristics and classroom structure on interpersonal affection and appreciation are complex. Some of these influences will be examined in later chapters. In general, however, teachers can encourage more wide-spread appreciation and a greater sense of classroom community by (a) using flexible seating arrangements and frequent peer interaction; (b) openly encouraging students to appreciate each other; and (c) acting in ways that model support and appreciation of all students (Epstein, 1983).

Forming, Storming, Norming, Performing, Adjourning: Why Do Groups Experience Conflict?

According to Tuckman and Jensen (1977), groups progress through five rather predictable stages of development. These stages describe both how group members relate to one another and how groups go about their tasks. These stages can be identified both in the yearly cycles of school life and in the shorter cycles of changing work groups within a classroom. For instance, early in a project or early in the year, during the *forming* stage, students look to the teacher for assurance, structure, and authority. A great deal of time is spent defining learning tasks and supplying needed information about those tasks. "What does she want us to do?" is a common question in this stage. *Storming* follows. As individuals feel increasingly comfortable, they begin to question the authority of the teacher, they respond more openly to their tasks, and they experience interpersonal and intrapersonal conflict. "I don't like this" and "I want to do it this way" become important means of testing authority. Greater order develops in the *norming* stage. The class becomes more cohesive by developing norms for how members should behave towards each other and how interpretations and perspectives should be shared. "In this class we listen and make sure everyone has an opportunity to share ideas" is an example of a sophisticated norm designed to build cohesiveness. With norms and roles in place, the class focuses increasingly on *performing* its academic tasks. Attitudes like "How else might we solve this problem?" indicate that class members are committed to working towards high levels of thinking, problem solving, and decision making. Finally, as members finish their tasks and prepare for a transition in their interpersonal relationships, there is a need for closure to facilitate *adjourning*. "What have we learned?" "What have we appreciated about working together?" and "How can we apply these skills to new settings?" are all appropriate questions for reflection and closure.

How about that classroom you enjoyed? Can you remember a time when the class disagreed with the teacher? What happened? Try to describe both of your classroom situations using the concepts of forming, storming, norming, performing, adjourning.

The Individual-Group Maturation Model: How Do We Build Trust, Communication, Shared Goals, and Interdependence?

The Individual-Group Maturation Model (J. Gibb & L. Gibb, 1978) suggests that groups express four basic concerns. These concerns, which are interdependent and hierarchical, are reciprocal trust, feedback, the formation of goals, and interdependence. The first and most important concern is *reciprocal trust*. In early stages of group life, individuals tend to be mistrustful, uncertain, cautious, and fearful. They worry about their personal adequacy and group membership. Conformity and structure are important and are used to help reduce uncertainty. When groups are able to build trust, fear diminishes and groups have the opportunity to build *communication and decision-making systems* that are honest and responsive to group problems and tasks. When groups are able to develop an adequate system of communication, they are usually able to establish goals that satisfy the needs of individuals and make sense for the group. Groups then concern themselves with issues of freedom, control, and *interdependence*. When groups have established trust, good communication, and shared goals, members are often able to feel simultaneously independent and interdependent.

Richard and Patricia Schmuck (1996) describe how these four concerns might manifest in different classrooms. In some classrooms, for instance, students may be afraid that their peers and teacher will reject them. To minimize this fear, students limit public discussion. Lack of sharing decreases opportunities to personalize learning and increases feelings of alienation from learning and school. This alienation makes it less likely that students will adhere to the academic norms of the school and more likely that clashes with authority will result. These clashes reinforce fear and mistrust. In other classrooms, however, students are encouraged to express themselves and move past fear of rejection. When they do, their ideas and behaviors are greeted with respect. They feel rewarded. Interpersonal communication becomes increasingly genuine and complex. Collaborative decision making becomes possible. Students become more responsible for their own behavior and begin to set both individual and collaborative learning goals. They feel both more autonomous and more connected with peers. Self-confidence and intrinsic motivation increase and fear decreases.

How about that classroom you enjoyed? How interdependent did you feel? Try to describe both of your classroom situations using the concepts of trust, feedback, goals, and interdependence.

❧ RECURRING THEMES IN GROUP ❧ STRUCTURE AND DEVELOPMENT

Values, norms, and roles. Inclusion, control, and affection. Trust and shared goals. Conflict. So many principles, theories, and vocabulary may seem overwhelming. To begin to integrate these into useful schemas that can be used to build an understanding of the group nature of classroom life, it may be helpful to view some of the themes that seem to be shared among different principles and theories.

First, when people are together in all sorts of groups—including classrooms—important and predictable interpersonal issues tend to surface. For instance, if you have ever felt anxious when you entered a new class, you are not alone. What you felt was most likely related to issues of group formation, trust, and inclusion.

Second, and perhaps most important, interpersonal issues that are expressed in groups are not only somewhat predictable, but often related sequentially to each other. That is to say, things tend to happen when it is time for them to happen and not until other things have been addressed. Both group theory and Maslow's theory of psychological health tell us that the need for shared values, basic trust, and feelings of inclusion and belongingness need to be addressed early in the life of a classroom. Group theory also tells us that if these needs are not addressed and the relationships among group members are not nurtured, groups will be less successful at completing their tasks. In other words, if students do not feel genuinely included in the life of the classroom, classrooms will be not only less friendly and pleasant but less successful places for learning as well.

Third, and related to number two, conflicts—storming and control issues—are natural. People seek not only to be included in groups but also to differentiate themselves from others. Conflicts help groups clarify values and define roles. Conflicts give groups energy. Conflicts can be important sources for learning; students need to learn (a) how to negotiate interpersonal conflicts (D. Johnson & R. Johnson, 1991) and (b) how to engage in a genuine academic disagreement to develop high-level reasoning and listening skills (D. Johnson & R. Johnson, 1992). Working together is not always about being "nice" and "going along to get along." Disagreement and differentiation are natural and can be exciting and productive.

Fourth, balance is key. All groups, including classroom groups, need to work towards balance (a) between task and maintenance, (b) between teacher talk and student talk, (c) between initiation and response. Balance changes. *What may seem right one day might not work the next. Sensitivity and flexibility are essential.*

🍂   A PRACTICAL THEORY: USING THEORY   🍂 AS A FRAMEWORK FOR LEARNING TO LOOK AT CLASSROOMS

Kurt Lewin once said that there is nothing as practical as a good theory. And, in fact, intelligent work and problem-solving behaviors may be more dependent on the availability of good theoretical frameworks and "habits of mind" than on specific knowledge about the task or problem. The availability of *multiple* frameworks—frameworks that enable a person to view a situation from more than one perspective—is key. Or, conversely, as Abraham Maslow is supposed to have said: "When the only tool you have is a hammer, every problem tends to look like a nail." Group theory offers many exciting frameworks and perspectives that can be used to build a rich understanding of classroom life.

"Learning to look" is a challenge. Learning to look at classroom life might mean participating as a student in a class and using theory to reflect on that experience. Learning to look might mean using a theoretical framework to structure a classroom observation while simultaneously remaining open to the nuances and surprises of daily classroom life. Learning to look might mean collecting information about classroom climate and using that information for reflection and planning. In this section we examine the challenges of learning to look through structured classroom observations and questionnaires, and we begin to learn how to use such theory-based tools.

Preparing to Look

If you want to observe classroom life in a systematic fashion, there are many details—the who, what, where, when, why, and how—that need to be determined. Where and when are often determined by availability and convenience. Who, what, and why invite considerable reflection and, depending on their conceptualization, might vary widely. For instance:

Take a minute to think of a time you observed in a classroom situation. Whom did you observe? What did you look for? How did you decide?

Who might be:
"I am going to observe Ms. Peach."
"I am going to observe Ms. Peach's class."
"Ms. Peach and I have agreed to observe each other's classes."

What might be:
"I am going to observe how Ms. Peach uses a balance of task and maintenance statements."
"I am going to observe how the students in Ms. Peach's class get along together."
"I am going to observe how the students in Ms. Peach's class use both task and maintenance statements in their small-group, problem-solving lesson."

Why might be:
"I am going to observe Ms. Peach because it is an assignment for this course. "
"I am going to observe a small group in Ms. Peach's class to learn how to identify task and maintenance statements in small-group discussion."
"Ms. Peach and I have agreed to observe each other's classes and help each other plan how to coach students to use both task and maintenance statements in small-group problem solving."

Think about each of these statements and ask yourself what they imply about the immediate purpose of data collection and, perhaps more importantly, what they imply about teaching, learning, and life in classrooms.

- Are you observing Ms. Peach, her class, or one small group?
- Are you informing Ms. Peach about the purpose of your observation or deciding together what and how you will observe?
- Does the class know you are going to observe? Is the class told about the purpose of your observation? Do they have an opportunity to discuss the *possibility* of your observation, to express curiosity, to indicate discomfort?
- Do you have a specific purpose for your observation? Is your purpose to judge whether a behavior is appropriate, to learn to identify a specific behavior within the context of real classroom life, or to help collect data that might be used to inform instructional decisions?

As you prepare to collect data, be as open, inclusive, and collaborative as possible. Aim for shared planning and decision making. When observing, aim for reciprocal observations. Learn to identify and describe what you see. Try not to judge—good or bad—what you find. Learn as much about the classroom context as you can. And remember to relax and have a good time!

Learning How to Collect Data about Interpersonal Behavior

One way to learn about classroom life—especially how individuals and groups interact—is to observe behaviors and keep track of what you see. To do this, you must first decide what you will observe. For instance, perhaps you would like to structure a classroom observation to learn about roles. To do this, you might observe teacher and student talk and compare how much a teacher talks with how much the students talk, or you could collect data to determine who initiates interaction and who responds, or you could observe a small-group problem-solving session and look specifically for how group members use task and maintenance roles. There are many possibilities, and you will need to decide, specifically, what to look for. Second, you will need to construct an observation instrument to keep track of what you observe. Remember to start simple. If you try to look for too many behaviors at once, you will end up feeling frustrated and unsure of the information you have collected. Here are some basic guidelines for how you might proceed. Do not expect the process to work perfectly the first time.

1. Choose a theoretical framework on which to base your instrument and observation.

2. Choose a time to observe when people are working at a task and you expect them to talk frequently.
3. Decide whom to observe. Will it be the teacher, the teacher and the class, or a small group?
4. Prepare an observation instrument. Tally sheets are common. (Figure 2.1 contains two examples that might be used to observe verbal task and maintenance behaviors. Figure 2.2 contains an example of how you might use the Verbal Interaction Category System to observe.) If you are going to observe more than one person, keep the observation sheet simple.
5. Make sure you are comfortable with the observation sheet—that you understand the categories clearly enough to recognize them and that you can be reasonably consistent when you tally what you hear. Remember that not everything a person or group says will necessarily fit into one of your categories.
6. Explain to the person or group that you are interested in how groups talk when they are working together on a task. Decide if it is appropriate to show the person or group you are observing the instrument you will be using. If you share the observation instrument before you observe, will you also share the data you collect? Try to decide before you begin.
7. Decide where to sit or stand. Make sure you can both see and hear the subject(s) of your observation clearly.
8. Observe. Do not enter the conversation or make comments (verbally or otherwise). Be as inconspicuous as possible. The length of your observation may depend on the length of time the person or group works on the task. It may also depend on your stamina. Most people find it difficult to observe carefully for more than about twenty minutes at a time.
9. Sit back and look at the data you have collected. Be descriptive, not evaluative. "What categories were used frequently and infrequently?", not "How well did they do?"
10. If you have decided to share the data you have collected, do so. Remember not to analyze and evaluate the data for the subjects of your observation.

Learning How to Collect Data about Values, Norms, and Climate

Another way to learn about classroom life—especially about the perceptions of individuals—is to ask teachers or students to respond anonymously to a series of statements. This technique works well when investigating classroom values, norms, and climate. Here are some basic guidelines for how you might proceed. (See Figures 2.3 and 2.4; D. Johnson & F. Johnson, 1994; D. Johnson, R. Johnson, Buckman, & Richards, 1985; and R. Schmuck & P. Schmuck,

	Name	Name	Name	Name
1. Gives information or suggestions				
2. Encourages others to participate				
3. Asks for information or suggestions				
4. Paraphrases others				
5. Summarizes				
6. Supports or praises others				
7. Helps clarify the task or directions				
8. Uses humor that does not put others down				

	Name	Name	Name	Name
1. Gives information or suggestions				
2. Encourages others to participate				
3. Summarizes				
4. Supports or praises others				

Directions: When you observe a whole class discussion, you could observe the teacher or both the teacher and the class. When you observe both, tally teacher behavior in one column and all student behavior in a separate column. When you observe a small group discussion, you could observe just one student or the entire group. When you observe an entire group, keep a separate column of tallies for each person.

Figure 2.1
Sample Observation Forms for Task and Maintenance Statements.
Note. Odd-numbered statements are examples of task behaviors. Even-numbered statements are examples of maintenance behaviors.

	3-minute segment	3-minute segment	3-minute segment	3-minute segment	3-minute segment
Teacher initiates— Information					
Teacher initiates— Directions					
Teacher initiates— Narrow questions					
Teacher initiates— Broad questions					
Teacher responds— Accepting ideas, behaviors, feelings					
Teacher responds— Rejecting ideas, behaviors, feelings					
Student responds— To teacher					
Student responds— To another student					
Student initiates— Talking to teacher					
Student initiates— Talking to another student					
Silence					
Confusion					

Directions: When you observe a whole class, try to make one tally about every five seconds (about twelve a minute). Place your tally mark in the cell that you think best describes what is happening in the class. Shift one column to the right about every three minutes.

When you observe a small-group discussion, the procedure will be somewhat different. Start your observation when the teacher explains the task to the class. For this segment of the observation, observe the teacher statements and student statements of the whole class. Make about twelve tallies a minute. When the small groups begin to work, shift your attention to one group. Begin a new column on your observation sheet or use a separate observation sheet. During the small-group segment of the lesson, tally only teacher talk that is directed to the whole class or to the small group you have chosen to observe.

Figure 2.2
Sample Observation Form for Verbal Interaction Category System.

Life In This Classroom

All classrooms are different. What do you think about life in this classroom? Put an *X* in the box that best describes what you think about each statement.

	Almost Never	Seldom	Sometimes	Frequently	Almost Always
1. In this class, students usually get to work with other students.					
2. In this class, other students like to help me learn.					
3. In this class, I do most of my work by myself.					
4. In this class, I like to share my ideas with others.					
5. In this class, I learn important things from other students.					
6. In this class, I have good friends.					
7. In this class, students share ideas and materials with each other.					
8. In this class, all the students know each other well.					
9. In this class, I get to talk with other students.					
10. In this class, the students like being together.					

Figure 2.3
Sample instrument, using Likert-type scale, to gather information about how students perceive cooperation in the classroom.

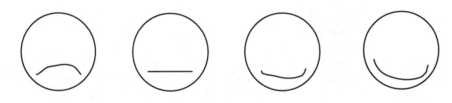

Circle the face that best describes how you feel about each statement that is read to you.

Figure 2.4
Sample Response Sheet for Students without Strong Reading Skills.

1996, for examples of response instruments.) Do not expect the procedure to work perfectly the first time.

1. Decide what you want to know more about and whom you will ask.
2. Decide what statements might help you learn more about what people are thinking. Decide how many statements to use. Start simple.
3. Design a response scale. A "Likert-type" response scale is most common (see Figures 2.3 and 2.4). It is common to reverse the response tendency for one or more items (see item # 3 in Figure 2.3).
4. Decide how the instrument will be "delivered." Do students have sufficient skills to work uninterrupted with their own copies of the instrument? Do you need to design a simple response form with no statements (see Figure 2.4), and have each student respond to each item as you read the statement? Perhaps each student can be given a complete copy of the instrument, but you will want to read each item aloud and have students fill in their responses one item at a time.
5. Explain to participants what you are interested in learning more about. Keep it simple. Make sure that participants understand that their responses are anonymous—that they will not put their names on the instrument. Decide ahead of time whether or not you will share the results of your data collection.
6. When you look at the data you have collected, be descriptive, not evaluative.

WORKING WITH PEERS

We do not always have to "go somewhere else" to observe and learn about group behavior. Sometimes we can learn by observing ourselves.

Using a *Fishbowl* to Learn about Task and Maintenance Behaviors

1. Chairs are arranged in a "fishbowl"—two circles, one inside the other. Half the class sits in the inside circle and the other half sits in the outside circle. Each student in the outer circle uses the observation instrument in Figure 2.1 to observe one classmate—or "fish"— in the inner circle.
2. Students in the inner circle have twenty minutes to complete "What Employers Want" (see Figure 2.5).

The American Society for Training and Development, with the assistance of the US Department of Labor, surveyed Fortune 500 firms to determine what skills employers want. Below, in no particular order, are listed ten skills that employers consider to be "workplace basics." Your task is to rank these skills in order of importance from highest to lowest. Place by the number 1 the most important, by the number 2 the next most important, and so forth. You have 20 minutes, as a group, to complete your task and create one rank ordering.

1. _____
2. _____
3. _____
4. _____
5. _____
6. _____
7. _____
8. _____
9. _____
10. _____

interpersonal skills
leadership
writing
teamwork
oral communication
reading
computation
problem solving
listening
creative thinking

Figure 2.5
What employers want.

3. Reflection and Planning:
   Individual:
   - After twenty minutes, students in the inner circle are asked to spend a moment reflecting by themselves:
   - On a scale of 1 (low) to 5 (high): How confident am I about my group's final decisions?
   - How comfortable am I with the process my group used to determine these decisions?
   - How satisfied am I that other members of the group listened to my ideas?

   Students in the inner circle are also asked (again, there is no public sharing):
   - What do you predict the observation sheet will indicate about your own use of task and maintenance behaviors in the activity?

   - What do you think the data for the entire group will indicate about the use of task and maintenance behaviors?

4. Students in the inner and outer circles change places. Students in the new inner circle are asked to spend about five minutes discussing, without using judgment words like good and bad and without using names of other students, (a) how they think the group they observed went about making decisions, and (b) how both task and maintenance behaviors were used in the group.

5. Each observer and fish pair face each other. The observer gives the fish the observation sheet and answers questions the fish might have about the data. Questions should be restricted to the data.

6. Original fish come back together in the inner circle and spend about five minutes discussing (a) how they made decisions and (b) the use of both task and maintenance behaviors in their group.
7. Students switch roles and repeat the process, completing "The Nine Work Strategies of Successful Engineers at Bell Labs" (Kelley & Caplan, 1993) in Figure 2.6.

Using Our Memories, *Group Interview* (Kagan, 1992), and *Gallery Tour* (Kagan, 1992) to Examine Norms

1. Using a *Group Interview* in a randomly-assigned group of four, students each take two minutes to describe a class situation in which they enjoyed participating. Procedure is repeated, with students describing situations they did not enjoy. While each student is speaking, other group members "interview" the speaker by asking clarifying and probing questions to build an understanding of the norms in each of these situations.
2. Using large paper and markers, each group of four makes a two-column chart of "Norms That Help" and "Norms That Hurt." Each column should contain at least one norm that helps describe the experiences of each member.
3. Groups hang their charts around the room. Students participate in a *Gallery Tour*—they travel around the room with their group members, visiting and discussing each chart in turn.
4. Reflection and Planning:
   Group:
   • When groups return to their own work, they re-examine their own lists and try to add one idea that they learned from the work of another group.
   • Groups then discuss what kinds of group norms the use of *Group Interview* and *Gallery Tour* might help to establish in their class.
5. Papers can be used to focus a discussion about "norms that will help in our work together."

Using Ourselves to Learn about Values, Norms, Roles, and Group Development

1. In a randomly-assigned group of four, students decide (or are assigned) to examine values, norms, roles, or a stage theory of group development.

2. Individually, members each write approximately four statements that might be useful in a response instrument designed to explore the concept chosen.
3. Members bring their ideas to their group, and the group constructs a response instrument of approximately ten items.
4. Reflection and Planning:
   Group:
   • What kinds of different skills did members of the group need so that the group could work together to complete its task?
5. Each group provides copies of its instrument for all class members. All students complete instruments from each group except their own.
6. Groups collate and present data from their own instruments.
7. The class uses data to examine the classroom. Questions might include "What have we done that has helped create these norms (or values, or roles)?" "Are these norms (or values, or roles) that help?" "What developmental issues (inclusion, trust, etc.) seem most important to us now?" "How can we use this data to create the kind of classroom in which we want to participate?"
8. Data collection might be repeated near the middle and end of the class's time together to examine changes and development.

Using a *One-Minute Paper* and *Inside-Outside Circle* (Kagan, 1992) to Reflect on Group Theory

QUESTION: What is one thing you learned in this chapter that you think might influence you as you learn to look at groups in classrooms?

1. Each student writes a response.
2. Class stands in two concentric circles with the inside circle facing out and the outside circle facing in.
3. Students in the outside circle take one minute to share their responses with their partners. Students in the inside circle take one minute to ask their partners clarifying and probing questions. They do not share their own responses.
4. Students reverse roles. Students in the inside share and students on the outside listen and clarify.

Below, in no particular order, are nine skills that researchers found described the "stars" at Bell Labs. All skills are considered important, but your task is to decide which skills go in each area of the diagram. The "most important" goes in the inner circle and the "least important" go in the outer circle. You have 20 minutes, as a group, to complete your task and create one figure.

Followership: Helping the leader accomplish organizational goals.

Leadership: Formulating, stating, and building consensus on common goals and working to accomplish them.

Networking: Getting direct and immediate access to coworkers with technical expertise, and sharing your own knowledge and expertise with others.

Organizational savvy: Navigating the competing interests in an organization to promote cooperation, address conflicts, and get things done.

Perspective: Seeing your job in its larger context and taking on other viewpoints.

Self-management: Regulating your own work commitments, time, performance level, and career.

Show-and-tell: Presenting your ideas persuasively.

Taking initiative: Accepting responsibility above and beyond your stated job, volunteering for additional activities, and promoting new ideas.

Teamwork effectiveness: Assuming joint responsibility for work activities, coordinating efforts, and accomplishing shared goals with coworkers.

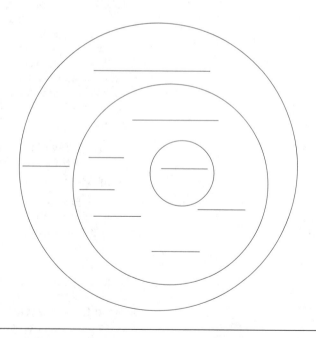

Figure 2.6
The nine work strategies of successful engineers at Bell Labs.
Adapted and reprinted by permission of *Harvard Business Review* (Exhibit: The Nine Work Strategies).
From "How Bell Labs Creates Star Performers" by Robert Kelley and Janet Caplan, July–August 1993.
Copyright © 1993 by the President and Fellows of Harvard College; all rights reserved.

5. Students exchange papers.
6. Students in the outside circle rotate one person clockwise. Each student is now facing a new partner.
7. Students in the outside now share with their new partners what their old partners have told them. Students in the inside then do the same.
8. Students again switch papers, and students in the outside circle rotate.
9. Students repeat sharing and switching.

Answers to Working with Peers Activities in Chapter 2

What Employers Want

1. Teamwork
2. Problem solving
3. Interpersonal skills
4. Oral communications
5. Listening
6. Creative thinking
7. Leadership
8. Writing
9. Computation
10. Reading

The Nine Work Strategies of Successful Engineers at Bell Labs

Outer Circle: Organizational savvy, Show-and-tell
Middle Circle: Self-management, Perspective, Followership, Networking, Leadership, Teamwork effectiveness
Inner Circle: Taking initiative

CHAPTER 3

Building an Understanding of the Power of Diversity in Groups

🦋 As you read, you might want to ask yourself:

To help students become empowered learners, why must both teachers and students understand that people are smart in different ways?

How might social categories and status differences affect what we see and how we act in groups?

Why do teachers in classrooms that empower learners have high expectations for all students?

Why have schools historically tracked students? How might tracking impact the rights of all students to become empowered learners? How might cooperative learning provide an alternative to tracking?

I remember my grandmother making me a chopped liver sandwich on rye for my school lunch and how when I took it out of its aluminum foil in the cafeteria, the kids sitting around me, holding peanut butter and jelly, or Kraft yellow cheese, or baloney sandwiches, yelled, "Ick!" and held their noses. I felt ashamed. That sandwich held my whole heritage. I was a Jew in a school of mostly Irish and Italian Catholics. I put the sandwich back in its foil, stood up, and headed for the girls' room. I was torn between tossing the sandwich in the garbage and purchasing a cellophane-wrapped Drake's crumb cake from the cafeteria woman, who had gray hair in a fine net and wore a white uniform and white sturdy shoes, or going into the bathroom stall and eating my ethnic sandwich, hidden from view. I loved my grandmother's chopped liver, and I chose the stall.[1]

[1]From *Long Quiet Highway* (p. 7), by Natalie Goldberg. Copyright © 1993 by Natalie Goldberg. Used by permission of Bantam Books, a division of Bantam Doubleday Dell Publishing Group, Inc.

To function optimally in school, students need positive peer relations. As schools, the workplace, and society become increasingly diverse, building shared values and building and maintaining positive peer relations become both increasingly important and increasingly challenging. A cooperative context is of primary importance to the building of shared values and the appreciation of differences. Competition or the expectation of competition—for resources, jobs, or the recognition and approval of a teacher—increases an individual's sense of solidarity with his own identity group and simultaneously increases bias against other groups. Competition tends to foster a "we're better than they are" (Miller & Harrington, 1990, p. 54) comparative social evaluation, in which personal characteristics are compared and seen as better or worse than others. A shift away from competition creates opportunities to move away from "up-down comparisons." A shift from "better or worse than" to "different from" is important because it lowers the personal threat that people often feel when confronted with diversity.

Think back to the earliest time in your life when you realized that people were "different." What happened that made you realize this?

Because diversity is a fundamental characteristic of life in classrooms, classrooms are ideal places to build an understanding and appreciation of human differences; appreciation and understanding of differences are essential characteristics of classroom communities that empower students as learners. Is there a best way to build an appreciation of differences? Is it a good idea to "celebrate diversity" with costumes, festivals, and food—to eat matzo on Monday, tacos on Tuesday, and wonton on Wednesday? How crucial are differences in academic ability? Is it best to separate students into different groups so that instruction can be tailored to meet the perceived unique needs of each group? Or should we de-track schools and include students of different perceived academic abilities in the same classrooms? Does unintentional bias develop as a result of our perceptions of differences? Is it important to develop an awareness of, and pedagogy for, the effects of possible bias? How *does* diversity impact on life in classrooms? And, perhaps most fundamentally, should diversity concern us at all?

Educating students to become productive citizens in a diverse world is an important, multifaceted, and complex process. Banks (1993) suggests that it requires a focus on five basic dimensions: content integration, knowledge construction, prejudice reduction, equity pedagogy, and an empowering school culture and social structure. In this chapter we will focus on four of these dimensions to help us build an understanding of how a cooperative context might help to create classrooms that (a) provide equitable educational opportunities for all students to help them reach high levels of achievement and (b) give all students opportunities to become productive members of a diverse, democratic society (Nieto, 1992). The discussion of each dimension will be introduced by one or two questions. The purpose of these questions is to focus on issues specifically related to building cooperative contexts, not to imply that these are the only issues relevant to the dimension.

🦋 MULTICULTURAL EDUCATION AND THE 🦋 CONSTRUCTION OF KNOWLEDGE

- How might culture influence what we know and how we know it?
- How can we learn to recognize and value knowledge, ways of knowing, and ways of learning that are different from our own?

The Importance of Cognitive Style in Understanding How Individuals Learn

People differ in the ways they process information; each individual, how-ever, has a fairly consistent approach, which is known as *cognitive style.* Evidence suggests that cognitive style may be influenced by race, gender, and culture; therefore a brief examination of cognitive style is important to building an understanding of how diversity may impact life in classrooms. Many models have been developed to describe differences in cognitive style. We will explore two: field-dependent versus field-independent and reflective versus impulsive. Both of these sets of style variables are considered to be independent of intelligence or "ability"; both are best viewed as continuums rather than as either/or distinctions.

Field-Independent and Field-Dependent Learners   Field-independent individuals tend to prefer situations that require analytical approaches to problem solving and to prefer material that is less imbedded in social con-text. Field-dependent individuals tend to prefer situations that require global approaches to problem solving and to prefer material that is more imbedded in social context. In general, European American students tend to be more field independent while Mexican American, Native American, and African American students tend to be more field dependent. Cooper-ative learning tends to provide a rich social context for learning, and this may explain, to some degree, why Mexican American and African Amer-ican students are likely to experience greater academic success in cooper-ative than in competitive or individualistic learning environments (Kagan & Zahn, 1975; Kagan, 1980). It does not follow, however, that students of European descent experience greater success in environments that do not emphasize social context and cooperation. Both Sharan and Shaulov (1990) and Light (1990) have investigated students' self-reported pre-ferred styles and have found that even when students do not express a preference for learning cooperatively, they tend towards higher achieve-ment in learning environments that are structured around substantive co-operative work.

Impulsive and Reflective Learners   In addition to preferring either ana-lytical or global approaches to problem solving, it appears that some people

Would you describe yourself as more field dependent or field independent? More impulsive or reflective? Why?

respond to problems rapidly while other people respond more deliberately and consider alternative solutions before settling on a response. These two types of problem solving have been labeled impulsive and reflective. Both styles have advantages. (This may seem surprising, given the fact that the word "impulsive" tends to have negative connotations. Perhaps the label itself suggests a subtle form of style bias.) Impulsives tend to excel in tasks that require broad analysis; reflectives tend to excel in tasks that require detail. The deliberate, "wait your turn" atmosphere of many classrooms may disadvantage students with impulsive styles; short teacher "wait time" may disadvantage students with highly reflective cognitive styles.

The Importance of Intelligence in Understanding How Individuals Learn

Do you know your IQ? What does IQ mean to you?

The works of Howard Gardner (1983) and Robert Sternberg (1988) demonstrate that intelligence is not a singular idea that can be measured adequately using a written test. In their views, what makes people smart is not a simple and fixed profile of abilities but a complex and flexible profile that is unique to each individual and that individual's life circumstances.

Learning and Multiple Intelligences In 1983 Gardner tentatively identified seven basic intellectual abilities that are relatively independent of each other. He identified these abilities, or intelligences, through observations of product development and problem solving within specific social and cultural contexts. *Linguistic Intelligence* is related to the production of language. *Logical-Mathematical Intelligence* includes both inductive and deductive reasoning and often involves numbers or patterns. *Bodily- Kinesthetic Intelligence* involves the use of the body in learning, in emotional expression, or in play. *Spatial Intelligence* is related both to sight and to the ability to form images in the mind. *Musical Intelligence* includes sensitivity to sounds and the ability to recognize and use rhythmic tonal patterns. *Interpersonal Intelligence* helps individuals communicate and work with others. *Intrapersonal Intelligence* helps individuals to communicate with themselves—to understand their own feelings and thinking processes. More recently (1995) Gardner has identified an eighth intelligence, a *Naturalist Intelligence,* which he relates to the ability to make and use acute discriminations.

Logical-Mathematical and Linguistic Intelligences represent "ways of knowing" that are essential to success in school; the acquisition of high-status school knowledge demands logical and linguistic "smarts." Other ways of knowing—and the people who excel in these other kinds of smarts—are frequently undervalued and underdeveloped in schools. Gardner's framework can be used to help create learning environments that value and develop the abilities of all students—environments that provide students with opportunities (a) to learn in ways that will give them access to knowledge that might otherwise be less accessible; (b) to learn *how* they are smart—not *if* they are smart; (c) to learn how *others* are smart; and (d) to learn how *different smarts,* and different students, can work together in ways that optimize success for everyone.

Learning and the Triarchic Mind   Like Gardner, Sternberg (1988) suggests that intelligence is related to real-world performance. He defines intelligence in *everyday* life "as the purposive adaptation to, selection of, and shaping of real-world environments relevant to one's life and abilities" (p. 65). He believes that there are three components, or mental processes, in thinking. Metacomponents, or *book smarts,* are used for analysis and critical thinking. They are used to plan, monitor, and evaluate solutions to problems. Performance components, or *practical smarts,* are used to implement the solutions to problems. Knowledge-acquisition components, or *creative smarts,* help individuals learn how to solve problems and develop new ideas. Sternberg believes that *how* these three components come together is a product of socialization and the culture in which a person is brought up. Like Gardner, he believes that, while all kinds of smarts are quite useful in real life, schools tend to reward some profiles of smarts—and some cultural backgrounds—more than others.

Using Gardner's and Sternberg's ideas, how do you think you are smart?

🌿 MULTICULTURAL EDUCATION AND 🌿 THE REDUCTION OF PREJUDICE

- How might the attitudes of teachers towards their students influence the school experiences of these students?
- How might the attitudes and behaviors of teachers be influenced by race, class, appearance, and cognitive style?

The Importance of How Teachers View Students

In 1968 the idea of *self-fulfilling prophecy*—the idea that behavior based on an expectation can actually cause that expectation to become true—was popularized when Rosenthal and Jacobson published *Pygmalion in the Classroom.* In this controversial study, elementary school children in a working-class community with a significant Mexican American population were given a test at the beginning of the school year. Teachers were told that the test could measure potential for intellectual growth. In truth, the test was not designed for that purpose at all, and students were identified randomly as potential "intellectual bloomers." By the end of the year, some of

Take a moment to think about two teachers—one who liked you and one who did not. Why do you think they did (or did not) like you? How could you tell?

these students did show significantly greater gains on achievement tests than other students in their classes. Gains were most dramatic in the primary grades and for children who would normally, on the basis of test scores, have been thought of as children of low or medium ability. The researchers asked teachers to evaluate the classroom behavior of all students. Intellectual bloomers were described as more curious, interesting, happy, and more likely to experience future success than their nonidentified peers. This study provided an impetus for many studies that examined how teacher expectations affect life in classrooms.

In one of these studies, African American and white students, when labeled "gifted," were treated differently from their peers and differently from each other as well. White students received preferential treatment, but African American gifted students were treated not only worse than their gifted white counterparts but also worse than nongifted black students (Rubovitz & Maehr, 1973). In a second study, Chambliss (1993) described how two groups of adolescent boys—the Saints and the Roughnecks—were treated differently in the same high school. The Saints—a group of upper-middle-class whites—were never arrested during a two-year study, even though they were constantly truant, frequently drunk, and involved in wild driving, theft, and vandalism. The Roughnecks—a group of lower-class whites—were constantly in trouble, although they had a pattern of delinquency that was no more serious than that of the Saints. In a third study, a kindergarten teacher, after less than two weeks of school, grouped her young students by perceived ability. All the students and the teacher belonged to the same racial group, and it seems that class distinctions and cultural literacy were the primary determiners of group assignment. Quality of clothes, hair styles, the use of standard English, dependence on public assistance, and the like determined whether students were expected to succeed or not. These initial perceptions and groupings remained intact throughout the year. Perceived high-ability students were called on for calendar, to lead the Pledge, and for activities that required no specific academic abilities—activities like show-and-tell and descriptions of Halloween costumes—more often than perceived middle- or low-ability students. By the end of the year, perhaps in imitation of the teacher, high-ability children treated their low-ability classmates poorly, and low-ability students treated each other poorly. When these children went on to first and second grades, their new teachers kept these same "ability groups" intact (Rist, 1971).

In addition to race, class, and physical appearance, cognitive style may also influence teacher preference and behavior. Two studies suggest that teachers tend to prefer children (Westby & Dawson, 1995) and adolescents (Getzels & Jackson, 1962) with more convergent, linear styles of thinking over their divergent, creative peers—even when the achievement of both groups is essentially equal (Getzels & Jackson).

Teacher Expectations and Teacher Behavior   A teacher does not necessarily have a "typical" style and may not interact with all students equally or, perhaps more importantly, equitably (Carew & Lightfoot, 1979). For instance, based on their expectations for student success, teachers may behave quite differently when they question different students. Teachers tend to call on perceived high-achieving students more often than on perceived low achievers. They ask high-achieving students more interesting questions. When a student is called on, wait time may depend on perceived ability. When teachers expect correct answers, they tend to give more clues and wait longer for responses— as much as five times longer. When students respond to questions, teachers are less likely to comment on the responses of perceived low-ability students. When perceived low-ability students answer questions correctly, they receive less praise. Not only do teachers tend to alter their questioning styles based on the perceived abilities of the students, they tend to seat perceived high-ability students in more advantageous classroom locations, they spend more time in their proximity, they give them more personal attention, and they touch them more frequently (Kerman, Kimball, & Martin, 1980).

High Expectations and Student Success   High teacher expectations for *all* students are essential to high levels of achievement. Understanding different cognitive styles and multiple intelligences is not a substitute for high expectations. "It is one thing to recognize a child's special artistic strength, but it does not serve that child well to [always] make him the illustrator for a group science project and excuse him from research and writing" (Oakes & Lipton, 1990, p. 58). Wheelock (1992, pp. 94–97) lists ways that teachers and lessons can communicate both high expectations and opportunities for students to approach learning in different ways.

Teachers communicate high expectations when they create an environment where

- Making mistakes is part of learning
- There is mutual trust and cooperation among students and between students and teacher
- Seating is arranged so that no student is invisible
- Students have enough time to answer questions
- The classroom becomes a partnership in the uncovering of knowledge
- All students become involved—even the quiet ones
- Students see themselves in the role of teacher

  Lessons communicate high expectations when they encourage students to

- Recognize their prior knowledge and experience
- Construct their own knowledge
- Communicate information in more than one way
- Enter into dialogue and give more than one-word answers

- Use thinking skills such as comparing, contrasting, and applying knowledge
- Acknowledge their own cultural backgrounds
- Use different kinds of intelligence
- Become invested in the group effort

Trust, Empathy, and Respect   Rogers (1969) believed that *genuineness, trust* and *acceptance,* and *empathy* are qualities of teachers who are able to facilitate high levels of learning for all students. How important are these seemingly intangible qualities? Studies suggest that, in classrooms with high levels of trust, students believe that others are working towards learning and towards the best interests of the group. In classrooms with high levels of trust, proportionately more student and teacher time is spent on learning than in classrooms with low levels of trust; in low-trust classrooms, organizational and relationship issues consume more time. Schmuck (1963) found that when teachers were high in understanding and empathy, "liking" was more evenly dispersed among their students—there were fewer status and "in-group/out-group" problems. Later in this chapter we will examine how student status influences student success.

How would you describe your first-grade teacher? What was that teacher's name?

In 1978, Pedersen, Faucher, and Eaton published a compelling portrait of one teacher who seemed to embody the essence of high expectations and the qualities that Rogers identified. "Teacher A" taught in an impoverished inner-city school for thirty-three years. Students were randomly assigned to her first-grade class or to classes taught by "Teacher B" or "Teacher C." While investigating archived school records, the researchers began to notice a pattern; the IQ scores of some students tended to increase during their years in elementary school while the scores of other students tended to decrease. Upon further investigation, they learned that the IQ scores of students who spent a year with Teacher A were likely to increase throughout elementary school; after a year with Teacher B, the scores of girls were likely to increase, but the scores of boys were more likely to decrease; after a year with Teacher C, the IQ scores of both boys and girls were likely to decrease. Researchers wondered if changes in IQ scores in elementary school would have any impact on these students in adult life. They did follow-up studies to find out. They found that about two-thirds of Teacher A's students were high-status adults, but only about one-third of Teacher B's students and 10% of Teacher C's students were considered high status. Something Teacher A did must have made a difference in the lives of students, and the researchers set out to discover what it might have been.

Most students remembered Teacher A as "good or excellent," but few students of Teacher B and Teacher C rated their teachers so highly. Teacher A had an excellent memory for former pupils; she was able to recognize them and call them by name even after twenty-five years! Teacher A was described as being able to give "students the profound impression of the importance of schooling, and how one should stick to it" (Pedersen et al., p. 19). Teacher A had high expectations—she believed that all children could learn to read.

When asked to describe her teaching style, one former colleague said simply that she taught "with a lot of love" (Pedersen et al., p. 20).

Martha, the teacher in the following description, also conveys both respect and high expectations—even when a student is particularly challenging.

> Robert was a challenge from his first day in Martha's class. He was a pudgy boy who had spent the previous school year at a special school for youth with severe behavioral problems. During the two years prior to that he had continually been removed from classrooms for exhibiting "inappropriate and aggressive" behavior.
>
> Martha invested herself in helping him. She waited daily at the classroom door to greet Robert, and she always told him goodbye in the afternoon. She spent a few moments every day talking with him about anything and everything, from TV shows to his mother. And she firmly insisted that he participate in classroom activities—especially cooperative learning groups with other children.
>
> Because of the attention she paid to him, Robert slowly began to realize that Martha was committed to him. By November Robert had become a marginally accepted and fairly productive member of this class. He was still ornery and still had small outbursts in class, but he responded to Martha and to the other students in much more positive ways. Not once was Robert sent to the principal or suspended, a dramatic reversal for him. Martha was able to help Robert become a more academically and socially competent person despite the stigma of being labeled behaviorally disordered.
>
> What was significant about Martha's influence on Robert was her dogged determination that he be given the opportunities to succeed in school and to attain social competence. There were no magic tricks, no technical fixes—just consistent, day-in and day-out, hour-to-hour, even minute-to-minute reminders to Robert to complete his work and respect others. She simply refused to give up on him.[2]

New York's Central Park East is an example of a high school where high expectations are coupled with high levels of respect. The principal, Debra Maier, says that respect for *all* students is the essential quality that leads to success.

> I think respect is an essential thing that is missing everywhere—schools in this city in which there isn't toilet paper in the bathrooms, or a mirror for people to look at, or towels to wash their hands, or doors in the boys' stall. . . . Those are petty aspects, but they are very important statements of our disrespect for the young people who go to school. Often there is not a place for young people or for adults to engage in a conversation. That is a sign of disrespect. We don't treat schools as if they are essentially respectful relationships. [At Central Park East] . . . we work very, very hard in order that all the relationships in this school are respectful. (Smith, 1995, pp. 159–160)

[2]From "In the Meantime: The Possibilities of Caring," by G. Noblit, D. Rogers, and B. McCadden, 1995, *Phi Delta Kappan, 76* (9), pp. 681–682. Copyright 1995 by Phi Delta Kappa. Reprinted with permission.

It is hard to overestimate the potential power of educators like Teacher A, Martha, and Debra Maier to empower students as learners.

🍂   MULTICULTURAL EDUCATION 🍂
AND EQUITY PEDAGOGY

- How might teachers teach to empower all students as learners?

> An equity pedagogy exists when teachers use techniques and teaching methods that facilitate the academic achievement of students from diverse racial and ethnic groups and from all social classes. Using teaching techniques that cater to the learning and cultural styles of diverse groups and using the techniques of cooperative learning are some of the ways that teachers have found effective with students from diverse racial, ethnic, and language groups. (Banks, 1993, p. 27)

Placing students in groups and telling them to cooperate is not cooperative learning; neither is it equity pedagogy. In fact, without careful structuring, the petty tensions, interpersonal conflicts, and status issues associated with diversity may actually escalate and achievement decrease when students from different backgrounds or students with different cognitive styles work together. For cooperative learning to be an effective equity pedagogy, there must be, among other things, (a) interaction that helps participants learn about themselves and each other as individuals and (b) conditions that encourage equal-status interaction.

Helping Individuals and Groups Learn about Themselves and Each Other

How much do you know about the other students in this class? How did you get to know them? Did anyone surprise you? Was anyone different from what your first impression led you to expect?

Everyone has a need for a strong, positive identity. Identity has both personal and social aspects. The social aspects of identity—those that are established through interaction with others—are influenced by basic principles, including the principles (Miller and Harrington, 1992) that

- Identity is comparative: We are smart, creative, industrious, or funny in comparison to others.
- Identity is fluid: We feel and act differently in different situations.
- Identity is relational: Our self-identity depends on how we see ourselves and act towards others and on how others see us and react to us.
- Identity has emotional significance: We feel anxious when our identity is threatened.

When individuals or groups first come together, interpersonal responses tend to be based on social identities and categories—categories of race, gender, class, ethnicity, age, and the like. These categories are easy to recognize and are rich with associations; they influence how individuals act towards each other, and they are used to predict future behavior. Unlike social identity, personal identity features are harder to recognize and are less rich in associations. Therefore, social identity often serves as the basis for initial action, re-action, and interaction in groups.

The Importance of Time   It takes time to move past behavior based on social identity and social stereotypes. It takes time to learn to get to know someone as an individual rather than as a representative of a social group. It takes time, but time is not enough. Even after six months of being to-gether, for example, bias will not decrease, and students will not necessarily respond to each other in less stereotypic ways, unless they are encouraged to do so. In classrooms teachers must structure time so that students have genuine opportunities not just to get the job done but to get to know each other as people and to build and maintain their relationships. The impor-tance of both task behaviors and maintenance behaviors was discussed in Chapter 2. Time must also be structured so that students have opportunities to learn *how* to get to know each other—to learn *how* to build and maintain their relationships. This will be discussed again in Chapter 7 when we ex-amine how to help students learn the interpersonal skills they need to be ef-fective group participants.

The Importance of Heterogeneous Grouping   When students are per-mitted to choose whom they will work with in the classroom, existing social identities and boundaries tend to be maintained. Therefore, it is important that assignment to groups be based not on personal preference but on het-erogeneity. This does not necessarily mean heterogeneity by any one par-ticular social category such as race, gender, or ethnicity. Nor does it neces-sarily mean heterogeneity by ability, even though this is a common interpretation of grouping strategies and cooperative learning.

In general, it is helpful if groups cross categories—if individuals share different characteristics with different group members. It is best not to iso-late members of "minority" groups from each other. For instance, if there are five females (or Asians, or students with physical handicaps, or any other group that is easy to identify) in a classroom of twenty-five students, it is probably best not to place each female in a different group—even though, at first glance, this practice would seem to follow the principle of hetero-geneity (Miller and Harrington, 1992). To empower all students, eventually everyone in a class should have opportunities to work with everyone else and to learn about them as individuals—not as representatives of a partic-ular social group. Grouping strategies will be discussed again in Chapter 10.

The Importance of Safety   A feeling of safety is a fundamental charac-teristic both of psychologically healthy people and of groups where individ-uals are able to move past behavior based on social identity and stereotypes

What helps you to feel safe in a group?

towards an understanding and appreciation of others as individuals. In classrooms teachers can help create feelings of safety by (a) reducing time pressures, (b) structuring tasks that provide both challenge and opportunity for success, and (c) eliminating competition for rewards or recognition among members of the same group and among different groups. The threat of failure that results from structuring competition into group life decreases feelings of safety, attention to the task, and interpersonal appreciation. It increases blaming, scapegoating, and bias.

Helping Individuals and Groups See Each Other as Equals

Individuals do not like to feel less able or less included than others. But in classrooms, unless teachers are very careful to structure opportunities for equal-status interactions, this tends to happen.

> Small task groups tend to develop hierarchies where some members are more active and influential than others. This is a *status ordering*—an agreed-upon social ranking where everyone feels it is better to have a high rank within the status order than a low rank. Group members who have high rank are seen as more competent and as having done more to guide and lead the group (Cohen, 1994, p. 27).

Very seldom is group participation equal. This is true in experimental groups that have been selected to eliminate race, gender, and age differences and in classrooms where students seem to be trusting and friendly toward each other (Cohen, 1994). Unequal participation is a problem because members often agree that the person who has talked the most has made the most important contributions and the person who has talked the least has made the least important contributions (Berger, Conner, & McKeown, 1974).

Types of Status Differences In Classroom Groups   Students tend to know how competent each of their classmates is in "important" subjects such as reading and math, and, based on this knowledge, are able to rank order their classmates by *academic status*. Students with high academic status will dominate when their group is given a task in that subject area. Students who are seen as less able tend to be more passive. Academic status in reading is so important that students with high reading status will dominate their group even when reading is irrelevant to the group's task. When, independent of actual ability, experimenters label some students "high ability" (as Rosenthal and Jacobson, 1968, did in *Pygmalion in the Classroom*), these students tend to dominate. Some students enjoy high *peer status*. These students, like high academic-status students, tend to dominate classroom groups. Peer status may depend on athletic or physical ability, attractiveness, good social skills, cheerfulness, or other characteristics that the peer group values. Classroom groups are also affected by *societal status*— status differences that mirror the preferences found in the larger society and are based on differences such as race, gender, and class.

Recognizing Status Differences In Classroom Groups   It is important to learn to recognize status differences in groups. Teachers can learn to recognize status differences through behavioral observations. When looking for status differences, for instance, it is helpful to realize that low-status students

- Tend to talk less
- Have their ideas ignored or undervalued by other group members
- Have difficulties with access—they tend to appear physically removed from their group and from relevant materials
- May seem passive and uninvolved
- As a result of the ways they are treated, may experience frustration and misbehave

Teachers can also use sociometric data to help them determine status differences in their classes. Later in this chapter we will learn how to collect sociometric data from students.

Have you ever felt as if you lacked status in a group? How did you know?

The Educational Disadvantages of Status Differences   In Chapter 1 we examined briefly the importance of peer discussion to learning. During small-group discussions and activities, status differences disadvantage groups and their members in several ways. First, students with high academic status have more opportunities to participate than students with perceived low abilities. When this happens, academic differences are reinforced by classroom interaction because high-status students have more opportunities to learn. Second, students with high social status have more opportunities to participate than students with low status. When this happens, social bias is reinforced rather than remediated by classroom interaction, because relationships with low-status students continue to be based on social, not individual, identity. Third, the overall quality of work suffers when a variety of opinions and skills are not available to a group—either because some members are silenced or dominant or because members struggle against each other for dominance rather than work with each other towards equity (Cohen, 1994).

Changing Status Expectations—The Low-Status Student as Expert
An obvious way to change low expectations is to create a situation in which a low-expectations student is able to be an expert (Cohen, 1994). One way to do this is to find a task that the student is already good at and is able to teach others. Every student is an expert at something. It is a worthwhile challenge to identify these areas of expertise and build them into classroom life. For this intervention to be helpful, you must prepare the student care-

fully to be the teacher, and you must prepare the class carefully so that they understand that teaching the class is, in itself, an important skill.

Another way to help the low-status student become an expert is to design a situation so that the low-status student is in control of and understands the initial materials that are needed for a group task. Individuals who talk early in a group's task tend to be seen as influential. If, early on, a low-status student has an opportunity to talk, that student may become more influential. Again, it is important to prepare students carefully for this role so that they will be successful (Cohen, 1986).

Changing Status Expectations—the Multiple Abilities Treatment
When the tasks that students work on cooperatively require many different abilities, there is an increased likelihood that students from diverse backgrounds or students with different profiles of ability will be able to assume important roles in their groups. Or conversely, when students work on cooperative tasks that require a very limited profile of abilities, it becomes likely that some students will find it difficult to fit in. Even young students know that Logical-Mathematical and Linguistic Intelligences tend to dominate traditional classroom life and are, therefore, the common currency for high status and academic success.

The essence of the Multiple Abilities Treatment is for the teacher to tell students that the task they are about to undertake requires many abilities: that "None of us has all of these abilities. Each one of us has some of these abilities" (Cohen, 1994, p. 122). The effectiveness of the Multiple Abilities Treatment lies, first of all, in the nature of the task. It must require many abilities. Second, the teacher must alter the expectations of all students. They must all believe that they have some but not all of the abilities needed for optimal success. Normally low-status students must believe that they can contribute something significant to the work of the group; normally high-status students must also believe that, although they have something to contribute, they do not have *all* the necessary skills and they need the unique contributions of others. All students must understand what the different abilities are that are required by the task. The teacher needs to provide class time and help students list and describe these abilities in ways that make them seem both "real" and important.

Maria describes the potential power of the Multiple Abilities Treatment quite well:

> As you see people working together, you see all of the abilities that other students have that you didn't see before. There was this one kid, and he was really shy. He was always, like out of everything. He was never doing something or speaking out until we had an art project we had to do and he—like he just *visualized,* just got a pencil and piece of paper and like acted and draw [sic] a lot things that people didn't even see in him until that one time that we saw another part of him. (Maria, a seventh grade student) (Cohen, 1994, p. 122)

Changing Status Expectations—Assigning Competence   Once students are working together on a multiple-abilities task, a teacher can observe for the use of these abilities. During group work, when the teacher sees a low-status student contribute significantly to the work of the group, the teacher can "assign competence" to that student. When a teacher assigns competence to a student, this tends to influence both the individual student's expectations for him- or herself and the expectations of other students towards the individual (Cohen, 1994). For assigning competence to work, the comments from the teacher must (a) be honest, (b) refer to the group's task, (c) relate to a particular skill or ability, and (d) describe the specific actions of the student.

Looking for multiple abilities in action can, potentially, change life in classrooms for students and teacher alike. It can help students learn how they are smart and can change their perceived status. It can help teachers learn to look for what students can do rather than to look for what they cannot do, to look for what is going right rather than what is going wrong.

🐸   MULTICULTURAL EDUCATION   🐸
AND AN EMPOWERING SCHOOL
CULTURE AND SOCIAL STRUCTURE

- How might the existing structures and norms of school influence the school experiences of students?
- How might these structures facilitate or impede opportunities for all students to become empowered learners?

> Mr. Berke didn't know how crazy I was about the class. He was blind to my young heart and to what he had opened in it. At the end of the year when we were promoted to sixth grade, we were put into tracked classes. I was not in 1A, 1B, or 1C, the top tracks. Mr. Berke placed me in 2A . . . the average group. . . . When I was handed my fifth-grade report card and the letter saying I was promoted to 2A, I went home weeping. . . . [I] cried because I wouldn't be able to learn a foreign language in 2A.[3]

The creation of a school culture where all students are empowered as learners is an extraordinary challenge that requires fundamental rethinking and refeeling of many aspects of school life. Banks suggests that, among other things, assessment, tracking, and teacher expectations must be rethought. Earlier in this chapter we discussed the power of teacher and fellow student expectations. In Chapter 9 we will examine assessment. In this section we will examine a powerful institutional norm—tracking.

[3]From *Long Quiet Highway* (pp. 9–10), by Natalie Goldberg. Copyright © 1993 by Natalie Goldberg. Used by permission of Bantam Books, a division of Bantam Doubleday Dell Publishing Group, Inc.

How and Why Schools Track Students

Tracking is the process whereby students are divided into categories so that they can be assigned in groups to various kinds of classes. . . . Tracking, in essence, is sorting—a sorting of students that has certain predictable characteristics.

First, students are identified in a rather public way as to their intellectual capabilities and accomplishments and separated into a hierarchical system of groups for instruction. Second, these groups are labeled quite openly and characterized in the minds of teachers and others as being of a certain type—high ability, low achieving, slow, average, and so on. Clearly these groups are not equally valued in the school; occasional defensive responses and appearances of special privilege—i.e., small classes, programmed learning, and the like for slower students—rarely mask the essential fact that they are less preferred. Third, individual students in these groups come to be defined by others—both adults and their peers—in terms of these group types. In other words, a student in a high-achieving group is seen as a high-achieving *person,* bright, smart, quick, and in the eyes of many *good.* And those in the low-achieving groups come to be called slow, below average and—often when people are being less careful—dummies, sweathogs, or yahoos. Fourth, on the basis of these sorting decisions, the groupings of students that result, and the way educators see the students in these groups, teenagers are treated by and experience schools very differently. (Oakes, 1985, p. 3)

Think about a school (or classroom) that you attended that used tracking. How and why was it done? What track were you in? Who was in the same track? A different track?

Schools have offered a tracked curriculum for more than seventy-five years. In high schools tracks may be labeled "accelerated," "college prep," "regular," or "basic." Elementary schools and middle schools track, too. Some students are labeled "gifted" while others are diagnosed "learning disabled." In elementary schools children are sometimes tracked into academic and developmental kindergartens; children as young as first grade change classes and are grouped together by perceived ability for reading and math. In elementary schools tracking is sometimes accomplished within single classes. When within-class groupings are used, groups generally choose cute names for themselves; in spite of this, everyone in the class knows who are the bluebirds, bluejays, and buzzards.

Tracking: The Historical Context   At about the beginning of the twentieth century, the immigrant and school populations increased tremendously. Secondary schools became social centers and holding tanks for unemployed and unemployable adolescents; they became symbols for immigrant families of the hope for a better life in the next generation. As student populations grew increasingly diverse, the purpose of education was debated widely. While some believed that "becoming educated" was the same for *every* person, others argued that some curriculum was inappropriate for some students—especially immigrants and girls, who were often considered to be intellectually and morally inferior. Tracking became part of a system of education to "fit the young for their niches" (Powell, Farrar, & Cohen, 1985, p. 247); it "promised something for everyone, but . . . did not promise the same thing for everyone" (Oakes, 1985, p. 21). Ironically, tracking was seen by some as a new kind of equality, an "opportunity for all to receive education as will fit them equally well for their particular life work" (Oakes, p. 34). This idea seems to have had some lasting appeal. In 1994 Sapon-Shevin described a gifted class where the students were studying the stock market. When questioned about the purpose of the curriculum, the teacher responded: "These children are the intellectually elite group and they will be the ones making the most money so they need to learn about the stock market" (Sapon-Shevin, p. 181). To some, cultural capital and investment capital are hard to separate.

Assumptions about Tracking

The existence of tracking has been supported not only by tradition and a notion that schools should prepare students for their life's work, but by several widely-held assumptions about the nature of teaching and learning as well (Oakes, 1985). It is important to examine these assumptions in an effort to understand the nature of tracking and its alternatives.

The first assumption is that students learn better when they are grouped with others who are like them—that smart students learn better when they are with smart students and slow students learn better when grouped with other slow students. Research does not support this assumption. It has never been found that any one group of students benefits, *overall,* from learning in a homogeneous group. Worse yet, it appears that learning in homogeneous groups is least helpful to low and average students and that *achievement may depend much more on classroom environment than on who is in the class.* In Chapter 4 we will explore how to build a classroom environment that maximizes opportunities for all students; in Chapter 6 we will address how to develop learning goals in heterogeneous groups.

The second assumption is that slow students feel better about themselves if they do not have to compare themselves to smart students and that the best way to avoid comparisons is to separate students. This is not true. Ask anyone who has ever been labeled a buzzard and they can tell you that buzzards know they are buzzards, even if they do not come into daily contact with bluebirds. Research indicates that it is being placed in a low track—not being in contact with "smart" kids—that makes students feel negative about themselves and their futures.

The third assumption is that the test scores, recommendations, and parent and student choices that are used to track students are accurate. This is not necessarily true. It is very difficult to develop tests that are without cultural bias, and the reality of standardized testing and the standard "bell" curve is that half of the students taking the test will be identified, at least marginally, as deficient or below average, no matter how much they know or how well they have done on the test. Yet, despite difficulties with tests, poor and minority students are placed in lower tracks more often by recommendations than by test scores, and "African American, Latino, and some Asian students are most likely to be categorized by their supposed 'deficits' in the early grades, whereas White and other Asian students are most likely to be placed in programs emphasizing their 'abilities'" (Nieto, 1992, p. 70). This is not surprising, since, as we have seen, so many things other than ability influence the perceptions of teachers towards students and, therefore, their recommendations about students. Parent and student choice tends to be problematic because choice tends to be informed by test scores or the advice of teachers, guidance counselors, and principals.

The fourth assumption is that it is easier to teach when students are similar in ability. This may actually be true with traditional pedagogy. Throughout this book however, we will develop the knowledge and skills necessary to use more equitable and empowering pedagogy—pedagogy that has the potential to help *all* students learn—so that this assumption will no longer seem true.

What Tracking Looks and Sounds and Feels Like

When students are tracked, they tend to experience school very differently. High-track students are expected to learn high-status academic knowledge; teachers expect these students to work on projects and to acquire important high-status life skills and frames of mind such as critical thinking, self-direction, and creativity. In low-track classes—classes that are populated disproportionately with poor and minority students—students are often not exposed to the kinds of knowledge that high-track students take for granted. These curricular differences make it very difficult for students to move out of low-track courses. Teacher expectations for low-track students tend to be low status also. The life skills teachers target for low-track students include being punctual, conforming to rules and expectations, working quietly, being cooperative, and getting along with others (Bowles & Gintis, 1976; Oakes, 1985).

One might be tempted to conclude that the skills teachers target for different groups of students—the hidden curriculum—are part of a sorting machine that has been designed to socialize students quite effectively into the expectations of their social class and to prepare them for the jobs of that class. Upper-track students are being taught to be proactive leaders; lower-track students are being taught to be passive and compliant workers. If compliance, not critical and creative thinking, is a goal for students in lower tracks, it is doubly tragic. First, these students are obviously being denied access to skills that have traditionally been needed for upward mobility. Second, given the lessons of Levi Strauss and other companies, it is clear that success in the modern world of work requires much more from workers at all levels than passive compliance. However, while passivity may not lead to high levels of work success, passive compliance is useful in schools themselves; passive students are less likely to question the treatment they receive.

Alternatives to Tracking

What the best and wisest parent wants for his own child, that must the community want for all of its children. Any other ideal for our schools is narrow and unlovely; acted upon, it destroys our democracy. (Dewey, 1915/1956, p. 7)

Developing alternatives to tracking means more than business as usual with a new name. It means reorganizing schools to include high expectations for all students, instruction in predominantly heterogeneous groupings, a supportive climate with meaningful interaction between students and adults and among students, and instruction that is dynamic, meaningful, and offers "diverse routes to knowledge" (Wheelock, 1992, p. 149) to diverse students. Will all students achieve equally in these kinds of settings? Probably not, but many more will achieve at higher levels, and the differences will not be determined by the structure of the school itself. Will these changes make a difference in how students experience school? When one school compared students in heterogeneous teams to those grouped homogeneously, it certainly did.

- Only 7% of the students in the heterogeneous core team had ten or more absences per quarter compared with 23% in the control group.
- Thirty-three percent of the students in the heterogeneously grouped team were rated "exemplary" in terms of academic performance compared with 18% in the control group; 34% were rated "below standard" compared with 56% in the control group.
- Discipline referrals to the principal were "greatly reduced" in the heterogeneously grouped team, with teachers reporting that discipline "is not the time-and energy-consuming process it was in the past" (Wheelock, p. 57).

Cooperative Learning as Empowering Pedagogy

Cooperative learning is a pedagogy based on the assumption that heterogeneity and group interaction help create powerful opportunities for learning. Throughout this text we will learn how to use the power inherent in cooperative learning. In this section we will briefly examine concerns that have been raised about ability in relation to cooperative classrooms.

Creating Cooperative Learning Environments That Are Challenging to All Students Critics of cooperative learning sometimes claim that "gifted" students are "held back" by cooperative, heterogeneous, group work. This is possible, especially when group tasks are simple ones that require little discussion and a narrow profile of abilities. The challenge of cooperative learning, as in all instruction, is to create opportunities for learning that empower all students—high achievers, low achievers, and students in the middle. When group tasks are rich, high-achieving students are far less likely to be held back. In fact, it is possible to argue that high-achieving students, because they are most likely to provide elaboration, will learn even more than other students. When the top 5% and 10% of students have been evaluated in heterogeneous cooperative groups, their achievement has been higher than students who are not in cooperative groups (Slavin, 1991, 1995). When researchers (Coleman, Gallagher, & Nelson, 1993; Gallagher & Coleman, 1994) identified five school districts where cooperative learning has been implemented carefully, they concluded that the needs of the gifted could be met using cooperative learning. "Gifted students in this study clearly preferred CL [cooperative learning] to their experience of the 'traditional' teaching-learning method. Their preference for CL in homogeneous settings was unreserved; their preference for CL in any setting was strong" (Gallagher & Coleman, p. 25).

Following is an excerpt of a conversation I had with Steve—a high-achieving student in a heterogeneous tenth-grade English class. Steve is describing a discussion he had with three classmates about a poem. Arthur is a special-needs student who has been "mainstreamed" into the class.

Think of a time when the ideas of others helped you to understand. What was the incident?

Lynda:	In the conversation some people said things like "I don't get it, I don't think the poem means anything." Do you think the conversation helped you understand the poem?
Steve:	Yeah. You like share your feelings, your views, with others and they share theirs. And you put them both together. Other times if you have no idea what a line means and somebody else says something and then it like just clicks to you.
Lynda:	Did that happen in this conversation?
Steve:	Yeah.
Lynda:	Can you give me an example?
Steve:	I remember Arthur saying something about the rain being like the sadness. And it just clicked and a couple of lines just fell into place. I remember that.

Not only does Steve seem unconcerned that Arthur is classified as a special-needs student, he specifically mentions the "good group of kids" that are in this class and how helpful Arthur's contributions were during the group's conversation. Is this class unusual? I hope not. Arthur's teacher has provided high-quality instruction and high teacher expectations, and she continually works to build a sense of acceptance and community. These are essential for all students—including students with disabilities. In later chapters we will again address issues of inclusion and exceptionality.

🐞 A PRACTICAL THEORY: USING THEORY 🐞 AS A FRAMEWORK FOR LEARNING TO LOOK AT CLASSROOMS

In this chapter we have examined ways in which diversity might influence life in classrooms and might affect opportunities for all students to become empowered learners. One key to understanding how diversity impacts life in classrooms is to understand how students view each other.

Collecting Sociometric Data to Learn about Status Differences

One way to learn about classroom life—especially about how students perceive each other and about status differences among students—is to ask students directly about their interpersonal attractions and preferences. Data of this sort, which measures aspects of the social life of the classroom, is called *sociometric data*. Sociometric data provides a different "lense" on classroom life than behavioral data collected through teacher observation does; it can be used to provide teachers with glimpses into the "interpersonal underworld" of student life. Teachers frequently report that they are surprised by the sociometric data they collect.

To collect sociometric data, you must first decide what kinds of interpersonal attraction and status issues you want to know more about. In general, you can collect data that will give you clues about academic status or peer status or both. Once you have decided, you will need to construct a statement or two that will help you gather information. Remember to keep your statements simple. Do not try to learn about too many different areas of status at one time, or both you and your students will get confused. Here are some basic guidelines for the collection of sociometric data.

1. Choose a status issue that you want to know more about. Develop a statement, or statements, that are short and specific. (Figure 3.1 contains examples of statements that might be used to gather information about academic and peer status.)
2. Make sure students know the names of all class members and that a complete list of class names is visible.
3. Assure students that all responses are confidential. Classroom rapport is essential when collecting sociometric data.

Your name: _____

1. Select three students with whom working in a group on
   school work would be a plus for you.

   _____

   _____

   _____

2. Select three students with whom spending time in a social
   group would be a plus for you.

   _____

   _____

   _____

Figure 3.1
Sample statements for collecting data about academic and social status.

4. Explain why you are collecting data and how it will be used. (You might
   collect sociometric data to help you form groups, to plan future activities,
   and so on.)
5. Collect data.

   After you have collected sociometric data, you will need to organize your
data. When data is organized pictorially or graphically, it is called a *sociogram*. The type of sociogram you use will depend on the number of students in the group or class and the number of statements you use. Figures 3.2,
3.3, and 3.4 contain examples of how the same sociometric data might be
represented in different ways. There are advantages and disadvantages to
each. Here are some basic questions you might ask about the data you collect:

- Are there any surprises?
- What characteristics seem to describe isolates?
- What characteristics seem to describe students who are most frequently
  chosen?
- Does high (or low) status seem to be related to gender, race, ethnicity, or
  social class?
- Are there cliques of students who tend to choose each other in relatively
  "closed systems"?
- Is there a high correlation between high academic status and actual aca-
  demic performance?
- Is there a high correlation between academic status and peer (social) status?

	Audrey	John	Brie	Laurel	Mary	Peter	Alice	Muriel	Erin	Kristi	Mae	Dave	Jack	Liza	Kirsten	Ian	Lynn	Liz	Kate
Audrey		x						x									x		
John						x						x				x			
Brie		x			x										x				
Laurel							x			x	x								
Mary			x									x		x					
Peter		x										x				x			
Alice			x					x							x				
Muriel	x													x			x		
Erin	x							x									x		
Kristi				x										x			x		
Mae				x				x	x										
Dave		x				x										x			
Jack					x							x				x			
Liza		x		x	x														
Kirsten	x							x	x										
Ian		x				x						x							
Lynn	x								x							x			
Liz			x	x					x										
Kate		x	x									x							
TOTALS	4	7	4	4	3	3	1	5	4	1	1	6	0	3	2	5	4	0	0

Response statement: Select three students with whom working on schoolwork would be a plus.

Figure 3.2
Sociometric grid for academic status.

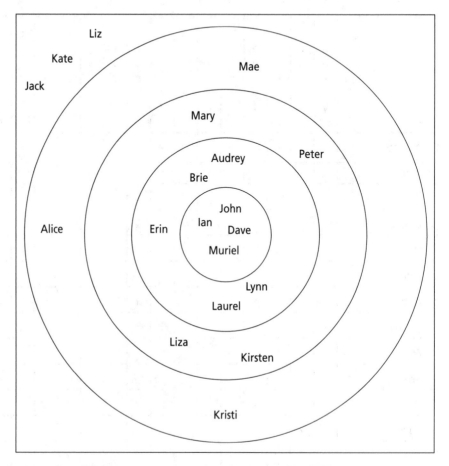

Response statement: Select three students with whom working on schoolwork would be a plus.

Figure 3.3
Target sociogram for academic status.
Note. Students near the center of the target received more peer nominations than students at or near the edge.

Once you have collected sociometric data, you can use it—in combination with social categories, test scores, information about cognitive styles, or students' preferences for subject matter—to assign groups. We examined how to relate basic grouping principles to social categories earlier in this chapter. You can also use sociometric data to help plan behavioral observations. To build a more complete picture of classroom life and a better understanding of how the class is developing as a group, it is helpful to collect sociometric data several times during the school year. Sociometric data is a versatile and valuable source of information about interpersonal life in classrooms.

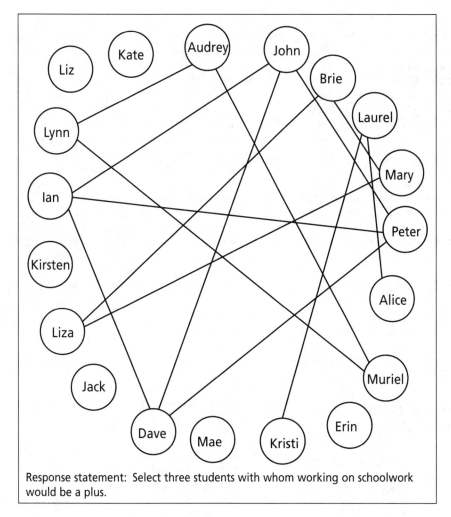

Response statement: Select three students with whom working on schoolwork would be a plus.

Figure 3.4
Circle-Line sociogram for academic status.

Note. The lines in this circle-line sociogram indicate *only* reciprocal choices (i.e., Audrey chose Muriel *and* Muriel chose Audrey).

🐝 WORKING WITH PEERS 🐝

Using *Jigsaw* (Aronson, Blaney, Stephan, Sikes, & Snapp, 1978) to Review Chapter Content

1. Students group in random foursomes. Students count off one to four. Each will specialize in a different section of Chapter 3: #1s specialize in

"Construction of Knowledge"; #2s specialize in "Reduction of Prejudice"; #3s specialize in "Equity Pedagogy"; #4s specialize in "Empowering School Culture and Social Structure."

2. Students each spend a few moments reviewing their own sections (This can be done outside of class.)

3. Students form "practice pairs"—each student joins with a student from a different group who is responsible for the same section of material. Students discuss their material, focusing on the questions: "What is fundamentally important?" and "How might we organize this material so that our group members will remember it?" (Graphic organizers are particularly effective with *Jigsaw.* This stage of the *Jigsaw* might last up to one-half hour.)

4. Reflection and Planning:
   Pair:
   - At the end of their time together, each member of the practice pair shares with his or her partner some aspect of the material that working together helped to clarify.

5. Students move back into their original foursomes. Students each take a few moments to teach their sections of material.

6. Reflection and Planning:
   Group:
   - At the conclusion of the teaching time, each group member, one at a time, shares with each other member:
   - One aspect of the material you presented that I want to think more about is _____.

Using *Simultaneous Stirring Up the Class* to Examine Sociometric Data and Review Status Concepts

1. Students group in random threesomes. Each student in the group is assigned a different one of the three sociometric figures—Figure 3.2, 3.3, or 3.4. Students each spend a few moments studying their assigned figures to answer the questions: "Given the information in this figure, what three students might I want to know more about in order to learn about the status issues in this class?" and "Why do I want to know about these particular students?"

2. Students share ideas in their trios, and together the students develop one list of three students to learn more about.

3. *Based on the information in Chapter 3,* the students work together to develop three questions that they would like to ask to learn more about these students—questions that they think might help them understand the status issues in this particular class. Students must agree on the three students and questions and be able to explain why the questions are important.

4. Reflection and Planning:
   Individual:
   - Students each describe one new idea or point of clarity that they got from working with their groups.

5. The students who examined Figure 3.2 stand and rotate one group clockwise around the room. Students who examined Figure 3.3 stand and rotate two groups clockwise around the room. Students who examined Figure 3.4 stay seated.

6. Students are now in reconstituted groups of three. In these new groups, students are each responsible for sharing the names of their three targeted students and the questions their original group decided were important. Students then work together to develop a new list of three questions that incorporate the best ideas and reasoning of each group member.

7. Reflection and Planning:
   Individual:
   - Students each describe one aspect of this new list that is different from the work they brought with them from their old groups.

8. One student in each group is chosen randomly to report one question and reasoning.

Using Our Memories, *Group Interviews* (Kagan, 1992), Graphic Organizers, and *One-Stay Three-Stray* to Examine Cognitive Preferences, Teacher Expectations, and Status

1. Using a *Group Interview* and the same randomly chosen groups of four that were used for the *Group Interview* in Chapter 2, students each take three minutes to expand their stories about class situations in which they enjoyed and did not enjoy participating. While each student is speaking, other group members "interview" the speaker by asking clarifying and probing questions. Interviews focus on four basic questions: (a) How does cognitive preference influence the kinds of class situations different individuals enjoy? (b) How were teacher expectations conveyed in each setting? (c) How were trust and safety established and maintained (or not established and maintained) in each

setting? and (d) How were status issues perceived in each situation? (Before students begin the *Group Interview*, it is useful if they spend a minute or two thinking, individually, about their experiences in relation to these four questions.) Interviewers may want to take notes.

2. After the *Group Interview*, students spend a few additional minutes discussing each of the four questions and building an understanding of common themes and principles. Then, sifting through the considerable detail that, most likely, will have been generated by the discussions, students work together—preferably with large newsprint and markers—to create a graphic organizer that summarizes information about all four questions.

3. Students count off one to four. All #1s rotate one group clockwise around the room. All #2s rotate two groups clockwise. All #3s rotate three groups clockwise. All #4s remain seated. Students are now in reconstituted groups of four. In these new groups, the #4s use the graphic organizer created by their original groups to summarize the discussion for their new groups. In turn, the #1, #2, and #3 students each tell the #4 people something that was interesting about what they shared and how their groups' conversation was represented.

4. Students move back into their original groups of four. First the #4s share what the "visitors" said they liked. In turn, the #1, #2, and #3 students each summarize what they saw when they "strayed" to other groups.

5. Reflection and Planning:
   Group:
   • Students take a few moments to examine *Group Interview* and *One-Stay Three-Stray*—the structures they have used in their conversations:
   • How might these structures be used to (a) establish high expectations for student participation and (b) influence status expectations?

Using a *One-Minute Paper* and *Corners* (Kagan, 1992) to Reflect on the Dimensions of Multicultural Education

QUESTION: *Of the four dimensions of multicultural education discussed in Chapter 3, which one are you most interested in learning more about? Why?*

1. Each student writes a response.
2. Each of the four *Corners* of the room is designated as the "meeting place" for one dimension.
3. Students move to their corners and learn from others who have expressed the same preference why they chose that particular dimension.
4. An individual in each group might be asked to report two or three reasons that were discussed.

CHAPTER 4

Building an Understanding of the Learning Community

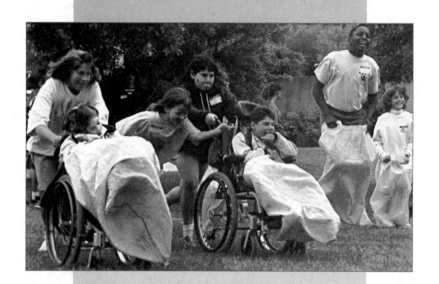

❧ *As you read, you might want to ask yourself:*

What is real learning?

Why do teachers who want to empower their students as learners take the time to build community?

How are values and rules different?

Why do teachers who want to empower their students as learners share influence and decision making with their students?

Why are celebrations important in a learning community?

How might learning communities reach out to include parents and neighborhoods?

Real learning does not happen until students are brought into relationship with the teacher, with each other, and with the subject. We cannot learn deeply and well until a community of learning is created in the classroom. (Palmer, 1983/1993, p. xvi)

In Chapter 1 we examined the power of a cooperative context for learning and living. In Chapter 2 we learned about the importance of shared values. In Chapter 3 we examined how, when students come together to learn, different cognitive styles, expectations, perceptions of status, and the structure of schools can make the building of shared values a challenge. The learning community will be our focus in this chapter. This focus reflects the belief that, for schools to survive and thrive, *learning and community must be essential values in schools.*

Costa describes three values as essential to schools and believes that

> recent efforts to bring intellectual, cooperative, and empowered focus to our schools will prove futile unless we create a school environment that signals the staff, students, and community that the development of the intellect, cooperative decision making, and the enhancement of individual diversity are of basic importance as the school's core values. (Costa, Bellanca, & Fogarty, 1992, p. 93)

Costa's core values—the development of the intellect, cooperation, and enhancement of diversity—complement L. Graves' (1992) definition of a learning community as a place where (a) all students feel they belong and are respected; (b) interaction is ongoing, face-to-face, regular, and focused around common goals; and (c) both cohesion and self-reflection are honored and encouraged. A sense of shared values and community is important at all levels of school life—the school level, the classroom level, and the small-group level. Shared values and community must include not just students or students and teachers, but students, teachers, parents, and surrounding communities alike. Some teachers have assumed that the building of shared values and community is tangential—an affective and perhaps "fluffy" addition—to the real purposes of schooling. Others have assumed that feelings of community will develop automatically if students work together to learn. Neither assumption is true; a sense of community and a focus on learning are essential but not automatic (Breitborde, 1996). In this chapter we will explore some basic principles that are important to understanding and building learning communities. We will focus primarily but not exclusively on the building of learning communities in classrooms. In Chapter 11 we will examine briefly how teachers can reach out to colleagues in efforts to build a sense of professional community.

❧   THE SIGNIFICANCE OF INCLUSION IN   ❧
THE BUILDING OF A CLASSROOM
LEARNING COMMUNITY

Especially in the early stages of building a learning community, individuals are concerned about trust and about finding their places—about feeling included. As described in Chapter 2, questions such as "Who will notice me?"

"Whom will I accept?" What do I have to do to fit in?" and "Do I want to fit in?" are often indications that individuals are concerned with feeling included.

> Everyone is eligible for inclusion in a truly cooperative community; no one is excluded because of race, religion, personality quirks, differences of perspective, or nonconventional attitudes or interests. In addition, if I feel I belong, I know . . . that I contribute something that is necessary to the group and is valued by the other members. I also know other members well enough to value and respect their unique contributions. Together we define who we are as a group. This definition may change, evolve, grow, but we construct its meaning together out of what we all have to give. This means we must find out what resources each of us brings and communicate this positively to the group as a whole, [and] not only at the beginning of building the group. . . . If this process is thorough, members of a community are seen as colleagues rather than as competitors. (L. Graves, 1992, p. 65)

For everyone to be eligible for inclusion in a learning community, it is important that differences—such as differences in cognitive styles, intelligence profiles, race, ethnicity, and social class—be viewed as *resources* to be balanced, reconciled, and integrated into a whole rather than isolated, "melted," or reduced by compromise or averaging. Frequent student-to-student contact—where students genuinely get to know each other as individuals—is essential to the building of inclusion. It is through frequent contact and self-disclosure that students move away from responses that are (a) based on categories and social comparisons and (b) evaluated along "better or worse" dimensions towards responses that are (a) based on personal characteristics and (b) evaluated using "same or different" dimensions (Miller & Harrington, 1990).

Building Feelings of Inclusion in a Class—Getting to Know You

Building feelings of inclusion, which are essential to building community, means providing intentional opportunities for students to learn about each other as individuals—about each other's lives, preferences, and talents. Simple fun and games—activities which are not integral to daily classroom life and the learning goals of students—are not optimal. *Inclusive learning communities are best built with activities that are authentic and relevant to the ages of the students and connected to meaningful learning goals and to the curriculum.* These kinds of focused activities are important throughout the year and, because of the hierarchical nature of interpersonal needs, are crucial in the early stages of classroom community building and when class membership changes.

Think of a classroom situation you enjoyed. (You could use the same one that you described in Chapter 2.) How well did you know the other members of the class? How did you get to know them?

To better understand how these types of activities might be integrated into the curriculum and daily classroom life, take a moment to visit Linda, Dana, Meg, and Susan in their classrooms.

In Linda's first-grade class, the children know a lot about each other—they know about each other's pets, siblings, and favorite flavors of ice cream. Each week they sit together in a circle and share information about an aspect of their lives. Often the topic for their sharing is related to a theme they are exploring in their work together. For instance, early in the year, after reading a story about siblings, they collected data about how many brothers and sisters each has. They used a bar graph to represent "how many" brothers and sisters; they used a Venn Diagram to show who has a brother, who has a sister, who has both a brother and a sister, and who has neither. Throughout the year, they learn many things about each other and many ways to report what they know.

Dana devotes a bulletin board in her fifth-grade classroom to "Stuff About Us." On the first day of school, she tacked a picture of her cat on this board. She told the class how much she liked her cat and then invited students each to place something on the board that was important to them. Throughout the year students are encouraged to bring in different important "stuff." The "Stuff About Us" board changes all the time. It includes pictures of visiting relatives, programs from ballet recitals, papers that students are particularly proud of, ticket stubs from sporting events, craft projects, and so forth.

Meg devotes a bulletin board in her seventh-grade classroom to "Classroom Classified." She wants the students in her seventh-grade team to reflect on the resources, needs, and learning goals they each bring to the classroom; she wants them to know about the resources, needs, and goals of others as well. The sections in the "Classifieds" include "Help Offered," "Help Wanted," and "Traveling Towards." Meg is working to build a learning community in which everyone has learning goals and where it is safe for everyone to state what he or she is good at and what he or she needs help with.

Early in the year, Susan wanted her third-year Spanish students to practice speaking and to learn more about each other. Susan used *Carousel* (Kagan, 1992) to structure an opportunity for each student to learn about the summer vacation of every other student. She divided her class into groups of five, and students numbered off one to five. On Monday, all the #1s took two minutes to tell about their vacations to the other members of their groups. The #1s then moved to the next group and repeated their two-minute descriptions. They continued to move, after each description, until they had described their vacations in each group. On Tuesday, all the #2s described their vacations, on Wednesday the #3s talked, and so on. By Friday, all the students in the class had heard about each other's vacations and had opportunities to practice and polish their stories and language skills.

How do you think it might feel to be a student in one of these classrooms? How do you think it might feel to be the teacher?

Building Feelings of Inclusion in a Class—The Class Identity

Once students begin to get to know each other as individuals, inclusion involves beginning to build a whole-class identity. Class mottoes, banners, songs, and group-created poems, if age and subject appropriate, serve this purpose well; so do noncompetitive celebrations and "events." Daily rituals such as singing, story time, or class meetings that focus on sharing; regular events such as cleaning up a neighborhood park, buddy reading with younger students, or poetry parties; and rites of passage such as the fifth-grade concert, the seventh-grade camping trip, and the tenth-grade community project all help to symbolize and sustain feelings of inclusion and whole-class identity while simultaneously incorporating an appropriate emphasis on learning.

Many teachers are surprised when they realize that the building of a whole-class identity is a process that must continue, simultaneously with the use of small cooperative groups, throughout the year. A few "getting to know you" activities in September are not sufficient to build and sustain a feeling of inclusive community throughout the year. In addition to mottoes, rituals, and events, *informal* learning groups are also used to help build and sustain a sense of the classroom as a learning community; these provide variety and balance for long-term, *formal* cooperative groups. The use of informal cooperative groups will be examined in Chapter 5.

Building Inclusion Throughout the School and Community

Daily rituals, regular events, and rites of passage can often be used to help build a sense of community that encompasses an entire school. An entire school, for instance, might explore a common theme or participate in an ongoing service project. Noncompetitive field days, all-school concerts and musicals, cross-grade and cross-discipline projects all have the potential to help build an inclusive sense of community based on learning.

In the following scenario, when Jean and Lynda work together, they plan, within the structure of their regular class schedules, to provide students with an interesting cross-discipline and cross-grade collaboration and to create a whole-school celebration.

Think of the different schools you attended from kindergarten through twelfth grade. How well did you know students in different grades? How often did different classes do things together (other than watch movies)?

Jean is a physical education teacher. Lynda teaches music. Each year, for three weeks, they combine their classes and students, and everyone in their elementary school participates in a Dancebration. They start with square dancing. Keeping groups as heterogeneous as possible, vests or "pinnies" are used to designate lead dancers and younger students assume lead positions as often as older students. When the older partners use tricks—such as rolled shirt cuffs and handkerchiefs tied to wrists—to help the younger ones identify their left hands, "allemande left" becomes a meaningful movement sequence for six-year-olds and a meaningful teaching experience for ten-year-olds. Students learn to box step and they learn the Charleston, Jitter Bug, Twist, Bunny Hop, and Limbo. Dancebration has become a proud school tradition. The entire school has "dress-up days" to coincide with square dancing, fifties music, and the like. These themes have spilled over into art class, social studies, concerts, and other events. Students invite their classroom teachers and their parents to dance; the principal, school nurse, and secretary participate also. As students grow older, they look forward to being "the teachers." Parents report that students practice at home and even waltz at family weddings (Baloche & Blasko, 1992).

With careful planning, school-based learning communities can be expanded to include parents and community members. For instance, as part of a study of numbers, an entire elementary school might explore the concept

Think of the different schools you attended from kindergarten through twelfth grade. Were parents welcome? What roles did they play in the life of the school?

of "one million" and enlist members of the community to help them read one million pages; families might be invited into a school to work with their children to create books based on family histories and traditions (McCaleb, 1994); or, as an alternative to a competitive science fair, a "Family Science Festival" can be organized to encourage families to work together in a hands-on exploration of kitchen chemistry (Lewis, Schaps, & Watson, 1995). Using community members as visiting experts or tutors, and organizing community-service projects are other avenues that can help build and extend a learning community. The key to involving parents and community members in learning communities is the intentional development of opportunities that are authentic, diverse, inclusive, and noncompetitive.

THE SIGNIFICANCE OF CONTROL AND INFLUENCE IN THE BUILDING OF A CLASSROOM LEARNING COMMUNITY

Democracy is much broader than . . . a method of conducting government. . . . It is . . . a way of life. The keynote of democracy as a way of life . . . [is] the necessity for the participation of every mature human being in formation of the values that regulate the living of men together. . . . The foundation of democracy is faith in the capacities of human nature; faith in human intelligence and in the power of pooled and cooperative experience. . . . Faith that . . . each individual has something to contribute, whose value can be assessed only as it enters into the pooled intelligence constituted by the contributions of all. (Dewey, 1968, pp. 57–60)

As individuals begin to feel included in the learning community, they tend to become increasingly concerned with issues of communication, decision making, control, influence, and power. As described in Chapter 2, questions such as "Am I competent?" "Will my voice be heard?" "What role can I play?" are often signs that individuals are concerned with issues of control and influence. These questions are fundamental to classroom life and, whether or not a teacher chooses to address them directly, they affect basic behavioral patterns and daily classroom management. Dreikurs (Dreikurs, Grunwald, & Pepper, 1982), for instance, indicates that misbehavior is directly related to issues of inclusion and influence, that students (a) want to belong (to be included) and to be recognized (to have influence) and (b) will misbehave if they cannot get recognition in positive ways. Glasser (1986) believes that behavior is deeply influenced by an individual's need for community and that all individuals have needs (a) to belong (to be included), (b) to feel powerful and be free (to have influence), and (c) to have fun.

When members of a classroom community are concerned with issues of influence, they tend to challenge classroom norms—often by focusing on the significance and fairness of rules and procedures. Issues of influence and control manifest in relation to academic work when students express concerns about assignments, time requirements, responsibilities, and the like. Conflict, or storming, is common when issues of influence and control are dominant. Teachers often become anxious when conflicts arise and when students question norms, procedures, and rules. As we learned in Chapter 2, however, conflict is necessary—it is developmentally appropriate—in the life of a group. Students and classrooms cannot develop and mature without conflict and questioning. Empowering teachers know this and help their students (a) learn to share influence for norm building and decision making and (b) learn the skills necessary to communicate their differences and manage their interpersonal conflicts productively.

Building Shared Influence Through the Shared Development of Rules and Values

> If we want children to make good values their own over the long haul—then there is no substitute for giving them the chance to become actively involved in deciding what kind of people they want to be and what kind of classroom or school they want to have. (Kohn, 1993, p. 11)

> Rules [imposed by external constraint] . . . remain external to the child's spirit. . . . Rules due to mutual agreement and cooperation, on the contrary, take root inside the child's mind. (Piaget, 1965, p. 362)

One way teachers might share influence with students is by involving them in the development of rules and in an exploration of the values behind these rules. Sharing influence with students does not meaning abdicating responsibility, and teachers who are skilled at sharing influence with students are careful to communicate what is "nonnegotiable."

As you read the next set of scenarios, notice how the teachers share influence and simultaneously structure their activities to communicate certain standards for bottom-line behaviors.

Think about that classroom situation you enjoyed. Were there rules? What were they? Were you involved in establishing these rules?

In Sue's second-grade class the process of shared influence is initiated early in the year with a discussion of the reasons for rules. Sue then has students brainstorm rules they think they might want. In the spirit of true brainstorming, Sue accepts and records all suggestions. In the beginning, many of these rules, such as "Don't run in the hall," are stated negatively. After a couple of weeks, Sue asks her students if there are things they *should* do; then she helps her class to gradually change negative rules into positive ones. Next, she asks students to group and categorize similar rules and helps students develop some general guidelines based on these categories. "We want our classroom to be a clean and quiet place where we can raise our hands and listen to others. We want it to be friendly and fun" is the statement Sue and her students developed to express the values and rules of their classroom (N. Graves & T. Graves, 1990).

In Kim's sixth-grade class she asks her students to develop rules that will help the class. These are the rules they developed together: (a) "Get our work done," (b) "Feel safe at school," and (c) "Be glad we're in school" (Lickona, 1990).

Ralph begins the process of rule building in his seventh-grade class by asking students what an ideal classroom would be like and how people would act so that the classroom would be safe and enjoyable for everyone. The "students typically talk about being helpful, quiet in class, courteous toward others" (Lickona, 1990, p. 5). This description of the ideal becomes the basis for the creation of class rules.

Early in the year Chris' eleventh-grade students study the play *Twelve Angry Men*. Chris uses detailed observation sheets and the movie to help students analyze behaviors that facilitate or block discussion and collaboration. The students use this analysis as a reference point for the development of rules that will inform their own classroom behavior and help them to build a community of learners capable of substantive discussion and cooperative decision making.

At Memorial High the overarching theme for the academic year has been democracy. Early in the year the students studied the constitution; among other things, they read original sources, researched the biographies of the participants in the original Constitutional Convention, and examined the economic circumstances that brought the colonies together. They held their own convention and drafted a constitution—complete with a bill of rights. They used this constitution and bill of rights throughout the year to guide their own community.

When teachers and students work together to formulate rules, this not only enhances feelings of shared influence and responsibility but also tends to produce more dispersed and diverse friendship patterns (Epstein, 1983). An increase in diversity of friendship patterns suggests a decrease in status issues; this is particularly significant when diverse populations of students are asked to work together cooperatively.

Think about your own family when you were an adolescent. Were there rules? What were they?

In addition to building perceptions of shared influence and diverse friendship patterns, the essential values behind the rules tend to become more apparent when rules are formulated jointly. Lickona (1991) suggests two essential values: (a) respect—for self, for others, and for the environment; and (b) responsibility—for self, for others, and for the environment. Dacey (1989) suggests that there may be a qualitative difference between a focus on values and a focus on rules. In a study of families with adolescent children, he found that the parents of highly creative adolescents had, on average, only one specific rule for behavior, while the parents of less-creative adolescents had, on average, six rules. This focus on values was described by one parent as: "I can't think of any rules we've had for our kids—we just tried to help each to become a *mensch* (Yiddish for truly admirable person)" (Dacey, 1989, p. 266). These parents of creative children worked to develop, through modeling and discussion, a well-defined set of values. They tended to expect their children to make decisions based on these values, and they helped their children reflect on the decisions they made.

Building Shared Influence through the Use of Class Meetings to Reflect on Rules and Values

Merely formulating rules and expressing shared values with students is not enough; regular reflection on these rules and values is also needed. A class meeting (Glasser, 1969) is one way to structure reflection, communicate perceived discrepancies between values and behaviors, and problem solve.

In general, class meetings (a) provide a time when a whole class meets together for an interactive discussion that is not directly related to academic content; (b) are conducted, ideally, in a circle so that everyone can make eye contact; and (c) are held both at regularly scheduled times and in response to special needs. Class meetings are not magical; they are hard work for everyone. The keys to successful class meetings are communication, trust, and shared influence; all individuals in the circle must feel that they have the right to contribute and that their contributions are treated with respect.

In their classrooms Patti, Jose, Jim, and Fran all use class meetings to help resolve discrepancies between expressed values and observed behaviors. As you read, notice that the students are an essential part of the problem-solving process—not just part of the problem.

When winter came, Patti's second graders began to have difficulty with the coat closet. There were so many coats, hats, and boots that the area was a mess; students began pushing each other in an effort to get to their belongings, and some even missed the bus because they couldn't find their belongings at the end of the day. Patti held a class meeting to discuss possible solutions. She wrote student suggestions on the board and, together, the class decided on a plan. Hooks in the closet would each be labeled with names, and students would place their belongings on or under their hooks. Students who did not use their own hooks would keep their belongings at their desks for the day. The plan worked; the coat area was well maintained, the pushing stopped, and students got to their buses on time (Lickona, 1991).

Jose became concerned that his seventh-grade class was getting too noisy and that students were not listening to each other. He held a class meeting and explained that while he was annoyed by this, he was also annoyed that he was spending time reminding them to be more quiet and polite. Several students admitted that they, too, were annoyed—by the noise, by the lack of peer respect, and by Jose's "nagging." The class discussed how the basic values of respect and responsibility were related to noise levels and listening and agreed to pay more attention to these issues during the next week. Jose noticed considerable improvement, and at the next class meeting, students reported that they did, too.

Holding a large ball of yarn, Jim begins a class meeting by saying: "Sometimes I notice that some members of our class are very quiet during class meeting and others talk a lot more. I wonder why that is?" As soon as a student responds, Jim holds the end of the yarn in his own hand and rolls the yarn ball to the student. When a second student speaks, the first student holds onto a piece of the yarn but rolls the ball again. The conversation, and the rolling of the ball of yarn, continue for about five minutes. The yarn creates a visual representation of who talked, and the class is then able to use the web to focus and continue their discussion. Jim calls his technique *Yarn Yarn* (Kagan, 1992).

Fran was concerned that his tenth-grade students were not completing their homework and that his students were not taking enough responsibility for their own learning. He held a class meeting; the first thing he did at the meeting was to tell the students that when they came to class unprepared, he felt less excited about teaching. They seemed genuinely surprised that their work or lack of work affected his attitude. Several students then described how difficult it was for them to enter into collaborative work if some members of the class had not done their work—how they felt both "geekful" for having done the work and resentful that others had not. Everyone in the class admitted that sometimes they came to class less than optimally prepared, and they explored reasons why this happened. By the end of the meeting, students agreed to take more responsibility for their work; Fran agreed to help students plan ahead by providing them with longer-range unit plans and to ask for student input when setting due dates for large assignments.

Building Shared Influence through the Use of Peer Negotiation and Mediation to Resolve Conflicts

Think about two interpersonal conflicts you were involved in—one that you felt you managed well and another in which you were not as pleased with your own response. What did you do differently in these two situations?

Although interpersonal conflict is inevitable and even necessary for development and learning, students are often not taught directly how to communicate their differences and manage their conflicts constructively. Learning how to communicate differences and manage conflict is essential to helping students learn to (a) increase control over their own behavior, (b) build shared responsibility and influence, and (c) establish a learning community. A six-step peer-negotiation and mediation procedure is one way students can learn to communicate their differences and manage their conflicts. In a six-step procedure, students learn to

1. Define what they want
2. Describe their feelings
3. Explain the reasons underlying those wants and feelings
4. Reverse perspectives in order to view the conflict from both sides
5. Generate at least three possible win-win agreements
6. Agree on a course of action (D. Johnson & R. Johnson, 1991, 1995)

In Figures 4.1 and 4.2, students are following these six basic steps to resolve conflicts with their peers.

Depending on the age of students, the overall school structure, and the subject matter of the classroom, students can learn and practice these steps in regularly scheduled, "stand-alone" lessons or integrated into academic content. These two methods are illustrated by Kecia and Laurie.

 To help her students learn to resolve conflicts using the six-step procedure, Kecia spends a few moments each day directly teaching the *specific skills* that her students need to use to negotiate successfully. Among other things she has helped her students (a) learn to distinguish between facts and feelings and extend their feeling vocabulary; (b) practice "I messages" and listening skills; and (c) generate alternative resolutions to interpersonal problems and recognize good resolutions.

Laurie, a tenth-grade English teacher, knows that conflicts are essential in literature—that it is the conflicts in a novel that capture your attention and hold your interest. She integrates conflict-resolution training into her teaching by utilizing the conflicts imbedded in novels to help her students learn negotiation and mediation procedures. As they study a novel, they (a) examine incidents of conflict within the novel; (b) analyze the positions and interests of the characters involved; and (c) apply negotiation and peer-mediation procedures to write scripts and role-play constructive resolutions to these conflicts (Stevahn, D. Johnson, & R. Johnson, 1996).

The situation:

It is a rainy day, and Kecia's class is staying in for recess. Tommy and Tomeka both want to use the computer; Tommy wants to play a game, and Tomeka wants to make a birthday card for her father.

They have been learning—through regular instruction and practice—how to negotiate their own conflicts; they decide that negotiation is the appropriate way to resolve their present difficulties.

Step 1:

Tommy: I want to use the computer.
Tomeka: I want to use the computer, too.

Step 2:

Tommy: I feel frustrated because I haven't been able to use the computer all week.
Tomeka: I've been waiting a long time, too, and I am worried.

Step 3:

Tommy: I'm frustrated because we have this new game and everyone else has gotten to play it but me.
Tomeka: I'm worried because today is my father's birthday. I haven't made him a card yet, and I want to use the computer to make the picture.

Step 4:

Tommy: So, you need to use the computer to make your dad's birthday card?
Tomeka: Gee, you haven't had a chance to try the new game yet? Wow, what a shame, it's neat.

Steps 5 and 6:

Tommy: Go ahead—since today is your dad's birthday.
Tomeka: Thanks.
Tommy: Do you want help?
Tomeka: No. I really want to tell my dad I did this all by myself.
Tommy: OK. But if you get done before the end of recess, can I have the computer to play the game?
Tomeka: Yeah, sure.

Figure 4.1
Example of a six-step peer-negotiation session.

When teaching students how to negotiate and mediate their conflicts, it is important to allow them to practice their skills regularly with the use of nonthreatening material. The use of nonthreatening material is crucial. Teachers sometimes wait until the heat of the moment to try to teach the skills of negotiation. Negotiation is best learned as a routine and is best practiced with material that does not have a built-in emotional content for students.

The situation:

Fran and Terry are quite upset. Fran had a serious disagreement with a friend and told Terry, another friend, the story. A couple of days later, Fran realized that several students not only knew details of the story that only Terry should have known, but that many details were exaggerated as well. In unpleasant language, Fran accuses Terry of being a big mouth.

In addition to learning to negotiate their own conflicts, all the students in Fran and Terry's school have learned how to mediate conflicts for their peers. They go to Jesse, one of the two designated mediators for the day.

Jesse: Fran and Terry, do you both want me to mediate your conflict?
Fran and Terry: Yeah.

Steps 1 and 2:

Jesse (who decides that Fran and Terry are still angry and need to cool off):
I want both of you to fill out the mediation form. You each need to describe what you think the conflict is and how you feel about it.

After a few moments have passed, Jesse brings Fran and Terry back together. Fran starts.

Fran: I thought when I told you my story that we were having a private conversation. I am embarrassed and angry to find out that everybody knows about me and Jordan.

Terry: I am embarrassed and angry, too. I told Chris about you and Jordan, but I didn't expect Chris to tell everybody else *and* exaggerate the details besides. But I am also angry at you. You didn't even ask me what happened. You just accused me of blabbing and then threatened me besides.

Jesse: Terry, what do you want?
Terry: Well, first of all, I want to explain to Fran what I think happened.
Jesse: OK.

Step 3:

Terry: I talked to Chris because Chris is having a similar difficulty. I thought your story might help. I never dreamed Chris would tell anybody else—much less exaggerate the story. I guess I should not have told Chris; but Fran, I thought we were better friends than for you to say those things to me.

Jesse: Fran, what do you want?
Fran: I want to tell Terry how ridiculous I feel that none of Jordan's friends are talking to me—they think I am spreading rumors, and I'm not. I don't spread rumors, and I thought that Terry was.

Jesse: Can you each describe what you think the other is feeling?

Figure 4.2
Example of a six-step peer-mediation session.

Step 4:

Fran: I think Terry is angry at me for my accusations, and I think Terry is probably angry at Chris for spreading rumors and for violating their friendship.

Terry: I think Fran is angry at me for violating our friendship and isn't sure
what to do about those rumors.

Step 5:

Jesse: What do you each think you can do?

Terry: Well, I could talk with Chris. I could also talk with Jordan and say that
Fran didn't say vicious things.

Fran: I guess I could talk with Jordan and try to explain that I didn't say
those things—but I'm not sure Jordan would listen.

Terry: Maybe we could both talk to Jordan at different times. If I went and
talked first, maybe Jordan would be more likely to listen to you.

Fran: OK. Terry, I also need you to understand how upset I was that you
talked with Chris at all.

Terry: And I need you to understand how upset I was that you accused me
of spreading rumors.

Step 6:

Jesse: So what can you two do?

Fran: Well Terry, I am sorry that I didn't ask you what happened before I
went off.

Terry: And I really am sorry that I talked with Chris—just like you must be
sorry you talked to me. I guess we had better speak with Jordan
soon—but it is going to take some time to repair the damage.

Figure 4.2
(continued)

When students are learning basic negotiation skills, they must learn to determine (a) what conflicts are negotiable and what conflicts are not negotiable because they violate basic values and (b) when it is appropriate to negotiate conflicts, when peer mediation is a good option, and when teacher or principal arbitration is necessary. In classrooms where shared responsibility and influence are *not* the norm, and students have *not* been taught how to manage their own conflicts skillfully, arbitration is common. When students receive careful skill training in peer negotiation and mediation, the need for arbitration tends to decrease. In one study, for instance, once students developed skills in negotiation and mediation, the frequency of student-to-student conflicts that had to be managed by a teacher dropped by 80% and the number of conflicts that were referred to the principal dropped by 95% (D. Johnson & R. Johnson, 1995).

Building Shared Influence through Shared Decision Making about Academic Issues

Think of a time you were able to make significant decisions about your own academic learning. What was the situation? Were you pleased with the decisions you made?

Teachers can invite students to share academic influence about what, how, in what depth, and why they learn. Sharing influence through shared academic decision making is potentially quite powerful. Various studies indicate that when students are given some choices about their learning, they (a) tend to complete more learning tasks (Wang & Stiles, 1976); (b) spend more time engaged in academic work (Rainey, 1965); (c) produce work that is considered "more creative" (Amabile and Gitomer, 1984); (d) develop more sophisticated reasoning strategies (Cobb et al., 1991; Yackel, Cobb, & Wood, 1991); and (e) are more interested in pursuing similar work at a later time (Amabile, 1983; Boggiano et al., 1992). Shared academic decision making, like shared rule development, does not mean that teachers abdicate responsibility for academic decision making; teachers who are skilled at sharing academic decisions are also careful to develop boundaries for these decisions.

Notice how the teachers in the following examples structure decision making—within boundaries—for both what and how students will learn.

Brenda is getting ready to begin a unit on Native Americans. She asks her students what they want to learn about Native Americans. She writes down all their ideas on big chart paper, uses this information to inform her planning, and refers to it throughout the unit.

Joyce announces to her fourth grade: "Here are five books that are available for us to read in our literature study groups. Look through them this week, and on Friday we'll decide together which one to read next."

Rich begins his unit planning by asking: "What's the *most* exciting way we could study this next unit?" If, together, he and his students decide that their "most exciting way" is not feasible, he asks: "Okay, what's the *next* most exciting way we could study this?" (Lickona, 1991, p. 148)

Building Shared Influence Throughout the School and Community

Just as students and teachers can share influence in a classroom, shared influence can be expanded to include teachers and administrators throughout a school or parents and community members as well. Merely inviting others to participate in aspects of school life does not necessarily suggest the sharing of influence; issues of resources, respect, and status are crucial. Inviting parents to serve hot dogs is not enough. Parents and community members must believe that their voices will be heard and respected and that they have important roles to play. Projects such as family science festivals and family history books are successful when schools provide the resources for all families—regardless of income, language differences, and the like—to participate equally in activities that are designed to validate and dignify parents, children, and parents and children learning together. When schools, parents, and children plan these kinds of projects jointly, the sharing of influence is even more significant.

🐾   THE SIGNIFICANCE OF AFFECTION,   🐾 APPRECIATION, AND CARING IN THE BUILDING OF A CLASSROOM LEARNING COMMUNITY

As individuals feel more included and influential and learn to handle their differences and conflicts skillfully, honestly, and empathically, they become increasingly concerned with issues of interpersonal affection, appreciation, caring, and interdependence. As described in Chapter 2, questions such as "Who will like me?" and "Whom will I feel close to?" are often related to these issues. Accomplishing significant goals, building shared memories, creating a joint history, celebrating good times, and reaching out to others—in both good times and bad—are all important aspects of community building that are related to appreciation and caring, and these need to be carefully integrated into classroom life.

> If we had to pick a logical setting in which to guide children towards caring about, empathizing with, and helping other people, it would be a place where they would regularly come into contact with their peers and where some sort of learning is already taking place. The school is such an obvious choice that one wonders how it could be that the active encouragement of prosocial values and behavior—apart from occasional exhortations to be polite—plays no part in the vast majority of American classrooms. (Kohn, 1991, p. 499)

Building Feelings of Interpersonal Appreciation and Caring—Learning How to Say Nice Things

Learning to say nice things and learning to express public appreciation are important to constructing a public narrative about community and caring; learning these skills also helps students build authentic examples of these important behaviors. It is not sufficient to assume that students know how to say nice things to each other in even the most superficial ways. In Chapters 8 and 9, when we examine reflection and planning, we will explore ways students might learn to express appreciation to their peers within the context of learning in small groups. Building opportunities for expressions of caring and appreciation into whole-class special events and into routines are important also.

In the following scenarios Julie, Jose, and Ravi all develop routines to provide students with opportunities to say and hear nice things. Tara uses a special event to help her students learn to express appreciation.

Julie uses morning rug time in her kindergarten class to celebrate "the person of the week." Every child in the class has the opportunity to be "special" for a whole week. When it was Juanita's week, for instance, she brought something to share each day—a baby picture, a picture of her sister, a favorite toy, and so forth. Julie wrote "All about Juanita" in a special, teacher-made big book that Juanita took home at the end of the week. Each day all the base groups (see Chapter 5 to learn more about base groups) put their heads together and talked about what they liked about Juanita. Julie wrote each group's contribution in Juanita's book. Among other things children said that Juanita "is funny," "has a nice dog," "is a good helper," and "always remembers her homework."

At the end of the week, in his class meetings, Jose sets time aside for students to share appreciations. He usually begins; he models the process by saying: "I appreciated it when ___ did ___." With practice, his students have become quite good at expressing their appreciations and seem to enjoy both thinking of positive, descriptive things to say about their peers and hearing what others say about them.

Ravi keeps a box in his room labeled "Good Stuff That Happens Here." Students are encouraged to notice when their peers are being helpful and caring, to write about these incidents in descriptive language, and to place their "stories" in the box. Periodically Ravi opens this box and reads the contents to the class.

At the beginning of February, in preparation for a Valentine's Day celebration, Tara gives each student an opportunity to decorate a plain paper lunch bag. These bags are hung on a bulletin board called "Things We Like About Each Other." Each day every student in the class thinks about two designated classmates and writes a sentence of appreciation about each one. During the day, Tara helps students edit their sentences, and they rewrite them on strips of colorful paper. At the end of the day, Tara collects the strips; she reads each one again, places it in the appropriate bag, and ties the bags shut with colorful ribbon. By Valentine's Day every child's bag has been filled with a sentence of appreciation from every other child in the class and, instead of exchanging commercially produced cards, each of Tara's students receives a bag full of nice things his or her classmates have written about that student. Kira's sentences, for instance, include "I like Kira because she is creative and kind to other people"; "Kira is nice, thoughtful, and cute"; "Kira is friendly"; "Dear Kira, I think you are good at math"; "Kira, you are polite, pretty, and nice to other people. I like you"; "I like you Kira because you never make anyone feel bad"; and "Kira is a great person."

Building Feelings of Interpersonal Appreciation and Caring—Learning How to Build Memories and Celebrate

Shared memories, celebrations, and events are essential to the building of interpersonal appreciation, affection, and community. Memories might be shared and "stored" in Nostalgia Corners, on Class Time Lines (Moorman & Dishon, 1983), or through collections of pictures on a special bulletin board. A sense of class or school history is important; a historic context helps a group understand how "we got to where we are." Part of shared history is shared good times. It is essential that members of a learning community work together to share good times and celebrate success.

Think back to your own school experiences. What celebrations do you remember?

Class celebrations often involve planned events and special occasions. Holidays and seasonal celebrations are wonderful opportunities to build memories and celebrate. Never underestimate the power of events such as Halloween or Thanksgiving to help bring joy into a learning community.

Events such as Backwards Day, Hat Day, Weird Sox Day, and Fifties Day can be fun, noncompetitive opportunities for students to express and build appreciation of abilities and talents that might not typically be emphasized in daily schoolwork. Sometimes events that seem to be unplanned are a genuine treat and an important way to build a sense of appreciation. Sharing learnings from a unit or project is an obvious choice when planning celebrations that center on learning. A class might share its successes with the class next door, at a home for the elderly, or at a community center. These types of sharings help students develop a sense of pride in their class and work, provide opportunities for students to learn important planning skills, and create opportunities for community outreach as well.

The following scenarios illustrate how three teachers use academic content to build memories and celebrate learning.

Angela and her sixth-grade students enjoy their study of poetry and decide to transform their classroom into a sixties coffee house and invite parents to a poetry reading. They use tie-dyes, fringe, dark lighting, and flowers to create the mood; students provide the entertainment with poetry readings and performances of both class favorites and original work.

Sherry and her chemistry students celebrate "Mole Day" on October 23rd (10-23). "Poetry, music, comic strips, cooking, drawing, painting, singing, and woodcarving are just some of the media that have been utilized. . . . Some understanding of the mole concept must be incorporated . . . [and projects have included] "The Lincoln Mole-Memorial," "A Bat-Mole-Bile," "Great Mole-ments in Chemistry History," and "The Mole-A-Lisa." . . . Projects are displayed throughout [the school building]" (Berman-Robinson, 1991, p. 999).

George enjoys planning "unplanned" celebrations when he senses his seventh-grade English students have been working together well. He likes to read short stories to his students, and they enjoy being read to. When his students walk into his classroom and see that the lights are out and there is a candle flickering on his desk, they know they are in for a special treat.

Field trips and other out-of-school events are often quite powerful ways to build a sense of community. Remember Steve in Chapter 3—the student who described how great his tenth-grade English class was and how the students were really good friends? I asked him how he got to be friends with everyone in the class.

Lynda: How did that happen?
Steve: I don't know, but it was just some of the activities that just brought us together.
Lynda: Do you remember any of them?
Steve: Well, last night we all went on a field trip together.

The field trip that Steve mentioned was a trip to see a special movie in the city. Steve, his classmates, and their teacher planned and enjoyed this event together and, one suspects, they will all remember it for a long time.

Building Feelings of Interpersonal Appreciation and Caring—Learning How to Help When the Going Gets Rough

Think back to your own school situations. Were you ever in a class where something very sad happened to another student (or to you)? How did the class respond?

In classroom learning communities, members need to learn to express appreciation, affection, and caring for each other in bad times as well as good times. Carol, for instance, knew that the students in her class were learning to care about each other when, one day, a student came up to her and said: "We need to be extra nice to ____ today because she is worried because ____." A community circle can be used, not just to express appreciation in the good times, but for problem solving and to express support during the bad times. A classroom community can work together, not just to build pride and share successes, but to provide needed services in the community as well.

Building Community Partnerships—Learning How to Care for the "Children We Share"

> The way schools care about children is reflected in the way schools care about the children's families. . . . When parents, teachers, students, and others view one another as partners in education, a caring community forms around students and begins its work. . . . As support from school, family, and community accumulates, significantly more students feel secure and cared for, understand the goals of education, work to achieve to their full potential, build positive attitudes and school behaviors, and stay in school. The shared interest and investments of schools, families, and communities create the conditions of caring that . . . [increase] the likelihood of student success. (Epstein, 1995, pp. 701–703)

Research into school and community partnerships indicates that (a) partnerships tend to decline as children get older; (b) contact with parents in affluent communities tends to focus on positive issues, and contact with parents in poor areas tends to focus on problems; and (c) most teachers, parents, and students believe that partnerships are valuable but are not sure how to create them. If teachers and schools want to involve families, they must learn to create partnerships that address issues of inclusion, influence, and appreciation: partnerships that (a) include all parents; (b) are based on respect and reciprocal influence, and can be maintained—and even strengthened—through disagreements; and (c) build feelings of genuine appreciation and caring for all involved. When working to establish partnerships with parents, it is important to remember that some parents when they were students themselves did not have positive experiences in school and, therefore, may need special encouragement to become involved positively in the life of the school. Epstein (1995, pp. 704–706) suggests a framework for six types of involvement that might be used to help build caring partnerships. His ideas are summarized in Figure 4.3.

Focus on Parenting	Focus on Communicating	Focus on Volunteering	Focus on Learning at Home	Focus on Decision Making	Focus on Community Collaboration
Purpose: Help all families establish a home environment that supports children as learners. Help families share relevant information about the culture, background, talents, and needs of their children.	**Purpose:** Establish clear two-way communication channels for communication from home to school and from school to home.	**Purpose:** Recruit volunteers from homes and community in such a way that all families know that their time and talents are welcome and valuable. Provide information (and training); match time and talent with school, teacher, and needs; recognize efforts.	**Purpose:** Provide information to parents about how to help students at home. Provide regular interactive homework that gives students responsibility for discussing what they are learning. Involve families in decisions related to curriculum.	**Purpose:** Develop parent leaders—involve them in decision making and information dissemination. Include parents from all racial, ethnic, and socioeconomic groups.	**Purpose:** Identify and integrate resources and services between the school and community to strengthen programs and partnerships. Insure that access is available for all students.

Figure 4.3
Building a caring learning community: six types of school, family, and community partnerships.

❧   WORKING WITH PEERS   ❧

Using Our Memories and *Rotating Interviews* to Review Chapter Content and Consider How One Might Build Inclusion, Influence, and Affection into Classroom Life

1. Students group in random trios. Students count off one to three. Each will be responsible for facilitating and recording a conversation based on a different topic that relates to chapter content, the building of learning communities, and personal memory. Each student needs a blank sheet of paper, and each records one of the three topics listed below at the top of his or her page. (All #1 students record topic A, etc.) When topic A is being discussed, student #1 acts as both facilitator and recorder for the conversation.

   Students will work together to record memories from when they were students, when they were observing classes, or when they were teaching. As a group, they should try to describe at least one memory for each item under each topic and should agree that the memory "fits" the topic and item before the group facilitator/recorder describes the memory in writing.

   The topics and items are

   a. Inclusion
      (1) "Getting to Know You" activities
      (2) Whole-class identity-building activities
      (3) School and community-building activities
   b. Shared Control and Influence
      (1) A time when students participated in the development of rules
      (2) A class meeting
      (3) A time when students participated in decisions about how to learn academic content
   c. Appreciation and Caring
      (1) A "Learning How to Say Nice Things" activity
      (2) A whole-class celebration *that centered on learning*
      (3) A time when things got rough and the classroom community showed that it cared

2. Discussion begins with item #1 of topic A and continues through items #2 and #3. Student #1 facilitates and records the conversation (~10 minutes).

3. Reflection and Planning:
   Individual:
   • How did this conversation help me understand how to build feelings of inclusion into a classroom learning community?

   Group:
   • How easy was it for us to use our own memories to describe inclusion activities?

4. Group changes (rotates) for the next discussion topic. All #1 students stand and rotate one group clockwise. All #2 students stand and rotate two groups clockwise. The #2 students now serve as the facilitators/recorders for topic B (~10 minutes).

5. Reflection and Planning:
   Individual:
   • How did this conversation help me understand how to build feelings of shared control and influence into a classroom learning community?
   Group:
   • How easy was it for us to use our own memories to describe ways to build feelings of shared control and influence?

6. Group changes (rotates) for the next discussion topic. All #1 students stand and rotate one group clockwise. All #2 students stand and rotate two groups clockwise. The #3 students now serve as the facilitators/recorders for topic C (~10 minutes).

7. Reflection and Planning:
   Individual:
   • How did this conversation help me understand how to build feelings of appreciation and caring into a classroom learning community?
   Group:
   • How easy was it for us to use our own memories to describe ways to build feelings of appreciation and caring?

8. Groups change again. This time all #1 students gather together—as do #2 and #3 students. Students in each group synthesize the best ideas from each conversation. Synthesis can be reported orally, or groups might use newsprint, markers, and webs or other graphic organizers to display the ideas.

9. Reflection and Planning:
   Group:
   • What happened when groups rotated for each topic? How might the conversations have been different if groups had remained together for all three topics?

Using Brainstorming to Explore Possibilities for Celebrations

1. Students group in random trios. Each student receives about thirty index cards or small strips of

paper. Students think and write *by themselves* ideas for building celebrations into a classroom learning community. Students use a different index card for each idea.

2. Students combine their cards and categorize them by type of celebration.

3. Reflection and Planning:
   Group:
   - What kinds of celebrations do we tend to think of most frequently? Least frequently? What ideas reinforce that learning is valued? Are there ideas that do not suggest that learning is valued?

4. Ideas might be shared among groups. For instance, while students continue working, each group could send a *Roving Reporter* (Kagan, 1992) to gather ideas from other groups. After the groups have completed their sorting, all members might simultaneously *Roam the Room* (Kagan, 1992) to gather ideas and then come back and report what they have seen. The entire class could use *One-Stay Three-Stray* to find out about the ideas of other groups.
   (*Note.* This activity provides students with considerable time to think by themselves, and all students have equal opportunity to share their ideas. The generation of ideas is separated from the process of categorizing and evaluating ideas; this is an essential characteristic of brainstorming.)

Using *Paraphrase Passport* (Kagan, 1992) and *Team Statements* (Kagan, 1992) to Reflect on Values and Rules

1. Students group in random trios. Students think and write *by themselves* lists of three to five rules that they think might be reasonable in a classroom.

2. Students share these rules and together build a list of three to five rules that they all agree are important.

3. Students then use *Paraphrase Passport* to discuss the question: "What are the values embedded in these rules?" During *Paraphrase Passport,* the ticket for talking and sharing one's own ideas is the ability to paraphrase the person who has just spoken.

4. Students think and write *by themselves* one- to two-sentence statements that they think represent clearly the values embedded in the rules that the group thought were important.

5. Students share statements and work together to build one team statement. It may be useful to use *Paraphrase Passport* again for this step of the discussion.

6. Students share statements—using newsprint or the blackboard—with the whole class.

Using a *One-Minute Paper* and *Value Lines* (Kagan, 1992) to Reflect on the Relative Importance of Building Community in the Classroom

QUESTION: *On a scale of one to five (one is the lowest score and five is the highest), how essential do you think it is to "take time" to build community into classroom life? Have at least three reasons to support your number.*

1. Students position themselves on a line from one side of the room (the "1" side) to the other (the "5" side), based on their numbers and reasons. To do this, students have to explain their numbers and listen carefully to the numbers and reasons of other students.

PART II

Developing Small-Group Cooperation

CHAPTER 5
Base Groups and Informal Groups: Building Stability and Variety Into Small-Group Cooperation

CHAPTER 6
Formal Learning Groups: Building Positive Interdependence

CHAPTER 7
Interpersonal and Small-Group Learning Skills: Teaching the Basics

CHAPTER 8
Reflection and Planning: Examining Interpersonal and Small-Group Learning Skills by Looking Back and Planning Ahead

CHAPTER 9
Individual Responsibility and Assessment: Checking for Understanding

CHAPTER 10
The Role of the Teacher: Guiding Learning in the Cooperative Classroom

CHAPTER 5

Base Groups and Informal Groups: Building Stability and Variety Into Small-Group Cooperation

✿ *As you read, you might want to ask yourself:*

Why is it important to see the use of cooperation as a "discipline"?

What are the barriers to high-quality cooperation?

What are the basic elements of high-quality small-group cooperation?

Why might teachers who want to empower their students as learners "take the time" to build base groups into their daily and weekly routines?

How might an empowering teacher form base groups and nurture their development?

Why is longevity a key to base groups?

How do base groups contribute to a classroom learning community, and how are they different from whole-class community-building activities?

How are informal learning groups different from base groups? How are they different from whole-class discussions?

Why do teachers who want to empower their students as learners take the time to build the use of informal learning groups into direct instruction?

How does the use of informal learning groups help to develop and sustain a learning community?

How might the use of base groups and informal learning groups look and sound and feel in a classroom that empowers students as learners?

In the introductory chapter of this book, we examined the power of a cooperative context for learning and living. In Part I—Chapters 2 through 4—we learned how to develop the whole classroom as a learning community. We learned that building an understanding of the classroom as a developing group and an understanding of the power of shared values in classrooms are both essential to teachers who are committed to creating classroom communities that empower all students as learners. In Part II of this text we will learn how to use small-group cooperation.

🐝   BUILDING AN UNDERSTANDING OF   🐝
COOPERATION AS A DISCIPLINE

Everyone who has ever used small groups for learning knows that merely placing students into groups and telling them to work together does not insure either high-quality cooperation or high-quality learning. Barriers to high quality include (D. Johnson & F. Johnson, 1994)

- Lack of group maturity: Groups need time and experience to develop into high-functioning groups.
- Going with the first, and often dominant, response: Groups need time and encouragement to generate many possible answers and solutions that include the efforts of all members, and they need to learn how to recognize and choose which ideas to pursue.
- Goofing off: Groups need to help all members learn to work hard so that everyone contributes and no one feels taken advantage of.
- Fear of disagreement or conflict: Groups need to learn to manage differences of opinion and use differences to build better understanding.
- Lack of ability or motivation to attend to both task and maintenance aspects of group work: Groups must learn how to get the job done while simultaneously building and maintaining their interpersonal relationships.

Five Basic Elements of High-Quality Small-Group Cooperation

"There is a discipline to creating cooperation" (D. Johnson, R. Johnson, & Holubec, 1993, p. 4:8) and a discipline to overcoming the barriers to cooperation. According to the Johnsons, teachers should consider five basic principles—or elements—when designing opportunities for small-group cooperation. These elements are

- Positive Interdependence
- Simultaneous Interaction
- Individual Responsibility

- Interpersonal and Small-Group Learning Skills
- Reflection and Planning

Beginning in Chapter 6 we will carefully examine each of these elements as we learn how to use the discipline of cooperation. In this chapter we will develop our understanding of small-group cooperation by learning how to build both stability and variety into classroom life through the use of base groups and informal learning groups.

🐜   BASE GROUPS: A HOME AWAY FROM HOME   🐜

What Are Cooperative Base Groups?

Base groups (Clarke, Wideman, & Eadie, 1990; D. Johnson, R. Johnson, & Holubec, 1992) are long-term, heterogeneous groups with stable membership that meet regularly throughout a school year. The primary purposes of the base group are to

- Provide student-to-student support, encouragement, and assistance.
- Provide students with a sense of home and routine within the classroom.
- Build long-term relationships and interpersonal communication systems.
- Encourage all members to make academic progress and strive for excellence.

Think about a group that you enjoy and have been a member of for a long time. Why has this group been enjoyable?

How Are Base Groups Formed?

Longevity is a key to the use of base groups. Ideally, base groups remain together for at least a year and provide an essential network of support. Therefore, careful assignment of students to these groups is important. Teachers often find it useful to wait two or three weeks, until they know their students well, to establish base groups. For the groups to work well, both heterogeneity and compatibility are necessary. Membership should be diverse in terms of academic ability, socioeconomic status, social status, gender, race, ethnicity, and possibly age. To build compatibility, teachers can use sociometric data about peer social status to help them determine groupings. For instance, a teacher might ask students to write the names of four or five others with whom they would like to spend time and assure each student that one of these people will be assigned to his or her group. (Sociometric procedures were described more fully in Chapter 3.) Sometimes interest surveys are useful. For instance, a teacher might use an interest survey to help place a shy, socially-unskilled student who likes to roller blade in a group with a student who also likes to roller blade and is more socially skilled. Grouping procedures that place students in groups so that they cross categories—so that members share some important characteristics with

What kind of interest survey do you think might be useful for a class you have worked with?

some group members but not all characteristics with all group members—were discussed in Chapter 3; these procedures are useful for maximizing both heterogeneity and compatibility.

Cross-age base groups are one particularly intriguing way to build heterogeneity and to expand feelings of community and appreciation past the walls of a single classroom. In an elementary school, for instance, one student from each grade might share membership in the same base group. In one school where this is the norm, base groups meet on Monday mornings, and each child sets both a personal learning goal and a behavioral goal for the week. Following the Monday morning meetings, members meet at the end of each day to update each other on their progress. On Friday afternoons members report a major learning for the week and whether or not they have meet their goals. When a goal has not been met, the base group helps problem solve—perhaps a goal was set too high, or perhaps the member needs to take his or her schoolwork more seriously, or perhaps the base group can offer more support. Mixed-grade base groups are possible in middle and high schools if homerooms—and base groups—are assigned to include students from each grade in the school. In mixed-age base groups, membership changes yearly as older students graduate and younger students enter the school. Mixed-age base groups can greatly ease the transition into and out of a school. Younger students learn important roles and norms from older students, while older students have the opportunity to watch out for younger group mates. As older students make the transition from elementary to middle school, from middle school to high school, or from high school to college or the world of work, they share their excitement, fears, and planning processes—both receiving support from and providing models for younger members.

What Do Base Groups Do?

The establishment of routines is a second key to the successful use of base groups. Base-group routines should provide opportunities for personal and academic support and should be somewhat independent of constant teacher facilitation. In elementary schools, for example, it is typical for base groups to meet at the beginning and end of each school day, and students stay with the same four- or five-member base group for the entire year. Morning meetings often last five to ten minutes, with a similar agenda each day. Morning base-group agendas commonly include (a) routine tasks, (b) academic support tasks, and (c) personal support tasks. For instance, students might take lunch count; make sure everyone is ready for the day—homework completed, supplies ready, and heads on straight; and find out what each person has done for fun since the previous day. Base groups often share answers to a question the teacher presents: personal-analogy questions such as "What color best represents your brain today?";

divergent-thinking questions such as "How is a mouse like a mousse?"; content-related questions such as "Who was your favorite character in *The Wind in the Willows?*". Afternoon meetings are likewise short and have well-established agendas; their tasks, too, include routines, academic support, and personal support. For instance, students make sure everyone knows what to do for homework; share reflections on the day and focus on a closure question supplied by the teacher; and remind each other to have some fun before school starts the next day. Classroom jobs are often completed by base groups—instead of individuals—at the end of the day. If a group member has been absent, other members arrange to call the student to wish him or her well and encourage him or her to return to school as soon as possible.

Some middle and high schools have integrated base groups into the fabric of school life by providing a structure for base groups to meet during homeroom. These base groups, like base groups in elementary schools, often follow simple agendas which include (a) routine tasks such as taking attendance, handing out notices, and collecting money; (b) academic support tasks such as sharing study strategies or sources for library research; and (c) personal support tasks such as sharing information about school clubs and helping individual members through turbulent times. When base groups are used throughout a school, they also provide a time for students to learn specific, "real-life," interpersonal and small-group skills—skills such as taking turns, paraphrasing, and asking others to explain their answers—that are then practiced within the context of academic classes.

When base groups are not used in homerooms, middle and high-school teachers sometimes use base groups in their content-area classes. When teachers choose this option, they tend to have students meet in base groups on Mondays and Fridays and use base-group meetings to help establish an anticipatory set and provide closure to the week. Again, base-group agendas commonly include routine tasks, academic support tasks, and personal support tasks. For instance, members of content-area base groups might share folders that are used for handling routine paperwork; assume responsibility for collecting handouts and making copies of notes for absent members; report progress on, and difficulties with, long-term individual projects such as term papers, reading, or volunteerism; and share important events from their school and personal lives.

Why Are Base Groups Important?

All children and adolescents, in all schools, have the right to believe that they are valued by peers—that peers notice and care when they come to school and that peers notice and care when they do not come to school. Base groups are one way to build a sense of inclusion, respect, appreciation, and community into classroom life.

In college classrooms how often have you felt that other students noticed whether or not you came to class?

Maslow's classification of the needs that motivate human behavior, described in Chapter 1, and Schutz's theory that individuals express three basic interpersonal needs, described in Chapter 2 and discussed again in Chapter 4 within the context of building learning communities, are two perspectives that can be used to build an understanding of why base groups serve important purposes in empowering classrooms. Base groups are a complement to—not a substitute for—whole-class community-building activities of the kind that were discussed in Chapter 4. Base groups are powerful for several reasons:

- Base group routines help establish a sense of consistency and familiarity —both essential to feelings of safety.
- The consistent membership in base groups helps students build a sense of belongingness or inclusion. When students come to school, they know they have a place in their base group; they know that their presence or absence will be noticed—not just by the teacher but, more importantly, by peers.
- Base groups can be used to help decentralize the control of basic classroom routines and to help students build reciprocal support and influence systems—both essential characteristics of empowering classrooms. These aspects of base groups have the potential to influence positively students' self-efficacy and sense of prestige and mastery.
- The long-term nature of base groups provides both the opportunity and the need for students to learn to value their differences and work through their conflicts.
- The long-term nature of base groups provides opportunities for authentic interpersonal sharing—sharing that moves past stereotypical perceptions and responses and creates both a need for shared values and opportunities to build shared values.
- The long-term nature of base groups provides opportunities for students to focus on problems outside of themselves and to develop compassion, affection, and appreciation for others; these are essential qualities of psychologically healthy, self-actualizing people.

Simon's story is a poignant example of why base groups might be a valuable aspect of life in schools.

 ### Simon's Story

When I was young, I looked to my family for protection, guidance, love, encouragement, affection, security, self-confidence, social skills, and intellectual growth. I looked for these things within and from my family. What I ended up getting was, oh, so different than my hopes and desires. In fact, I came out of this family situation with emotional scars that I am still, to this day, trying to carve away.

My mother had some serious problems with mental illness and was separated from my family shortly after my birth. She was prone to violent episodes. When she was out of the hospital, she frequently hung around outside our house. This was confusing, embarrassing, and dangerous. I knew that there was no way to predict what my mother might do. I vividly remember occasions when I was attacked by my mother. After these episodes, the parents of other children would bar them from having any contact with me. I understand now that they did this for their children's welfare. I also realize that when you grow up in the midst of danger and insanity, you never look upon it as such, because it is all you know.

It seemed that the rest of my family was burned out with the experience they went through with my mother, and they were trying to work out their own situations—leaving them with minimal energy to deal with a child. I felt unloved and unwanted. I was introverted and withdrawn. My outlook was dim. I tried hard to always act happy. My father drank. My concern was so great for my father's dilemma that I hardly ever made a peep about the tremendous pain that I felt inside. I guess this was the beginning of my road to becoming an alcoholic and a drug addict myself. There was simply nobody to turn to. My communication skills were nonexistent.

School was painful and embarrassing. Keeping close friends was difficult. Taunting from other children was unbearable. I got jumped and beaten up regularly. Before and during these fights, there were comments about my mother. I began to gravitate towards the gang members who lived around the corner. They welcomed me. I was a member of the gang, but I knew I would have to fight in order to stay a member in good standing. One day during school, one of the guys who always taunted me started up in front of some of my gang. I did not do anything but take his insults. The next thing I knew, one of the gang members said "After school!" This meant we were going to fight. I was scared to death. I wanted to run but I knew I could not. If I did I would be kicked out of the gang and shamed forever.

When the fight started, I hit the boy between his eyes. He fell back. I expected him to come back at me. He did not. His friends grabbed hold of him and took him away. The guys cheered for me. "Way to go man, you kicked his ass. He won't mess with you no more."

I can still hear their accolades. I had arrived. I was a full-fledged member. I put the timid child to death that night. We celebrated with booze and cheap wine. I was high. In addition to the buzz I had from the booze, I felt accepted. Whenever the guys cut school, I was invited. I had brothers. I had a family. I looked out for them and they looked out for me. They replaced the brother and family I never really knew. I had a family.

What do you think Simon meant by "family?"

In this chapter we have explored how base groups might be used to create a "home away from home" and enhance feelings of stability, safety, and belongingness in a classroom learning community. Next we turn our attention to three classroom scenarios. Julie, Mary, and Dale have all become experts in the use of base groups in their classrooms; they use these groups to facilitate classroom routines, build community, and encourage students to become empowered learners. Take the time to read these scenarios carefully—even those that do not represent age levels that are in your area of interest. As you read, ask yourself: "How has this teacher used base groups to enhance a sense of belongingness and community?" "Why has the teacher made these choices?" You might also think about how it would feel to be a student in Julie or Mary or Dale's classroom. How do you think it might feel to be the teacher?

❧ A VIEW FROM THE CLASSROOM: ❧
USING BASE GROUPS

Julie's kindergarten students burst into the room, hang up their coats, unpack their knapsacks, and move into their base groups. Each day the routine is similar. First, base groups work together to make sure all notices are placed in the "teacher's bin" and cards with each student's name are placed in the correct attendance pockets. Second, group members find out what each person has done for fun since the day before. Then all the base groups move to the story rug for calendar, weather, and other opening routines, including person of the week. On the day I visited Julie's class, the children had already gathered on the rug when Billy arrived—late, flushed, and upset. His base group, the Tigers, got up, asked him if he was OK, helped him with his coat and attendance card, and then brought him to the rug.

In Julie's class base groups sit together on the rug, and each week a different base group is in charge of opening exercises. When I visited, it was the Dragon-Pterodactyls' turn. Everyone knew this because their group name and paper-plate portraits of each child were displayed prominently near the calendar. Base-group members shared responsibility for flag salute, morning song, calendar, weather report, and, most important, for each other. At the end of "rug time," before the children left their base groups to move to their work tables, each base group held hands for a base-group handshake. Towards the end of the day, base groups eat their snacks together, and children share their favorite part of the day with each other.

Mary's fifth graders start the day in base groups. Early in the year Mary formed her students into groups of four or five. At the beginning of each day, groups meet in their own "spots"—one near the coat area, another by the reading corner, another near the entrance. Base groups have named themselves—Sharks, Pythons, Mountain Lions, Scorpions—and, using old boxes from copy paper, have created "environments" to match their names. These environments hang near where each group meets, giving each group a sense of place and heightening a sense of shared identity. Each group has also made a base-group poster. Posters include the names of each base-group member as well as personal information—number of siblings, pets, favorite colors, favorite flavors of ice cream, hobbies, and so forth. Throughout the year groups add information to their posters.

Mary has worked with her students to establish efficient base-group routines. After hanging up their coats, students take their book bags and go directly to their base groups. First, children share one thing each of them has done for fun since leaving school the previous day. Second, they take lunch count, and a student from each group delivers the lunch count to Mary's desk. (Early in the year Mary's students worked to design a chart that could be used to record lunch choices.) Third, base groups check to make sure all members have completed their homework, and members spend a few minutes discussing anything that was confusing or difficult. Fourth, students answer a question that Mary has written on the board. Questions vary widely. Sometimes Mary chooses questions that help students get to know each other. For example, she might ask: "If you could be any animal in the world, what would you like to be?" Answers to these questions are often added to base-group posters. Other times, Mary asks her students thinking questions such as "Which is taller, red or brown?" Questions like these help students learn to think divergently, to ask each other probing and clarifying questions, and to accept answers different from their own. Other times, Mary uses a question for review or as an anticipatory set. For example, she might ask: "What was the most interesting part of yesterday's science experiment?" or "What are three things you want to look for when we go on our nature walk this afternoon?"

Mary's students enjoy their base groups and take their base-group work seriously. Early in the year Mary emphasized "Getting-Together Skills" such as getting into groups quickly, using quiet voices, taking turns, and careful listening. At the end of each morning meeting, Mary reviews the content of the base-group meetings. When I observed, Mary focused the groups' attention and quickly asked: "Paul, tell us what the other members of your base group did for fun since yesterday" and "Maria, tell us what each member of your base group predicts. Will Julie ever be rescued from the island?" By taking a moment to ask these questions, Mary reinforces the idea that students are to participate equally and are responsible for listening carefully to their peers. She then signals her students to finish their meetings; each group shakes hands. Base-group meetings have lasted about ten minutes. Students move to their seats, ready for the rest of their day.

At the end of each day, Mary's students again meet in their base groups and follow an established routine. First, each base group completes a classroom maintenance job such as straightening the library area or erasing the board. Second, members check assignment books. Third, they discuss a closure question that Mary has written on the board. Fourth, students reflect on their day and briefly shares incidents in which they helped another person or another person helped them. Fifth, they say good-bye and remind each other to have fun.

Dale's entire seventh-grade team has decided to use base groups as part of homeroom, and students are "tracked" with their base groups throughout the day. Dale has established routines for base groups that include clerical, interpersonal, and academic tasks. Unfortunately, the students in Dale's school are quite mobile—as many as one third of the students in this class will move between September and June. Dale uses base groups to help students cope with these changes. When new students enter the class, for instance, Dale immediately assigns them to base groups. Base group members help new students by (a) teaching them classroom routines; (b) walking with them to classes for the first week; (c) introducing them to their subject-area teachers; (d) eating lunch with them; and (e) inviting them to get involved in specific school activities. When students leave the class, Dale encourages base groups to write letters and send news items about the school to their former members. Dale keeps a supply of large envelopes and stamps to facilitate this communication.

Thus far in this chapter, we have explored how base groups might be used to build a sense of stability into small-group cooperation. Next we turn our attention to the use of informal learning groups—groups that help to enhance learning and build a sense of movement and variety into small-group cooperation and the classroom community.

🐝 INFORMAL GROUPS: CASUAL AND EFFECTIVE 🐝

What Are Informal Cooperative Learning Groups? Why Are They Used?

Informal cooperative learning groups (D. Johnson, R. Johnson, & Holubec, 1992) are short-term, heterogeneous groups with membership that tends to be random. Informal cooperative learning groups are typically used during relatively long direct-teaching episodes such as lectures, teacher read-alouds, and movies or videos. The primary purposes of informal groups, when combined with direct teaching, are to

- Create a mood conducive to learning.
- Focus students' attention on the material that is to be learned by providing an anticipatory set and opportunities for students to share world knowledge.
- Maintain students' attention on the material that is to be learned by dividing the material into short segments.
- Create regular opportunities for oral rehearsal, semantic organization, and elaboration to help students process cognitively the material being taught.
- Provide opportunities for students to identify misconceptions and gaps in knowledge within the relatively safe context of a small group.
- Provide opportunities for students to benefit from giving and receiving peer explanations.
- Personalize learning.
- Provide closure.

Short term, random groups can also be used quite effectively in combination with other, more formal cooperative groups. The primary purposes of informal groups, when they are combined with formal groups, are to

- Provide a change of pace.
- Provide opportunities to move around the classroom.
- Structure an anticipatory set or closure for a lesson.
- Provide opportunities for frequent peer discussions and intergroup sharing to help build inclusion, communication, trust, and a focus on learning throughout the classroom community.

Have you ever "gotten lost" during a lecture? What happened?

For the remainder of this chapter, we will focus primarily on the use of informal learning groups. We will begin our careful examination of formal learning groups in Chapter 6.

How Are Informal Cooperative Learning Groups Used with Direct Instruction?

Using informal cooperative learning groups with direct instruction can be as simple as asking a question and, instead of having students raise their hands and respond in front of the entire class, asking students to turn to the people next to them for discussion. A typical format for informal groups, with direct instruction, is as follows:

1. Teacher asks a question that serves as an anticipatory set or advance organizer for the story, video, demonstration, or lecture that is to follow. Students discuss.

2. Teacher reads story, shows video, or delivers lecture—stopping every few minutes and asking students to discuss a teacher-prepared question or problem. Questions and problems might be factual or conceptual; they might focus on the material that has just been presented or might help students bridge to a new segment of the presentation. Students discuss.
3. Teacher asks a question that helps students summarize and synthesize the material that has been presented and provides closure for the lesson. Students discuss.

When using this basic strategy or another informal group strategy with direct instruction, it is important to consider how students will group and with whom they will talk. Some teachers find it useful to arrange the seating in their classrooms so that "turn to your partner" or "discuss in your foursome" is a simple process that does not require much movement. Seating arrangements that are conducive to the use of informal groups with direct instruction are described in Chapter 10. When teachers use seating arrangements to create informal groups, they often change seat assignments at regular intervals—each week, each marking period, or with each unit. Informal groups then change with seating assignments, and over time, students discuss their work with many peers. In learning situations where students do not have assigned seats, or when teachers want students to work with many different partners or groups, teachers might ask students to count off or use other pairing and grouping strategies to create informal groups. Novel and content-relevant ways to pair and group students are described in Chapter 10.

When using informal groups with direct instruction, it is useful to consider how students will interact with each other. The interpersonal and small-group learning skills that students will need—and will have opportunities to practice—in informal groups include using quiet voices, acknowledging a quiet signal, taking turns, talking one at a time, listening, paraphrasing, giving and asking for information, asking questions, repeating, and summarizing. These and other important skills will be addressed in Chapter 7.

The word *informal* can be deceptive as a description for the use of cooperative learning groups with direct instruction. Informal groups may look and feel quite casual, but teachers who use informal groups plan them quite carefully and often vary their plans to keep the use of these groups interesting and effective. These variations are commonly called *structures;* they add variety and excitement to the use of informal cooperative learning groups and provide students with many opportunities to practice important interpersonal skills. Spencer Kagan (1992) has collected, described, and named many structures that were developed by others, has developed many new structures, and has helped many teachers understand their power and usefulness. When they use structures frequently, teachers typically name the structures to facilitate and simplify directions. Following are several structures that many teachers find particularly useful when they want to facilitate the use of informal cooperative learning groups with direct instruction.

☀ ☀ ☀ ☀ ☀ ☀

Think-Pair-Share (Lyman, 1992)

Group size: two

1. Teacher asks a question or poses a problem. Students *think* by themselves.
2. Students *pair* and discuss their ideas.
3. Individual students are called upon to *share* their answers (or the answers of their partners) with the whole class.

What's good about *Think-Pair-Share:* It is simple to use. Students have an opportunity to think by themselves. All students have an opportunity to share their ideas and hear the ideas of others.

Interpersonal and Small-Group Learning Skills: Sharing an idea, listening carefully, asking clarifying and probing questions, and paraphrasing.

Think-Pair-Square

Group size: two and four

1. Teacher asks a question or poses a problem. Students *think* by themselves.
2. Students *pair* and discuss their ideas.
3. Each pair teams up with another pair and shares in its foursome—a *square.*

What's good about *Think-Pair-Square:* Students have an opportunity to think by themselves. All students have an opportunity to share their ideas and hear the ideas of others.

Interpersonal and Small-Group Learning Skills: Sharing an idea, listening carefully, asking clarifying and probing questions.

Pens in the Middle

Group size: three or four

1. Teacher asks a question or poses a problem. Students think by themselves.
2. In groups of three or four, students share their responses. When a student shares, he or she places a pen or pencil in the center of the group to mark a contribution. No student can share a second idea until all pens are in the middle.

What's good about *Pens in the Middle:* Students have an opportunity to think by themselves. All students have an opportunity to share their ideas and hear the ideas of others. Sharing is "equalized" to help lessen status problems. A teacher might monitor a group by picking up a pen, asking whose idea the pen represents, and asking a group member to describe that idea.

Interpersonal and Small-Group Learning Skills: Sharing an idea and taking turns.

Numbered Heads Together (Kagan, 1992)

Group size: three or four

1. Students count off in their groups.
2. Teacher asks a question or poses a problem. Students think by themselves.
3. In groups of three or four, students discuss their ideas.
4. Teacher uses numbers to call randomly on students to report their group discussions.

What's good about *Numbered Heads Together:* Students think by themselves. Students have opportunities to share their own ideas and to hear the ideas of others. Status issues are addressed, and responsibility is enhanced, because all students are equally likely to be asked to report. This structure helps teachers avoid typical questioning patterns that may be related to perceptions of ability or issues of race or gender. (These were discussed in Chapter 3.) It helps students move past perceptions of "She always calls on him" or "She only calls on me when she thinks I don't know the answer."

Interpersonal and Small-Group Learning Skills: Sharing an idea.

Roundrobin (Kagan, 1992)

Group size: three or four

1. Teacher asks a question or poses a problem. Students think by themselves.
2. In groups of three or four, students "go around" and, in turn, share their responses. Sometimes teachers find it useful to have students count off. They can then help organize the sharing by saying, "Start with person # 3 and share clockwise."

What's good about *Roundrobin:* Students have an opportunity to think by themselves. All students have an opportunity to share their ideas and hear the ideas of others. Sharing is organized to help lessen status problems.

Interpersonal and Small-Group Learning Skills: Sharing an idea and taking turns.

Roundtable with Roundrobin

Group size: three or four

1. Teacher asks a question or poses a problem. Students think and write by themselves.
2. In groups of three or four, students "go around the table" and, in turn, share their responses.

What's good about *Roundtable with Roundrobin:* All students have an opportunity to share their ideas and hear the ideas of others. Written responses help when groups have status problems, when students are not motivated, or when students find it difficult to express their own ideas and might be tempted to say, "I had the same idea as Chris."

Interpersonal and Small-Group Learning Skills: Sharing an idea and taking turns.

Group Interview (Kagan, 1992)

Group size: three or four

1. Teacher asks a question or poses a problem. Students think by themselves.
2. Each student is "interviewed" for a minute or two by the other members of the group.

What's good about *Group Interview:* All students, regardless of status, have an opportunity to share their ideas and hear the ideas of others. Students share one at a time and learn how to separate the asking of questions from the sharing of their own ideas.

Interpersonal and Small-Group Learning Skills: Sharing an idea, taking turns, listening carefully, and asking clarifying and probing questions.

Three-Step Interview (Kagan, 1992)

Group size: two and four

1. Teacher asks a question or poses a problem. Students think by themselves.
2. Students pair. Within pairs, students each spend a moment or two sharing their ideas and being interviewed by their partners.
3. Each pair teams up with another pair and creates a foursome. Within foursomes, students each share their partners' ideas with the other pair.

What's good about *Three-Step Interview*: Students have an opportunity to think by themselves. All students have an opportunity to share their own ideas, hear their ideas explained by a peer, explain the ideas of a peer, and hear the ideas of three peers.

Interpersonal and Small-Group Learning Skills: Sharing an idea, taking turns, asking clarifying and probing questions, and paraphrasing.

Stirring Up the Class

Group size: three or four

1. Students count off in their groups.
2. Teacher asks a question or poses a problem. Students think by themselves.
3. In groups of three or four, students discuss their ideas.
4. All #1 students rotate one group and share their old groups' discussion and answers with the new groups.
5. Teacher asks a question or poses a problem. Students think by themselves.
6. Students discuss their ideas.
7. Rotation procedure is repeated. This time, #2 students rotate two groups and share their old groups' discussion and answers with the new groups.

What's good about *Stirring Up the Class*: Students have an opportunity to think by themselves. All students have an opportunity to share their ideas and hear the ideas of others. Status issues are addressed, and responsibility is enhanced, because students have both an opportunity and an obligation to share their group's ideas with other groups. This structure is an organized way to alter group membership and encourage intergroup cooperation through the sharing of information among groups.

Have you ever used any of these structures to facilitate learning? When and how did you use them?

Interpersonal and Small-Group Learning Skills: Sharing an idea, taking turns, asking clarifying and probing questions, paraphrasing, moving in an organized way, and being responsible for the group's work.

How Are Informal Groups Used for Change of Pace and for Building Feelings of Inclusion and Community Throughout the Classroom?

Think of a classroom situation where you had an opportunity to move around and talk with other students. How old were you?

Like the use of informal groups with direct instruction, the use of informal cooperative learning groups for movement and change of pace, set or closure, or to build inclusion and community may *appear* casual but requires careful planning. When planning to use informal groups for these purposes, a teacher may want to consider (a) seating arrangements that include open spaces and room to move; (b) the interpersonal skills that students will need and will have opportunities to practice—including moving in an orderly fashion, using a quiet voice, and acknowledging the quiet signal; and (c) structures that might be used to help organize these active groups and teach these important skills. Structures are particularly important when students are asked to move around the room and talk with many different people; structures help insure that movement is orderly, that talk is purposeful, and that the use of informal groups does not reinforce any existing status problems. Following are several structures that might be used to help plan organized movement, change of pace, and purposeful talk in the classroom.

Corners (Kagan, 1992)

1. Teacher announces the corners. Corners are often related to student preferences or choices: "What is your favorite season—summer, winter, spring, or fall?" "Who is your favorite character in *Charlotte's Web*—Charlotte, Wilbur, Templeton, or Fern?" "Do you prefer Shelly, Keats, Byron, or Tennyson?" "For our science unit on plant growth, would you rather make observations about the effects of water, sunlight, temperature, or soil acidity on plant growth?" *Corners* might be used to ask students to make comparisons and applications: "What war most influences our policies today—the Revolutionary War, the Civil War, the First World War, or the Second World War?" "If dinosaurs came back to life today, which one might be most able to adapt to conditions in our community—the brachiosaurus, tyrannosaurus, ornitholestes, or compsognathus?" "The most important metal today is gold, iron, copper, or aluminum?" Corners might also be used to ask students to think in analogies and metaphors: "Would you rather be a rabbit, a fish, a bird, or a snake?" "Is research on the Internet 'A Highway To Heaven,' 'Easy Street,' 'A Long And Winding Road,' or 'A Road Less Traveled'?"
2. Students each think (and perhaps write) by themselves. Writing their responses helps them move past "I like the same corner that Chris likes."
3. Students move to their preferred corners.
4. Students discuss their reasons with others in their same corner. (*Three-Step Interviews* or *Group Interviews* might be used if students have a difficult time sharing and listening.)
5. Students are called on to paraphrase the different ideas they have heard in their corners. (Just because students have gone to the same corner does not mean they have the same reasons for doing so.)
6. Students might be asked to paraphrase—verbally or in writing—reasons for all four corners.
7. *Corners* might be used to form work groups: Students from the same corner—students with similar interests or preferences—could work together; students from different corners—students with different interests or preferences—could work together.

What's good about *Corners:* Students have opportunities to move around the room, think by themselves, declare their preferences publicly, and learn about the preferences of others. The parameters chosen can provide opportunities to use many kinds of questioning and thinking strategies.

Interpersonal and Small-Group Learning Skills: Stating an opinion, moving in an organized way, listening carefully, and paraphrasing.

Value Lines (Kagan, 1992)

1. Teacher announces a statement or question with two poles and implied "shades of gray" in between. As in *Corners,* these statements help students discuss preferences and choices, make comparisons and applications, or engage in metaphorical thinking: "If you were a member of the Swiss Family Robinson, would you want to be rescued?" "If you had been present at the Constitutional Convention, would you have argued for the Federalist or anti-Federalist position?" "Smoking should be banned." "Students should be allowed to play whatever games they want on the playground." "Learning quadratic equations is like learning to ride a bicycle or learning to brush your teeth."
2. Students think by themselves.
3. Students position themselves on an imaginary line—asking questions and explaining their positions so that they know where to stand.
4. Once students are in line, they might talk with those near them to hear why others have chosen similar views. The line might also be "folded in half" so that students with extreme positions have an opportunity to hear views that are different from their own.

What's good about *Value Line:* Students have opportunities to move around the room, think by themselves, declare their preferences publicly, learn about the preferences of others, and make careful distinctions between different opinions. The parameters chosen can provide opportunities to use many kinds of questioning and thinking strategies.

Interpersonal and Small-Group Learning Skills: Stating an opinion, moving in an organized way, listening carefully, asking clarifying and probing questions, and making distinctions.

Mix-Freeze-Pair (Kagan, 1992)

1. Students *mix.*
2. When the teacher says *freeze,* students stop.
3. When the teacher says *pair,* students form pairs—turning to the people closest to them.
4. Teacher asks question.
5. Students discuss question.
6. Process is repeated several times so that students have an opportunity to talk with several peers. (When there is an odd number of students in the class, each grouping will result in one trio. Part of the routine might be to ask the trio to raise their hands and then announce, "The next time we pair, make sure that these three classmates are all in pairs—not in a trio.")

What's good about *Mix-Freeze-Pair:* Students have an opportunity to move around the room and share with several peers. This structure is particularly good for review and closure.

Interpersonal and Small-Group Learning Skills: Sharing ideas and moving in an organized way.

Find Someone Who Knows (Kagan, 1992) or **Treasure Hunt**

1. Teacher creates a worksheet. Worksheet may be related to academic content *(Find Someone Who Knows)* or to personal information *(Treasure Hunt).*
2. Students mill around the room and gather information from their peers. When students are gathering academic information, it is common to have students sign worksheets when they provide pieces of needed information.
3. Students share information they have gathered. This can be done as a whole class, in base groups or work groups, or on some type of chart or graph.

What's good about *Find Someone Who Knows:* Students have an opportunity to move around the room and to talk with many peers. This structure is particularly good for personal sharing and for review.

Interpersonal and Small-Group Learning Skills: Sharing ideas, offering or asking for help or information, and moving in an organized way.

Inside-Outside Circle (Kagan, 1992) or **Mad Hatter's Tea Party**

1. Students form two circles—the inside circle facing out and the outside circle facing in. (If the classroom lacks floor space, two smaller sets of concentric circles will work.) In *Mad Hatter's Tea Party,* students face each other in two lines.
2. Teacher asks question or presents a discussion topic.
3. Students talk with their partners. This can be done freely or can be directed by the teacher. For instance, the teacher might say: "People in the outside circle, you have one minute to explain your position. If you are in the inside, you may ask questions but not share your own ideas."
4. Students move to new partners; it is easier for the outer circle to rotate. In *Mad Hatter's Tea Party,* either one line shifts, or both lines shift in opposite directions.
5. When students move to new partners, they might first paraphrase what their old partners said before beginning a new discussion.

What's good about *Inside-Outside Circle:* Students have an opportunity to move and to talk with many peers. Unlike *Mix-Freeze-Pair,* pairs are determined by the movement of the circles or lines. This may be preferable when there are inclusion or status difficulties in a classroom or when free movement may be too chaotic. This structure is particularly good for sharing, review, or closure.

Interpersonal and Small-Group Learning Skills: Sharing ideas, listening carefully, asking clarifying and probing questions, paraphrasing, moving in an organized way.

Rotating Review (Kagan, 1992)

Group size: three or four

1. Teacher asks a series of questions or presents several topics. These are posted around the classroom on large pieces of paper or on blackboards.

2. Each group of students is assigned to one topic or question. They move to that area, discuss the idea for a moment, and write a response.
3. The teacher signals, and all groups move to the next question or topic. They read what has been written, write comments or questions, and add something new. This continues until the groups return to their first positions. (It is helpful if each group uses a different color chalk or marker.)

Have you ever used any of these structures to facilitate learning? When and how did you use them?

What's good about *Rotating Review:* All students have an opportunity to share their ideas, see how their ideas relate to the ideas of others, and give and receive feedback. As the name suggests, this is a good structure for closure or review.

Interpersonal and Small-Group Learning Skills: Sharing ideas, adding to the ideas of others, giving and receiving feedback, moving in an organized way.

In this chapter we have examined how informal learning groups might be used with direct instruction and for variety and change of pace. Next we visit several teachers. They all use informal groups to help empower their students as learners. Take the time to read these scenarios carefully. As you read, ask yourself: "Why has the teacher chosen to use informal learning groups?" "How has the teacher structured these groups?" "How has the teacher used informal groups to empower learning and build community?" You might also think about how it would feel to be a student in one of these classrooms. How do you think it might feel to be the teacher?

A VIEW FROM THE CLASSROOM: USING INFORMAL GROUPS

Tom asks his second graders to gather on the rug and sit next to their story buddies. Yesterday, they began to study tropical rain forests and today they begin by reviewing the chart, "Things We Want To Know About The Rain Forest," that they worked on yesterday. To help them make a connection between yesterday and today, Tom asks his students to face their story buddies and share one thing from the list that they are most curious about. He waits a moment, asks his students to turn back to their "teacher positions" and, with all students now facing him, he begins to read the story *The Great Kapok Tree.* About every three to five minutes, he stops reading and asks a question. Questions are varied; some are designed to review what he has just read; some help the stu-

dents focus on information for their "Things We Want To Know" chart; other questions encourage students to predict what might happen next. Each time Tom asks a question, students turn to their story buddies. To encourage students to listen carefully to their partners, Tom takes a moment after the students discuss each question and asks a few students to "tell the class what your buddy said." Before he continues on with the next segment of the story, he reminds students to turn back to their teacher positions. By the time he has finished the story, his students have had several opportunities to talk with each other, and Tom has made sure that all students have had an opportunity to report one thing their partners have said.

Colleen's second graders have just completed a unit on dinosaurs. Working together—primarily in their dinosaur foursomes—they have learned many facts about many dinosaurs. Each carefully structured cooperative foursome has named itself after a different dinosaur; foursomes have read books about dinosaurs, they have written stories about dinosaurs, and they have plotted on the playground the sizes of different dinosaurs. Now Colleen wants her students to review these facts and talk with other classmates. She has created two worksheets that contain many questions about dinosaurs and distributed the worksheets so that each four-person group will have two copies of each worksheet. Her students roam about the room, interviewing each other and asking the questions that are on their worksheets. When they find someone who knows an answer they need, they stop, write the answer in their own words, and have that person sign their paper so that they can remember who helped them with an answer. After about ten minutes, Colleen has her students move into the four-person groups that they have worked in during their dinosaur unit. The students compare worksheets and answers, decide together if the answers they have written are correct and complete, and review their dinosaur facts once more. They quickly realize that they have learned a great deal about dinosaurs, that they are important resources for their classmates, and that their classmates are important resources for them.

Jane's fifth graders are reading *The Sign of the Beaver.* She knows that this is a challenging book for her students; she wants them to appreciate the dilemma that Matt faces and to practice their perspective-taking abilities. She knows that if she just asks her students to "share what you might do," they may not think through their own decisions carefully or listen to each other thoughtfully. So, Jane asks her students: "If you were Matt, would you go with Attean and the Beaver Clan or would you stay at the cabin?" and then has her students create a line from the front to the back of the room. Those at the front of the room are absolutely certain that Matt should obey his father and stay in the cabin. Those in the back of the room are absolutely sure he should go with the Indians. It takes Jane's students about five minutes to position themselves—to take a stance. During these five minutes, the students discuss characters and details from the story and (a) formulate and articulate their own positions and reasons carefully; (b) listen, compare, and differentiate the positions of others; and (c) realize that positions and decisions are often not as simple as they might first seem.

Marta is preparing to show a video about the human heart to a group of seventh graders. The desks in her classroom are grouped in fours, and students are seated at their desks. She begins by asking her students to "count off from one to four in your group." Next, she asks her students to put their heads together and list at least five things they know about the human heart; she gives them about two minutes to do this. Then, by using numbers, she calls on one student in each group to share items from that group's list; finally, she starts the video. The video is about twenty minutes long; twice she stops it and asks students questions that help them review what they have just seen and heard. Each time the procedure is the same; she gives them a moment to think by themselves; then she asks them to put their heads together and share with their group; and finally, she uses numbers to call on one person in each group to give a brief summary of the group's answer to her question. At the conclusion of the video, she uses the same procedure once again—this time asking students to list five new things they have learned about the human heart. Towards the end of her class, she explains the homework assignment and tells her students: "Make sure everyone in your group understands what he or she needs to do for homework before class tomorrow."

In Betty's tenth-grade chemistry class, students generally sit together in groups of four at lab tables for an entire marking period. Betty begins this class by having students number off from one to four. Betty has assigned a chapter of rather technical reading to her students, and she plans to spend the class period working with the concepts from the chapter. She begins by asking them to go around at their tables and respond to the questions "What is one concept you think you understand from your reading?" "What is one thing you need help to clarify?" She gives them five minutes to do this, reminding them that *each* member of the group needs to share responses to *both* questions within five minutes. While they talk, she walks around and listens; this gives her a good sense of where she needs to focus her work during the class period. She begins her lecture and demonstration and stops after about eight to ten minutes. When she stops, she uses an overhead to present her students with a problem that is related to the concept they are learning. She asks them to think by themselves about how they might solve the problem using the information they are learning. After a moment she asks them to share their ideas at their lab tables; she tells them they have three minutes to share ideas and decide on at least one possible way they might solve the problem. After three minutes, she asks all "persons #1" to stand, rotate one lab table around the room, and share their groups' ideas with new groups. She then continues with her lecture and demonstration. During the class, she repeats this process several more times. (The second time, she asks "persons #2" to rotate two groups; the third time "persons #3" rotate three groups; the fourth time, "persons #4" rotate.) At the conclusion of the class, students are all sitting at new lab tables in new foursomes. She gives them a few moments to reflect and asks them to discuss: "What is one concept that today's class helped you to clarify?" and "What concepts are still fuzzy?" Their homework is to reread the chapter, paying particular attention to the areas they still find "fuzzy."

Marilyn's students have been working together in formal learning groups for their entire study of *Huckleberry Finn*. Now she wants her tenth-grade students to review events and character development. She chooses to use informal groups so that her students can talk directly to each other—not through her—and so that they can talk with many of their classmates in a format that is well organized and nonthreatening. For homework, each student has prepared an index card that he or she can use to help describe an event from the novel and interpret what he or she thinks this event might indicate about the character involved. She asks her students to stand in two concentric circles—with the inside circle facing out and the outside circle facing in. The students in the inner circle begin sharing events and character interpretations with their partners in the outer circle. "Students in the outer circle listen intently and ask clarifying questions. Next, students in the outer circle share their events and interpretations. After both sets of explanations, the students trade cards, and the students in the outer circle rotate clockwise so that each student in the class now faces a new partner. Students must now explain the event and characterization represented by the new card they hold, the card given to them by their previous partner. With little teacher intervention, the students review many of the novel's critical events and share many interpretations of the characters as they continue to move around the circle—listening, offering explanations, and trading cards" (Kletzien & Baloche, 1994, p. 542).

Mike has just presented a lecture about events leading to the Revolutionary War to his eleventh-grade history class. He stops every few moments, asks a question, and has his students discuss their ideas with peers. At the conclusion of the class, Mike wants his students to talk with several peers—not just their lecture partners—and he wants his students to practice comparing, differentiating, and articulating several different ideas. He begins by writing four major events on the board and numbering them from one to four. He then asks his students to take a moment, think about each one, and decide—for themselves without discussion—which one they think might be the most significant. Students give a thumbs-up signal when they have made their choices. Next Mike points to the four corners of the room, numbers them one to four so that they correspond to the four events, and asks the students to move to the corners that represent their own choices. Once they are in their corners, he gives them a moment to find out why others have gone to the same corners. He randomly calls on one person in each corner to paraphrase some of the reasons that have been shared.

🐜 WORKING WITH PEERS 🐜

Forming Base Groups in the College Classroom

Participating in a base group is an important way to understand their subtlety and usefulness. In a college classroom, base groups can be formed using random assignment, interest inventories, sociometric data, or demographic information. Once base groups have been formed, members need opportunities to learn about each other and to establish routines. A common routine includes a base-group meeting at the beginning and end of each class. Meetings at the beginning of class often provide opportunities for students to discuss (a) information about personal events, (b) recent and upcoming tests and projects, and (c) a question designed to focus a review of readings or to provide an anticipatory set. Meetings at the end of class are designed to provide closure and reflection. One-minute papers are often shared in base groups. Starting in this chapter, the "Working with Peers" section of each chapter will include discussion questions or activities for base groups. It is helpful for base-group members to share phone numbers and information about schedules and for base groups to collect handouts and take notes for absent members.

Creating Base-Group Shields to Facilitate a Discussion of Commonalties

1. In four or five-person base groups, students work together to discover four or five commonalties that go beyond obvious choices such as "we all like pizza" and "we are all going to school."
2. Once lists of commonalties have been discovered, groups work together to create a shield, symbol, or picture that represents what they have in common. (If different-colored markers are available, each student might use just one color. Discussion and planning are encouraged when students each use a different color and all colors are incorporated into the work.)

3. Reflection and Planning:
   Group:
   - What strategies were used to discover commonalties? Did these strategies seem efficient?
   - Were we surprised about what we found?
4. So that students continue to learn about each other, each group might share its symbol with the whole class. Symbols can be used to decorate base-group folders; base-group folders are an efficient way to collect and return student work.

Using Our Memories and *Pens In The Middle* to Build an Understanding of the Nature of Interpersonal Support

1. In their base groups students each take one minute to describe a group in which they have felt support.
2. After each person shares, each other group member paraphrases one thing the person said. As group members paraphrase, they place pens in the middle of the group to "mark" their participation. (This encourages group members to listen carefully to one another.)
3. Reflection and Planning:
   Group:
   - What qualities did these different experiences have in common?
   - What qualities are helpful in building interpersonal support?
   - What qualities might we bring to our group to help build interpersonal support?

Using Base Groups to Review Chapter Content and Personalize Learning

QUESTION: *Which structure that you read about do you most want to use in a classroom with students? Why?*

1. Students think and write by themselves.

2. Students are to share with the other members of their base group. Before they share, they choose, as a group, an informal structure to facilitate their sharing. Choices include *Think-Pair-Square, Pens in the Middle, Group Interview, Roundrobin,* and *Three-Step Interview.*
3. Students use the chosen structure to share their responses.
4. Reflection and Planning:
   Individual:
   - On a scale of 1 to 5, how confident are you that you can explain why the other members in your group chose the structure they did?
   - How confident are you that they can all explain why you chose the structure you did?
   Group:
   - Was the structure we chose for our own discussion useful for our purpose?

Using *Blackboard Share* (Kagan, 1992) to Review Chapter Content

1. In groups of four (groups might be chosen randomly or base groups can be used), students count off one to four.
2. In their groups, students spend a few moments reviewing the chapter by discussing the question "What are the essential characteristics of base groups?" When groups seem to have had enough time, all #1 students move to the blackboard and write one characteristic that was discussed by their groups.
3. Groups read everything that has been written, paying particular attention to anything that is different from what their own groups discussed.
4. The procedure is repeated with students #2, #3, and #4 sharing at the blackboard in turn and responding to the questions "Why are base groups important in the development of a classroom that empowers students as learners?" "What are the essential characteristics of informal groups?" and "Why are informal groups important in the development of a classroom that empowers students as learners?"

Using Pairs and *Mad Hatter's Tea Party* for Analysis and Application of Chapter Content

1. Students group in random twos. Each pair is assigned one of the chapter scenarios that describes

informal groups. The scenarios are Tom, Marta, Betty, Mike, Colleen, Jane, and Marilyn. Each pair is to analyze its scenario, responding to the following questions:
   a. Why did the teacher choose to use informal cooperative learning groups in this lesson? What were the learning goals?
   b. Explain the teacher's choices using either a constructivist-developmental, information processing, motivation, or group development perspective.
   c. Did the teacher use any informal cooperative learning structure(s)? If so, what was the purpose of the structure? How did it fit with the goals?
   d. What other structure might the teacher have chosen?
2. Students then redesign the scenarios—working with partners, they decide how they could implement this alternative structure with the same academic content, goals, and students.
3. Pairs stay together and class stands (or sits) in two facing lines.
4. Pairs in one line explain to facing pairs in the other line what scenarios they analyzed—the goals, structure, and purpose. Pairs then explain what other structures might have been used, why, and how. The pairs who are listening are given an opportunity to ask clarifying questions.
5. Reflection and Planning:
   Pair:
   The listening pairs respond to the question:
   - Has your partner pair chosen a structure and explained it in a way that you are confident they understand how to use this structure with informal learning groups?
6. Pairs reverse roles: pairs who were formerly listeners now explain their analysis to their partner pairs and receive feedback on the Reflection and Planning question.
7. Reflection and Planning:
   Pair:
   All pairs caucus; they reflect on the feedback they have been given by their listening pairs, responding to the question:
   - How might we improve our ideas and/or our explanation?
8. One line of students shifts so that each pair now faces a new pair. Process is repeated one or two more times so that students have opportunities to

clarify their ideas and explanations and hear ideas from pairs who analyzed scenarios other from their own.

9. Reflection and Planning:

Individual:

- How has this activity helped me understand the subtleties of informal cooperative learning groups?

Pair:

- One way you helped me understand informal groups was _____.

Class:

- Was the *Mad Hatter's Tea Party* structure useful for our purpose in this exercise? What else might we have used?

Using a *One-Minute Paper* and *Stand and Share* (Kagan, 1992) to Reflect on the Purposes of Informal Learning Groups

QUESTION: *What one purpose of informal learning groups do you think is most crucial to their use in empowering students as learners? Why?*

1. Each student writes a response.

2. All students stand. Facilitator asks one student to share the purpose that he or she has decided is most crucial.

3. All students who have chosen the same purpose sit down.

4. A second student—one who is still standing—is asked to share. All students who have chosen this same purpose sit down.

5. Process is repeated until all students are sitting.

Using a *One-Minute Paper* and Base Groups to Reflect on Chapter Content

QUESTION: *What is one thing you learned in this chapter that you think might influence you as you reflect on the use of cooperative groups in classrooms?*

1. Each student writes a response.
2. Students share responses in their base groups.

CHAPTER 6

Formal Learning Groups: Building Positive Interdependence

As you read, you might want to ask yourself:

How are formal learning groups different from base groups and informal learning groups?

What is positive interdependence? Why is positive interdependence at the heart of high-quality cooperation? How is it structured into formal learning groups?

How might diverse groups of students be accommodated in formal learning groups in ways that empower all students as learners?

How does the use of formal learning groups help to develop and sustain a learning community?

What might the frequent use of formal learning groups look and sound and feel like in an empowering classroom?

In Chapter 5 we learned about base groups—long-term groups that provide interpersonal and academic support, encouragement, and assistance—and informal cooperative learning groups—short-term groups that are used to provide set, closure, and practice during direct teaching and movement and variety throughout the school day and year. In this chapter we will begin an investigation of a third type of group—the formal cooperative learning group. Used together, formal groups, informal groups, and base groups help to create rich, authentic learning communities that empower students as learners.

🐝   FORMAL GROUPS: CAREFUL   🐝
DESIGNS FOR LEARNING

Formal cooperative learning groups (D. Johnson, R. Johnson, & Holubec, 1992, 1993) are carefully designed, heterogeneous groups in which members work together on specific tasks. In formal learning groups students share:

- A goal to maximize the learning of all members.
- Both individual and group responsibility for their learning goals.
- Specific work goals that are to be accomplished cooperatively.
- Opportunities and obligations to learn and use the interpersonal and small-group skills that are needed to get the job done and build and maintain effective peer relationships.
- Opportunities and obligations to reflect on both learning and peer interaction.

Beginning in this chapter we will learn how to design formal learning groups and how to use the five basic elements of high-quality small-group cooperation—positive interdependence, simultaneous interaction, individual responsibility, interpersonal and small-group learning skills, and reflection and planning. In Chapter 7 we will examine how to identify and teach the interpersonal and small-group learning skills students need in order to work with others effectively. In Chapters 8 and 9 we will examine how to help students learn to reflect on and plan for their learning and their work together. In Chapter 9 we will also examine individual responsibility. In Chapter 10, we will explore ways to design learning opportunities that encourage positive simultaneous interaction. In this chapter we will focus primarily on positive interdependence.

🐝   POSITIVE INTERDEPENDENCE—   🐝
THE HEART OF THE MATTER

"The discipline of using [formal] cooperative groups begins with the careful structuring of positive interdependence" (D. Johnson, R. Johnson, & Holubec, 1993, p. 4:9). When positive interdependence is clearly structured and clearly understood, group members perceive that they—and their work—are linked for their mutual benefit, that the efforts of each group member will be unique, and that the unique efforts of all members will contribute to success. There are nine basic ways to structure positive interdependence into group work so that students will feel connected and committed to working together. The nine basic types of positive interdependence are goal, resource, role, identity, sequence, fantasy or simulation, outside-force, environmental, and celebration.

Goal Interdependence

Goal interdependence is fundamental to cooperative learning and is created when students understand that they share a mutual set of goals. The essence of shared goal interdependence is that students understand that they are working together to achieve a goal. This goal might be a shared product such as a list, a story, a picture or diagram, a report, or a completed experiment; the goal might be a better understanding of a concept, strategy, or procedure; the goal might be for every member of the group to achieve a certain criterion on an assessment. It is crucial that the teacher state the goal clearly so that the students understand it and understand that they are to work together to achieve it.

What may happen if students do not *understand their goals when they work together?*

Using Differentiated Goals to Accommodate Diversity and Increase Interdependence   Sometimes, when students with genuinely different educational needs, abilities, and backgrounds come together in cooperative learning groups, feeling of acceptance and interdependence may actually be increased by giving these students different but related and complementary goals. The use of differentiated goals is most successful when the goals communicate high expectations for all students and are combined with both careful attention to status issues and learning tasks that are multiability, multimodel, and integrated across subject areas. The importance of high expectations, perceptions of status, and complex, multiability tasks was discussed in Chapter 3. Here are two examples of how goals might be both differentiated and related as students work together:

> All students may be using the telephone book . . . but some students might be learning to dial 911 in case of an emergency, [others may be using the blue pages to learn about the resources available at their local government offices,] while others learn to compute and compare long distance charges and optimum calling times. Or, all students may be working on map skills, but at different levels. Perhaps Maria is learning about lines of latitude and longitude while Robin is learning the directions "up" and "down," "left," and "right." (Sapon-Shevin, Ayres, & Duncan, 1994, p. 51)

Teachers can differentiate and adapt goals, not only by level but by asking students to demonstrate their learning using different response modes and by adjusting the overall workload or time frame for an assignment (Nevin, 1993). For instance, instead of writing or speaking, a student might point, draw, or use a computer simulation to report what has been learned; or one group member might work to learn twenty words, another might be responsible for learning ten, and another might research how different language families have influenced this vocabulary.

K-W-H-L-S is one strategy that can be used with students of all ages to help insure that every student pursues goals that are congruent with the work the group is pursuing together and individually appropriate, interesting, and challenging. Figure 6.1 contains an example of a K-W-H-L-S worksheet that might be used for this purpose.

Pretending that differences do not exist makes it unlikely that all students will feel supported and included in the classroom learning community. Differentiating goals is *one* way to address directly the issue of differences—and it will often relieve the anxiety of all group members—but it is only a beginning to genuine cooperation. To empower students as learners, it is important to see that they share responsibility for (a) identifying the challenges that their groups face, (b) generating possible solutions that capitalize on the strengths of all members, (c) maximizing the learning of all members

Name of Student:				
K	**W**	**H**	**L**	**S**
What I know	What I want to learn	How I will learn it and work with others to attain our mutual goals	What I learned	How I shared, or will share, what I learned with others

Figure 6.1
Example of K-W-H-L-S (Know-Want to Learn-How Will Learn-Learned-Share with Others) worksheet that can be used to differentiate goals and build interdependence.

and the opportunities to share those learnings, and (d) building feelings of inclusion and shared goals for learning.

Once goal interdependence, which is essential, as been structured into a lesson, other types of positive interdependence can be added. These supplement goal interdependence and help to reinforce the message that students need to work together to maximize learning.

Resource Interdependence

When teachers structure resource interdependence, students share materials, information, or other resources. There are several basic ways to structure resource interdependence. A teacher might provide one set of materials to an entire group, giving each group member a different part of the needed materials. The teacher then makes sure that, when the group members put their materials together, they have a complete set. Large formats such as newsprint and markers are often useful when students share resources; these formats tend to convey a sense of shared ownership quite effectively. When markers are used, each student is usually provided with a different color. This encourages additional conversation and planning and provides the teacher with a way to monitor the contributions of each group member. Teachers may also want to structure resource interdependence so that students work independently to produce different pieces of needed information and then bring these pieces together to accomplish their group goal. When teachers structure resource interdependence, students often share materials and information within their groups; at other times, students share between groups. Sometimes, however, students do need their own materials for optimal learning—either during cooperative work or for independent practice—so it is important for teachers to plan the distribution of resources carefully.

Resource interdependence is more than just telling students to "share." What can teachers do to help insure that sharing resources encourages high levels of cooperation and learning?

Structures That Help Build Resource Interdependence Within a Group

Resource interdependence is most often built into a lesson *without* the use of special structures; there are, however, several structures, described in this section, that can be used to help build routine and add spice and variety to the sharing of resources.

Blind Hand can be used to help students understand that they, often literally, have part of the picture but not the whole picture; it can be used to help teach or review sequencing. *Blind Hand* can be used (a) with pictures—drawings photocopied from a picture book, illustrations of the stages in a life cycle, frames from a comic strip; (b) with written descriptions—events from a story or historical time period, the evidence needed to solve a "mystery" or problem, steps in a complex procedure; and (c) with representational symbols—steps in an equation or complex chemical reaction.

🐜 🐜 🐜 🐜 🐜 🐜

Blind Hand (Kagan, 1992)

Group size: three or four

1. Teacher divides material into pieces. Each student receives one (or two) piece(s) of material.
2. Students each examine their own pieces of material to make sure they can describe the details.
3. Students work together to determine the sequence or to describe the entire event that they each "have a piece of."

   The rules of *Blind Hand* are:

   a. You can tell (or read) what is on your paper, but you cannot show it.
   b. You can ask questions.
   c. You can take notes and share your notes.
4. Once students think they have determined the sequence or solved the problem, they put their resources together in sequence and look at "the whole picture." Before they check their work, it is often useful to ask students to reflect, as individuals, about how confident they are that their group's work is "accurate" or "makes sense."
5. Students reflect on their work together. Planning how to proceed is an essential skill with *Blind Hand,* and it may be useful for students to discuss: "Did we have a plan?" "Did our plan work?" "How did we decide what was important?"

What's good about *Blind Hand:* All students, regardless of status, have an opportunity to share their information and gather information from others. Students have an opportunity and obligation to practice many cognitive skills—including sequencing, descriptive language, deciding what is important, looking for details, comparing, contrasting, and synthesizing.

Interpersonal and Small-Group Learning Skills: Sharing information (and knowing when and what to share), listening carefully, taking turns, asking clarifying and probing questions.

🐜 🐜 🐜 🐜 🐜 🐜

In the following examples, all three teachers use *Blind Hand,* but with different content and for different purposes.

Gene wants to review the sequence in a story with second graders. He photocopies sets of six pictures and, using *Blind Hand* in groups of three, his students decide how to sequence these six pictures to retell a story they have read together.

Geri photocopies pictures from books her third-grade students do not know. They use *Blind Hand* to discuss the pictures and then create their own stories. Although all groups have the same pictures, their stories are often quite different, and groups can "compare and contrast" their work.

Pat uses *Blind Hand* in chemistry. She divides a set of symbols that represent a chemical reaction into pieces and, in groups, her students have to use their knowledge to decide what sequence makes sense.

Jigsaw is a commonly used structure that emphasizes resource interdependence—primarily within a group but across groups as well. *Jigsaw* is often used with written material. Dividing material into sections—sections of a chapter, stages in a life cycle, contributing factors to a major event, text sets about a particular theme, and so forth—is a common way to use *Jigsaw*. For instance:

Joe's students read Tennessee Williams' *Glass Menagerie*. "Joe then assigned each student to read one of five additional plays. In 'jigsaw' groups of five, the students presented their plays and discussed similarities in plot, character, setting, and theme" (Baloche, Lee Mauger, Willis, Filinuk, & Michalsky, 1993, p. 45).

Jigsaw can also be used with nonwritten material. Students might use different sets of manipulatives, conduct different experiments, solve different equations, work with different computer simulations, or act out different scenes in a play, and then come together to share their experiences and teach what they have learned. *Jigsaw* can be used (a) for an initial overview and input of information; (b) for review; or (c) to provide students with one in-depth experience and an overview of several other experiences—this is a particularly good use of *Jigsaw* when time and equipment are in short supply. As with all resource interdependence, when *Jigsaw* is used, the teacher always has to decide if, ultimately, students will need access to their own sets of materials or readings. The key to *Jigsaw* is not just that students do or read different things and then talk about them; the key to *Jigsaw* is interdependence.

Jigsaw (Aronson, Blaney, Stephan, Sikes, & Snapp, 1978)

Group size: three or four

1. Teacher divides material into sections—one section for each student.
2. Students prepare their own sections of material—they read, conduct experiments, solve problems with the help of a set of manipulatives, and so forth. This preparation might be done alone—in class or for homework—or with "preparation partners." This decision is made by the teacher, depending on the nature of the assignment and abilities of the students.
3. Students meet in "practice pairs." Each student meets with someone from a different group who has learned the same material. The purpose of this group is both to review and reconceptualize the material and to plan how the material might be best taught or presented to teammates.
4. Students present their work to the other members of their groups. Teacher encourages students to ask questions and to engage in genuine discussion, not just passive listening.
5. Students reflect on the presentations and the information they have learned. Sentences such as "You helped me learn this material when you _____" and "One new idea I learned today was _____" are useful prompts for reflection.
6. Individual mastery of students is assessed.

What's good about *Jigsaw:* Students have an opportunity to think by themselves. Students have opportunities to conceptualize, reconceptualize, and teach information or procedures to others.

Interpersonal and Small-Group Learning Skills: Sharing ideas and materials; listening carefully, organizing, teaching, and synthesizing information; asking clarifying and probing questions.

Academic Controversy is a structure that emphasizes perspective taking and consensus building within groups and resource interdependence both within groups and across groups. *Academic Controversy* is particularly useful when issues are complex and it is important for students to understand different perspectives; the structure helps students to develop both greater understanding of the subject matter and good skills for managing controversy constructively. The controversy structure can be used at any grade level. For instance:

Linda has used *Academic Controversy* with first graders to have them decide whether "Jack [from "Jack and the Beanstalk"] is a good boy" or "Jack is not a good boy."

Lauren has asked her second graders to decide whether to have junk food or healthy snacks at their Halloween party.

In Gail's fourth-grade class, students have discussed whether it is better to sit in rows or in small groups.

Arlene's students discussed "Everyone needs to know math" and "Everyone does not need to know math."

Valerie's English classes discussed "Holden Caulfield [from *Catcher in the Rye*] is selfish" and "Holden Caulfield is not selfish."

Academic Controversy (D. Johnson & R. Johnson, 1992)

Group size: four

1. Teacher prepares statements to be discussed.
2. Students are assigned to groups of four. Within each foursome, each student is assigned a partner and a point of view on the issue. Students work with partners to prepare reasoning for these positions.
3. Each student meets in a "preparation pair" with a student from another group who has prepared the same position. The purpose of this pair is to reconceptualize and to share materials and strategies.
4. Students meet again in their original pairs, compare notes, and finish preparing positions. "Our best case is _____."
5. Each pair of students presents its position while the other pair listens and takes notes. "The answer is _____ because _____."
6. The two pairs enter into an open discussion. "Your idea is wrong because _____. My idea is right because _____."

7. The two pairs reverse perspectives. Each pair now prepares a new argument.
8. The two pairs present their new arguments and points of view. "Our position now is _____ because _____."
9. The two pairs drop advocacy and work together to build a well-reasoned synthesis. "Given what we now know, our best reasoned judgment is _____."

What's good about *Academic Controversy:* Students have an opportunity to develop well-reasoned arguments and practice the skills of idea differentiation, perspective taking, and consensus building.

Interpersonal and Small-Group Learning Skills: Many skills are used in *Academic Controversy,* including the skills of perspective taking, building reasoned arguments, disagreeing in an agreeable way, extending the ideas of others, and integrating different ideas into coherent positions.

Structures That Help Build Resource Interdependence Among Groups

Sharing resources among groups helps to build intergroup cooperation and helps to build a learning community. When students work together in groups, it is useful for other groups to benefit from their work and learning. Both *Jigsaw* and *Academic Controversy* include some active sharing of resources among groups. When not carefully designed, group "sharing" often means "stand and report." This is time consuming and often boring; because it requires that only one group talk at a time, it does not provide opportunities for students to actively process and reconceptualize the work of their peers. Structures such as *One-Stay Three-Stray* and *Gallery Tour,* described in this section, can help create active, interactive alternatives.

How does sharing resources among groups help build a sense of community based on learning?

One-Stay Three-Stray

Group size: three or four

1. Students have worked together in their small groups to solve a problem, complete an experiment, or create a visual such as a story map, chart, or graph. This structure is best used when groups have produced a tangible product.
2. Students count off in their groups.
3. The #1 person in the group rotates one group, the #2 person rotates two groups, and, in a group of four, the #3 person rotates three groups. (Each one of these steps is best done one at a time to eliminate confusion.) One person stays "home." Students are now in totally new groups.
4. The person who "stayed home" now explains his or her old group's work to the visitors. Visitors often ask questions to make sure they understand and frequently take notes. The visitors give one piece of specific positive feedback to the home-group representative about that group's work. They thank the representative for staying home to explain the group's work.
5. Everyone moves back to his or her home group. First, the person who stayed home tells the other group members what positive things the visitors have said

about their work. Next persons #1, #2, and #3 explain what they have seen in different groups—comparing and contrasting the ideas and formats with their own.
6. Students reflect on their work together.

What's good about *One-Stay Three-Stray:* All students, regardless of status, have an opportunity and responsibility to share information and gather information from others. Students have an opportunity to practice many cognitive skills, including the use of descriptive language, deciding what is important, looking for details, comparing, contrasting, and synthesizing.

Interpersonal and Small-Group Learning Skills: Sharing ideas; moving in an organized way; asking questions; giving descriptive, positive feedback.

Gallery Tour (Kagan, 1992)

Group size: three or four

1. Students have worked together in their small groups to solve a problem, complete an experiment, or create a visual such as a story map, chart, or graph. This structure is best used when groups have produced a tangible product.
2. These products are hung or otherwise displayed around the room.
3. Work groups rotate to visit and discuss each display. (This is best done in an organized way with some signal from the teacher to indicate when it is time for students to move.) Sometimes students take notes, and often each group leaves a piece of descriptive feedback at each display. This can be done by using self-stick notes or by using feedback forms that have been specifically designed for the particular activity.
4. Students return to their own work. They might discuss the feedback that has been left by other groups; they might discuss how their work was the same as or different from other work they saw; they might add an idea to their work that they gleaned from the work of another group.
5. Students reflect on their work together.

What's good about *Gallery Tour:* Students have an opportunity to practice both giving and receiving feedback about work. Students have an opportunity to discuss the work of other groups and compare and contrast it with their own. Everyone gets to talk at once in an organized and productive manner.

Interpersonal and Small-Group Learning Skills: Sharing and comparing ideas; moving in an organized way; giving descriptive, positive feedback.

Using *Group Investigation* to Build Resource Interdependence in a Learning Community   *Group Investigation* is a complex structure that has been developed by Yael and Shlomo Sharan and their associates; it is based on Dewey and Thelen's ideas of education in, and for participation in, a democracy. It is designed to provide students with many opportunities to influence what and how they learn. When a class enters into an investigation, students "break a subject into specific questions, sort themselves into groups to explore these questions, plan and conduct an investigation, and figure out how to share what they have learned" (Kohn, 1993, p. 13).

Group Investigation (Y. Sharan & S. Sharan, 1992, 1994)

1. The teacher begins by choosing a problem that is multifaceted, can be investigated using a variety of resources, and has relevance to the lives of students both in and out of the classroom. In other words, the teacher chooses a problem that is worth investigating and can be investigated in a variety of ways. The teacher collects informational resources. This helps the teacher to determine if the overall problem is "doable" and to get organized. These materials help to motivate students and provide students with a starter kit of resources. The teacher presents the general problem, question, or topic that is to be investigated.
2. The class members scan their resources, discuss their interests and priorities, determine subtopics, and organize into research groups.
3. The groups plan their investigations. They further refine their questions, divide their work, and assign roles to help them manage their work as a group.
4. The groups carry out their investigations. During this phase, as in all phases of *Group Investigation,* the teacher is an active facilitator—helping groups plan, organize, and pace their work and helping them develop and use the skills they need to build and maintain their interpersonal relationships.
5. The groups plan their presentations. During this phase the groups must decide what they have learned in their investigations and how to organize and present their findings. Presentations need to be interesting and need to include all group members. Sometimes representatives from each group form a steering committee to coordinate the presentations of different groups into a coherent schedule.
6. The groups make their presentations.
7. The groups reflect on their work—as individuals, as groups, and as a class.

What's good about *Group Investigation:* Students have many opportunities to think for themselves, to make choices, to share information and experiences with others, and to participate in collective inquiry. *Group Investigation* is not a group project. The steps of the investigation, when well planned and facilitated by a skilled teacher, help create an experience in which students have both opportunity and responsibility to contribute to the classroom learning community.

Interpersonal and Small-Group Learning Skills: Many skills are used in *Group Investigation,* including the skills of making choices, planning, asking questions, and integrating ideas.

Role Interdependence

As a teacher, how important is it to you that students have opportunities to learn different small-group roles?

When teachers assign students complementary and interconnected roles that are designed to help groups get their tasks done and build and maintain their relationships with each other, they are structuring role interdependence.

Deciding When Assigned Roles Are Needed   In Chapter 2 we learned that when individuals come together in groups, different individuals tend to assume different roles, even when these roles are not assigned. When we examined Bales' theory, we learned that, in order to be successful, groups need members to assume both task roles—roles that help the group achieve its goals—and positive maintenance roles—roles that help group members build and maintain their relationships. In Chapter 3 we examined how status and other factors may influence the roles that people assume. These ideas all have practical implications for how and why teachers might use roles during cooperative group work. Teachers assign roles for several reasons: (a) to help insure that both the task and maintenance needs of a group are addressed, (b) to teach all members of a group the skills needed to assume both task and maintenance roles—and the sensitivity to know when these are needed, and (c) to provide all members of a group with opportunities to assume different roles. It is not acceptable if Arty Artist is always the drawer, Susie Scribe is always the secretary, Meticulous Matt is always the materials manager, Mary Marvel is always the mathematician, and Gracious Grace is always the encourager; students need to learn and have opportunities to assume a wide variety of roles. It is not enough just to assign roles to students; students need to be taught what these roles are and how, when, and why to use them in their group contexts. Definitions, role plays, modeling, and feedback are all important aspects of assigning and using roles. These will be discussed further in Chapters 7, 8, 9, and 10. It is important to remember that roles may seem artificial. Often a role seems artificial because it asks an individual or group to practice a behavior that is new or typically underutilized. When this is the case, the artificial feeling disappears as the behavior becomes more integrated into the repertoire of the individual or group. As the use of a specific behavior becomes more integrated or "natural," and as the use of both task and maintenance functions becomes well distributed in groups, roles become less necessary. In the following scenario, Joyce's students have developed a sophisticated understanding of how to use roles, and Joyce is able to share influence with her students by having them decide when to use them.

 Joyce, a fourth-grade teacher, has taught her students about ten basic group roles; these roles are listed and defined on a bulletin board in her classroom. She does not, however, always assign roles. Once she is confident that her students know different roles and know what it feels like to be members of a well-functioning group, she often lets her students decide if they need to use specific roles. One day, for instance, she began her math lesson by describing the academic task and then asking the math groups each to decide (a) if they needed to assign roles to accomplish their task and (b) what roles might be the most useful. At the conclusion of the class, Joyce first processed the academic content of the lesson to make sure her students had completed the task with a high level of accuracy and had understood the mathematical procedures they had used. Next, Joyce asked the groups (a) whether or not they had used roles—some groups had while others had not, (b) why they had made their choices, (c) whether or not they were pleased with their choices, and (d) what roles they had used if they had chosen to use roles. Joyce changes math groups about once a month, so groups made decisions based on their recent experiences together. This is how the spokesperson for one group described its decision.

Joyce:	Did your group use roles?
Joseph:	Yes.
Joyce:	What ones and why?
Joseph:	Well, we decided to use an encourager, accuracy checker, and time keeper because yesterday we had some problems . . . well . . . it seemed that maybe everyone didn't work all that much so we like needed someone to encourage everybody to do it and we didn't quite get done so we needed somebody to remind us to . . . well, you know, get done. And, well, we always kind of like need somebody to check— because it's math.
Joyce:	Was your group happy with their choices?
Joseph:	Yeah, we did better and we are happier with each other.

Roles That Help Groups Complete Their Tasks and Maintain Their Relationships   There are several "generic" roles that teachers frequently assign to group members. These include (Bennett, Rolheiser, & Stevahn, 1991).

- Checker: The checker's job is to ensure that everybody understands the work in progress.
- Scout: The scout's job is to seek additional information from other groups.
- Timekeeper: The timekeeper's job is to keep the group focused on the task and monitor the time.
- Active Listener: The active listener's job is to repeat or paraphrase what has been said.
- Questioner: The questioner's job is to seek information and opinions from all members of the group.
- Summarizer: The summarizer's job is to pull together the conclusions of the group so that they can be presented coherently.
- Encourager: The encourager's job is to provide support to members of the group so that they are more enthused about their participation.
- Materials Manager: The materials manager's job is to collect all necessary material for the group.
- Reader: The reader's job is to read material to the group.

These generic roles are a good place to start, but specialized roles may be useful also. If, for instance, the accuracy rate is low during a math problem-solving session, it may be important to develop the role of Accuracy Seeker.

Daniels (1994) describes eight roles for use with literature circles; these roles help to distribute different thinking tasks in a group and to encourage sustained, kid-directed discussions. Daniels provides his students with "role sheets" that help them organize their roles and responsibilities; he knows that, once his students become skilled, these role sheets become unnecessary. Daniels' eight roles are

- Discussion Director: The discussion director's job is to develop a list of questions that the group might want to discuss. The discussion director doesn't worry about the small details but helps people talk over the big ideas.

- Literary Luminator: The literary luminator's job is to locate a few special sections of the text that the group would like to hear read aloud and to decide how to present them.
- Illustrator: The illustrator's job is to draw some kind of picture related to the reading.
- Connector: The connector's job is to find connections between the book the group is reading and the world outside.
- Summarizer: The summarizer's job is to prepare a brief summary that conveys the essence of the reading.
- Vocabulary Enricher: The vocabulary enricher's job is to be on the lookout for a few words that are puzzling, unfamiliar, used in an unusual way, used a lot, or particularly important.
- Travel Tracer: The travel tracer's job is to describe the setting and to track where the action takes place.
- Investigator: The investigator's job is to dig up background information related to the book. For instance, the investigator might focus on geography, weather, culture, history, the author, the time period, or the illustrations. (pp. 77–84)

Using Flexible Roles to Accommodate Diversity and Increase Interdependence   Sometimes roles need to be assigned and interpreted flexibly so that students with different abilities can contribute meaningfully during group work. Take Kris for example:

> Kris, whose goals for math included writing numbers from 1 to 50 and using a calculator to compute problems, was given the role of writer/checker within her group. The other students in the group determined what mathematical function to use for the problem, helped Kris write down the problem on the worksheet by dictating the numbers, solved the problem, and dictated to Kris the numbers to write down for the answers. Kris was then responsible for checking the group's response on her calculator. (Sapon-Shevin, Ayres, & Duncan, 1994, p. 54)

The role of writer/checker is fairly common. Kris is assigned this role when her profile of abilities and her learning goals make her a "natural" for the role, not at a time when it might prove too difficult and without benefit to her or to other group members. Sometimes a role can be created or altered to provide a good fit with a student's unique profile of abilities. Sometimes it is necessary to provide individual coaching for a role before the student begins group work. Sometimes a student may need help to fulfill a role; this help might be provided by another student or an instructional assistant. When this approach is used, it is important for group members to relate directly with the student—not through the helper. Sometimes the assigning of roles is a delicate business—an art that can make a big difference both in how students perceive their capabilities and in how they are perceived by others. Eileen, for example, works with severely disturbed adolescents like John, a young man who reads at a preprimer level and came to her class with a long history of physical violence.

John's Story

Early in the year Eileen noticed that John became violent and had to be removed from class whenever books appeared. Eileen decided that John might be embarrassed about not being able to read. Eileen was committed to developing cooperative tasks where students are able to use a wide range of abilities. She was also committed to helping John learn to read, and she knew that John wasn't going to learn to read if he wasn't in class! Eileen began by asking John to work in a group of three and by placing him with students who were not easily frightened or prone to physical violence. She started with tasks that required no reading, and she kept books out of sight. When she began to use books, she assigned John the role of "reporter"; she knew that John loved to talk, and she didn't want him to worry about not being able to read. John's violent behavior subsided; he has not been excluded from the class for several months. He is a good reporter—and a good artist, too—and other students have learned to appreciate and count on these abilities. He has begun to pay attention when other members of his group read, he has begun to pick up books, and he has begun to read.

Identity Interdependence

When teachers want to build feelings of whole-class inclusion, they sometimes help a class develop a class name, slogan, cheer, or song. When teachers want to structure interdependence in small groups, they sometimes ask each group to create a unique name, motto, logo, shield, cheer, or special handshake. This is called identity interdependence and is typically used either for humor or when groups will be working together for relatively long periods of time. Special group identities sometime relate to the specific subject that the students are studying together. A math group might name itself "The Einsteins," "The Marvelous Multipliers," or "The Curious Calculators"; a social-studies group might name itself after an explorer; literature groups might name themselves after favorite authors or characters; in a music class, groups might develop theme songs, chants, or rhythmic motifs. At other times, students will choose names, logos, or mottoes that relate to their own characteristics or interests; these tend to be quite creative and give students opportunities to learn more about each other.

Have you ever been in a group that developed a special name? What was the group? What was the name?

Sequence Interdependence

When teachers structure sequence interdependence, a group accomplishes its overall task by completing a defined series of subtasks that need to be completed sequentially—one step at a time. In general, each group member is responsible for completing one step in the sequence. Some tasks are naturals for sequence interdependence. For instance, one student prepares a specimen on the slide and places it on a microscope, the second draws the specimen, the third describes it in writing. One student looks a word up in the dictionary, the second writes the definition, the third uses it in a sentence. One student gathers the ingredients for a recipe, the second measures, the third mixes.

Using *Simultaneous Roundtable* to Structure Sequence Interdependence The structure *Simultaneous Roundtable*, described in this section, can be used to design lessons that heighten (a) students' awareness of a step-by-step problem-solving procedure, (b) students' motivation to check work for accuracy and care if others learn, and (c) simultaneous interaction.

Mai uses *Simultaneous Roundtable* with her first-grade students when they are learning subtraction. Working with groups of four, she gives each student a blank sheet of paper. She asks her students to fold their pieces of paper in half and to draw five objects on the top half. Then she has her students pass their papers one person clockwise around their groups. She asks the second person to cross out one, two, three, or four of the objects the first person has drawn. Students pass papers a third time. She asks the third person to write the subtraction problem that is represented by the drawing on the bottom half of the paper. Students pass the papers again. She asks the fourth person to write the answer to the subtraction problem.

Simultaneous Roundtable (Kagan, 1992)

Group size: three or four

1. Teacher sequences material to be learned—often using a series of worksheets to organize the procedure.
2. Each student completes Step One.
3. Students rotate worksheets. (When using *Simultaneous Roundtable* with small children, learning to rotate papers is in itself a lesson. Small children sometimes get upset when they see the second person write on "their" papers. This becomes a lesson in sharing and resource interdependence as they learn that the worksheets are "our work," not "my work.")
4. Students check Step One and complete Step Two.
5. Process repeats until sequence has been completed.
6. Students reflect on learning.
7. What's good about *Simultaneous Roundtable:* All students are active. All students, regardless of status, have both an opportunity and an obligation to participate. Students learn to follow step-by-step procedures.
8. Interpersonal and Small-Group Learning Skills: Active participation, sharing materials, and (depending on activity) checking accuracy.

Fantasy or Simulation Interdependence

When teachers structure fantasy or simulation interdependence, they build scenarios that are related to a group's task and require a group to work through a hypothetical situation. Fantasy interdependence has traditionally been coupled with "survival" activities such as "Winter Survival," "Nuclear Shelter," or "Who Should Get the Heart"—activities that require groups to clarify their values and make "life and death" decisions. But fantasy or simulation interdependence may also involve students in other "pretend" situations. Students, for instance, might be part of a Conestoga wagon team, they might be a group of scientists or space travelers, or they might be travel agents planning a trip to an exotic location. Like identity interdependence, fantasy or simulation interdependence can be used to add spice to a lesson and to heighten the sense that "we are in this together."

Have you ever been in a group that used fantasy interdependence? What was the group? Was it fun?

Outside-Force Interdependence

Teachers structure outside-force interdependence when they place groups in competition with some outside force. In general, students should not compete against other groups within the same class, and competition between classes is counterproductive to school-based community building. Competition, if used at all, is probably best used sparingly—with students competing against their own individual or group scores or against the clock (when tasks are simple and speed and accuracy is important). In general, competition—even in the form of outside-force interdependence—should be used only when a class has built a strong sense of mutual respect and community, *not* as a motivator during rough times or for particularly difficult work.

Using *Student Teams-Achievement Divisions (STAD)* to Structure Outside-Force Interdependence into a Cooperative Context   *Student Teams-Achievement Divisions,* described in this section, is a structure that, if used carefully within a cooperative context, incorporates manageable competition and high levels of individual responsibility into learning. *STAD* can be used to add variety and interest when the material that students need to learn is factual, "right answer" information. *STAD* combines cooperative, competitive, and individualized learning into a single structure. It has a strong individual responsibility component that focuses on individual improvement and a strong group component that relies on group rewards.

Student Teams-Achievement Divisions (Slavin, 1995)

Group size: four

1. Teacher makes presentation of material to be learned and tested.
2. Students work together in academically heterogeneous teams to learn material and prepare for the quizzes and tests that they will each take individually.
3. Teacher provides guided practice.
4. Students take quizzes and tests individually.

5. Teams earn scores based on the "improvement points" of the team members. To determine team scores:

a. Calculate "base" scores of individual members. In general, base scores can be calculated by averaging scores on a few individual quizzes that are given before beginning *STAD*.

b. Determine improvement points.

Quiz Score	Improvement Points
more than 10 points below base score	5
10 points below to 1 point below base score	10
base score to 10 points above base score	20
more than 10 points above base score	30
perfect paper (regardless of base score)	30

c. Determine team scores. Individual students bring their improvement points to their team. The individual improvement points of all team members are added together and then averaged.

6. Teams are recognized for their achievements. Since it is possible for all teams to achieve awards, in essence, teams are not competing against each other. *STAD* encourages individual students to focus on—or compete against—their own past performance.

Criterion (Team Average)	Award
15	*Good Team*
20	*Great Team*
25	*Super Team*

What's good about *Student Teams-Achievement Divisions:* Students develop a strong sense of individual responsibility. All students have equal opportunities to contribute towards the success of the team. All teams can be successful since scoring is criterion, not norm, referenced.

Interpersonal and Small-Group Learning Skills: Helping others learn, seeking accuracy.

Environmental Interdependence

When teachers structure environmental interdependence, they plan the physical environment carefully to encourage students to stay together in the same space. In general, it is important for teachers to think about how they want to structure the environment and to express this clearly to students so that students know when they are "with their group" or "away from their group." Expressions such as these are helpful:

- "Sit in your partner position."
- "Sit eye to eye and knee to knee."
- "Sit so that you and your partner are inside your hula hoop."
- "Sit so that the legs of your chairs touch in a circle."

- "Stand shoulder to shoulder."
- "Work so that you can all see the material, can make eye contact, and can use 12-inch voices."

In Chapter 10 we will examine specific seating arrangements that can be used to manage grouping and encourage environmental interdependence.

Rewards and Incentives—Celebration Interdependence

When teachers structure celebration interdependence, students share a common incentive or reward, or they share a celebration when they reach their goal. The use of rewards is controversial. Some research indicates that (a) reward lowers motivation—especially the types of intrinsic motivation that are associated with psychological health and long-term success; (b) when students expect a reward, they tend to choose easier problems than when no reward is expected (Shapira, 1976; Pittman, Emery, & Boggiano, 1982); (c) when students have been rewarded, in subsequent unrewarded activity, they exhibit less interest and choose easier problems than nonrewarded students; and (d) rewarded students tend to confine their attention to information that is directly related to their goal (R. Johnson & Thomson, 1962; McNamara & Fisch, 1964).

Why is it important to think carefully about rewards and incentives? How might rewards have negative consequences? When are they important?

Rewards are best not used as a matter of routine. Nonetheless, teachers sometimes feel it is necessary to reward students—to offer them incentives when a job is well done or to encourage them to do the job at all. When incentives are linked with a group goal, interdependence is created. Whether this interdependence is positive or negative depends on how the incentive is structured. *When structuring incentive interdependence, it is important for students to believe that working with others can help but not hurt their chances to get the reward.* When differentiated goals have been established to accommodate diverse learners, these need to be acknowledged so that all groups and all individuals feel that they have access to the reward when the job is well done. When students do not believe that they have access to the reward or that others can help them achieve the reward, teachers tend to hear complaints about group membership such as "We don't want to work with ____ and ____. They'll keep us from getting ____."

Structuring Positive Incentive Interdependence   Bonus points are one way to link assessment and interdependence. When bonus points are used, *all* group members receive extra points when the individual score of *each* group member is above a certain criterion. Depending on the membership of the group, criteria might be the same for each group member or might be different and determined by base and improvement scores. This approach is quite different from simply giving a "group grade." (Assessment and grading issues are discussed in Chapter 9.) In real life, work is often collaborative, and rewards are often based on the output of the whole group; in class-rooms, however, this approach to rewards is often problematic and should be approached cautiously unless students, parents, and teachers alike have developed sophisticated understandings of the nature of cooperation and high-performance teams. When this happens, rewards will probably be un-necessary anyway.

When incentives are used, it is essential that all groups in a class can "win" the incentive; incentives should be criterion—not norm—referenced, and groups should not compete against each other. Whenever possible, build interdependence through whole-class rather than small-group incen-tives. For instance, each group that meets the criterion contributes three points to the class score, and when the class accumulates 100 points, they share a whole-class event—a celebration. The word *celebration* is key. In-centives should (a) be designed to encourage sustained periods of learning and collaboration—not connected with single pieces of work; and (b) help create a climate that encourages and celebrates the success of all class members. Grades and bonus points are not the only incentives that can be used to build positive interdependence. As we explored in Chapter 4, whenever possible, both small-group incentives and whole-class celebra-tions should be linked to learning, to collaboration, to joy, and to choices that students make themselves. For instance, appropriate incentives might include reading with friends or to younger students, computer time, or extra time for a cooperative game. A class might celebrate its work to-gether by listening to an extra chapter in a favorite read-aloud, by choosing which unit to begin next, by planning the next free-activity period or a night at the movies, or by deciding together what tie the teacher should wear on Friday.

In this chapter we have begun to learn the discipline of creating coop-eration through the application of five basic elements to lesson design; we have focused specifically on the careful structuring of positive interdepen-dence. Next, we turn our attention to several classroom scenarios. When planning their lessons, all of these teachers rely on their understanding of the five basic elements—positive interdependence, simultaneous interac-tion, individual responsibility, interpersonal and small-group learning skills, and reflection and planning—to inform their decision making as they de-velop and facilitate learning opportunities that encourage their students to become empowered learners who are capable of both meaningful coopera-tive inquiry and high levels of independent thought. Take the time to read these scenarios carefully. As you read, ask yourself: "What kinds of positive interdependence has this teacher used—goal, resource, role, identity, se-quence, fantasy or simulation, outside-force, environmental, or celebration? Why has the teacher made these choices?" You might also consider how you think it might feel to be a student in one of these classrooms. How do you think it might feel to be the teacher?

A VIEW FROM THE CLASSROOM: BUILDING POSITIVE INTERDEPENDENCE INTO LEARNING

Patrick is teaching beginning consonant sounds to his kindergarten children. This week they are learning *B*. Patrick has introduced the letter; the children have made *B* sounds, they have bounced balls, and Patrick has read a story about Bobo the Bear. Now they are going to work in pairs. Patrick gives each child an index card with a letter *B* on it—some of the letters are capital letters and some are lower case, and they are printed in a variety of colors. He asks the children to come to the rug and find their partners by finding classmates with letters written in the same color. When the children find their partners, Patrick asks them to sit on the rug, face their partners, shake hands, and say "Hey, Buddy." Patrick tells the children that, when they face their partners, they are in their partner positions. Then he asks all the students to face him and tells them that, when they face the teacher, they are in their teacher positions. He has them practice both positions a few times.

Patrick holds up several pictures that he has cut from a magazine. When he holds up each one, he asks the children to move to their partner positions and decide together if the object in the picture starts with a *B* sound. He gives them a moment to decide, asks them to turn back to their teacher positions, and then asks them to signal "thumbs up" or "thumbs down." Next, Patrick helps the children to discover that, although their letters are the same color as their partners', they are shaped a little differently—each pair has one capital and one lowercase letter. Patrick holds up a *B* and asks the children with similar letters to raise their hands. When he is sure that only one child in each pair has a hand raised, he asks these children to come to the front of the room and he hands each one a magazine. Once they have returned to their partners, he holds up a *b* and asks the children with similar letters to raise their hands. Again, after making sure that only one child in each pair has a hand raised, he asks these children to come to the front of the room, and he hands each one a large envelope. He moves among the pairs, handing each a single pair of scissors.

Patrick tells the children that they are going to work with their partners to find pictures that begin with the *B* sound. Patrick asks one pair of children to come to the front of the room; he coaches them through the procedure he wants each pair to follow. First, the "*B* child" looks through a magazine and finds a picture that she thinks begins with the *B* sound. Then, she says to her partner: "Do you think this begins with a *b* sound?" Her partner looks at the picture and says "yes" or "no." Finally, if they both agree the picture begins with the correct sound, the "*b* child" takes the scissors, cuts out the picture, and places it in the large envelope. The pair repeats the procedure, but this time the children reverse roles; the "*b* child" finds a picture, and the "*B* child" cuts it out and places it in the envelope. Once Patrick has completed this demonstration, he asks the children to turn back to their partner positions; he also reminds them to use quiet voices and to stay with their partners. He then asks the "*B* children" to pick up their magazines and begin looking for pictures. He walks among the groups to monitor the work and make sure the children switch jobs with each picture. The children work together for about ten minutes, and each pair finds several pictures. Patrick asks them to put their scissors and magazines aside. He then asks them to take all their pictures out of the envelope and pick one to share with the entire class. In turn, each pair shares a picture, and the other children signal whether or not the picture begins with a *B* sound. The children put all their pictures back in their envelopes. Patrick asks the pairs to shake hands once again—this time saying "Hey, Buddy, thanks for working with me." Tomorrow the class will create a collage from the pictures all the pairs have collected.

Linda's first graders have been working on sequencing skills. She reads them the story "Jack and the Beanstalk" and gives each child a green piece of paper that has the shape of a bean leaf drawn on it. The children are sitting at desks that are pushed together in groups of three. Each desk has a colored sticker on it—either red, yellow, or orange—and there is one of each color in each group. She tells the students that they are going to work together to review what happened at the beginning, middle, and end of the story and then write three sentences. First, she asks them to think, by themselves, of two things that happened near the beginning of the story. Then she asks them go around in their groups and each share one thing that he or she thinks happened near the beginning of the story. To facilitate this process and to insure that each person shares, she asks the children with the red stickers to begin. She reminds the children to use their "twelve-inch voices," to make sure that they listen carefully to what each person shares, and to share something different from what the other members of their group have shared. Next, she asks the children to think of things that happened in the middle of the story. The students repeat this entire process; this time the children with the orange stickers begin. Finally, they share things that happened near the end of the story, and the children with the yellow stickers begin the sharing. Linda now asks the children to make sure that everyone in their group knows at least one event from the beginning, middle, and end of the story; she asks the children to signal "thumbs up" when they are confident that everyone in their group is ready. Now Linda focuses the childrens' attention on the green pieces of paper, telling the children they are each going to write a sentence about the story. Children with red stickers are to write sentences that tell about an event near the beginning of the story; children with orange stickers are to write sentences that tell about an event near the middle of the story; children with yellow stickers are to write a sentence that tells about an event near the end of the story. The

students go to work eagerly; they signal when they are finished by putting their pencils down on their desks. Next, Linda asks the children to read their sentences in their groups. After each child reads, the other two children are to say something they like about the sentence. She asks the children to decide if, together, they have one sentence for each section—beginning, middle, and end—of the story. Again, she has them signal. Then she collects all the papers. She has created a huge beanstalk on one of the class bulletin boards. Tomorrow, all the children will gather at this bulletin board; together they will sequence the events from the sentences and place all the sentences in order on the beanstalk.

Molly's fifth-grade students are reading *Shh! They're Writing the Constitution* with their reading partners. The children are sitting in their pair-reading positions—away from their desks with their chairs facing each other. Each child has a copy of the book, and the children take turns, paragraph by paragraph, reading aloud. The students are to (a) partner-read a short section of about four pages; (b) discuss the three questions that Molly has written on the board; (c) make sure that both they and their partners are ready to answer the same questions individually; and (d) return to their own desks and, individually, write answers to the same three questions that they discussed together. Molly collects this written work and reads what each student has written.

The next day Molly places her students in groups of three. She wants her students to think more about the Federalist and anti-Federalist positions that they have read about the day before. She begins by asking the students to read, in their trios, their responses to a related question from the previous day. She asks her students to count off from one to three and assigns the #3 people to collect materials for their groups—one large sheet of newsprint, a black marker, and markers in three additional colors. Using their numbers, she assigns each student a different color marker. She then writes the question "What might happen if New Jersey were our country?" on the board and tells her students that they are going to work together to think about this question and to learn more about the Federalist and anti-Federalist positions. Each group uses its black marker to divide the paper into two columns, marking one column with a "+" and the other column with a "–." She tells the students they have ten minutes to work together to think of both positive and negative things about New Jersey being its own country and to write these ideas on the chart. Each person is to write on the chart using only his or her own color, and each column needs to have at least one idea in each color. Molly tells the students that, just as it was important for the writers of the Constitution to share lots of ideas and to make sure they understood the ideas of others, it is important for them as well. She asks the #2 people to make sure that each person has an opportunity to share ideas and write and the #1 people to make sure that everyone understands each reason that is written. The groups get to work quickly—with much discussion of taxation, currencies, stamps, and laws. Molly walks from group to group, reminding groups that each student needs to contribute, asking for clarification about ideas that seem unclear, and praising particularly good listening and questioning skills. When she senses the students have completed their task, she asks them to sign their groups' charts in their own marker colors. Next, Molly has the students hang their charts up around the room and, as if they were in an art gallery, the groups move clockwise around the room and discuss each chart. When they return to their own work, Molly asks each group to use its black marker to add one idea to its own chart that its members learned from another group. In their groups Molly asks the students each to complete the sentence: "Today I helped my group when I ____." She brings the class together and asks students to signal, individually, whether they think they might have been Federalists or anti-Federalists at the Constitutional Convention.

Dana and her fifth-grade students are beginning to study weather and are making wind-direction indicators. They begin by brainstorming as a whole class the question: "What are all the ways you might know where the wind is coming from?" Dana accepts all ideas without judgment and writes them on the board. When the students are finished generating new ideas, she and her students begin to categorize the ideas they have shared. She talks briefly about the importance of "yes-and thinking"—helping her students realize that it is important to share many ideas and to encourage others to share. Next, students divide into their three-person science groups and begin to discuss how they might, as a group, use recycled and found materials to construct their own wind-direction indicator. They write and draw a plan, create a list of needed materials, and decide together how each member will contribute materials, skills, and labor. Two days later, all the groups have assembled their materials, and they begin their construction efforts. Dana walks around and monitors the groups to insure that all members have opportunities to contribute during this hands-on construction phase and to encourage students to reflect on their initial plans. At the end of their work time, Dana asks the students to evaluate these plans: "Do they seem to be working?" and "What refinements have you made?" She gives the groups a few minutes to record how they have adjusted their plans and to decide what they need to do to finish their designs. After groups complete their work, Dana asks the groups to indicate how confident they are that their instruments will work and how comfortable they are that each group member participated in the design and construction of the wind indicator. Next the entire class—and its plastic bags, coat hangers, and assorted other junk—moves into the school yard to test its designs. As might be expected, some designs work better than others. The groups critique their own designs, discuss the designs of other groups, and decide—in a combination of whole-class and small-group discussions—how to refine their work. Again, they adjust their plans and work together to construct, test, reflect, and refine. Dana's students will go on to learn many things about wind and weather. Each day for several months, a different group will use its wind indicator to measure the wind direction in the school yard; its members will write their observations on a class chart.

When Arlene was marking homework assignments from her seventh-grade prealgebra class, she noticed that her students often left out a step when they solved equations and that they frequently failed to check their work. She has decided to review the step-by-step procedure that her students need to follow and to provide them with more guided practice. She begins the class by telling her students that they are going to continue to practice solving equations and that they will work together to insure that all students remember both to follow step-by-step procedures and to check their work. She completes a demonstration equation on the board—numbering each of the four steps in the procedure. Her students sit four to a table. (Arlene changes their seats each marking period.) She has prepared four different worksheets with a single problem on each side of each sheet. She distributes the worksheets so that each student at each table has a different worksheet. She instructs the students to begin to solve their problems and to stop after they have completed the first step. By putting their pencils down, students signal when they are ready to continue. Next, Arlene asks them to check the step they have completed, and they use a thumbs-up signal to indicate when they have done this. Now Arlene asks her students to rotate their papers one person clockwise around their tables. Each student now has a worksheet with a new problem. They read their new problems and check the first step. If they think the first step is correct, they are to turn to their partners and say "Good problem solving and good checking." If they think the problem is incorrect, they are to turn to their partners, say "Let's check this together," and, together, rework the step. Each student then completes the

second step of this second problem. The procedure is repeated; with each step, the students rotate papers, read the problem, check the steps that have already been completed, give feedback to the previous students, and complete the next step. When all the worksheets are completed, students turn them over and repeat the entire process with a second problem. When these problems are complete, Arlene has students check their answers one more time by comparing papers between groups. She then asks the students to respond, by using raised fingers, to each of the following questions: "On a scale of 1 to 5, how confident are you that you can remember all four steps in the problem-solving procedure?" "On a scale of 1 to 5, how confident are you that all the members of your group can remember all four steps in the problem-solving procedure?"

Arlene now asks the materials manager in each group to get the group math notebooks out of a bin near her desk. The math notebooks are identified by names that the groups have chosen for themselves. Each week her students work together in their math groups to discover different ways they might solve a thinking problem. Arlene uses an overhead to present the problem, she reminds her students that their goal is to think: "How else might we solve the problem?" Her students begin to work. Each week a different student is the recorder, and all the groups seem to know whose turn it is. First, each group discusses the problem; then the group members discuss one possible way to solve the problem. The recorder goes around, asks all group members if they agree that this is one possible way to solve the problem, and then writes the procedure in the notebook. The recorder then says: "How else might we solve the problem?" The group continues with the discussion. Within fifteen minutes, most groups have discovered about four procedures they might use to solve the problem. The recorder writes each one and puts wavy lines in between the ideas. Arlene has been walking around the room during this fifteen-minute problem solving session. She listens and sometimes asks a question to help a group clarify their thinking. Because she has been monitoring, Arlene knows that there is a fair amount of variation in the procedures described by different groups, and she decides to have the groups share their work. She asks each group to spend a moment reviewing its ideas; she asks the recorders to make sure they can explain each idea. Then she has the other three group members count off from one to three. She asks all persons #1 to rotate one group, persons #2 to rotate two groups, and persons #3 to rotate three groups. Each new group now has a recorder and three additional students—all from different groups. The recorders spend a few moments, with the help of the group notebooks, explaining the procedures their groups discussed. The other three members take notes and ask questions. Then Arlene asks all students to move back to their "home teams." She gives the members a few more minutes, both to describe what they heard when they traveled to different groups and to compare these ideas to their own. The materials managers place the group notebooks back in the bin. Before the end of the class, Arlene hands out pieces of scrap paper and asks each student to complete the sentence: "Working together to solve problems helps me because ___." Arlene collects their responses at the door.

The students in Ana's Spanish IV class are in their four-person work groups. They have been reading short stories in Spanish by different authors. She begins her lesson by telling her students that they are visiting their great-grandfather's estate on the coast in Spain; she then gives the groups a moment to consult a map and name themselves after coastal towns. One rainy afternoon they decide to explore the attic. Deep in the bottom of a trunk they find an old handwritten manuscript and they settle down to read. Ana now distributes a short story—written in Spanish—to each group of students. She has divided the story into four sections, and each student receives one section.

First, Ana tells her students to take a few minutes and read their own sections silently. Students signal when they are done. Then she asks each student to pair with another student who has read the same section. She gives the pairs a few minutes to work out difficult vocabulary and to practice reading. Next, Ana asks her students to read the story aloud in their foursomes. It is a great story—full of kings and queens and villains and intrigue. Her students soon realize, however, that the end of the story is missing. Ana tells her students that it will be their job, in their groups, to create an ending to the story and to work together to act out this ending. The students are excited and bursting with ideas. She tells them to put their heads together to share ideas in their groups. Because she is concerned that some of her more fluent students will take over, she asks her students to use *Pens in the Middle* to help them remember that each group member needs to contribute an idea. She encourages students to do several rounds of *Pens in the Middle* to insure that they generate many ideas (and practice their language skills as well). Ana walks around as her students work together; she listens, helps with particularly difficult vocabulary or grammatical constructions, and compliments good language use. When she senses that a group has generated sufficient ideas, she encourages its members to agree on an ending, to begin to write the outlines of the scripts which they will perform the next day, and to divide up the writing work so that each group member can complete a piece of the script for homework. She tells them she will collect their individual script work the next day.

The next day Ana gives her students about five minutes to complete their preparations. Many groups have organized simple props and costumes. Next, she has each group of four students join with another foursome, and each group in turn presents its "play." After each group has presented, the group that served as the audience gives two pieces of specific positive feedback and asks one question. The groups then separate to discuss their own performances and to decide what went well and what might be improved. Each foursome now joins with another foursome and, again, each group in turn presents its play, critiques the play of the other group, and discusses its own work. Each group presents its play a total of three times and, in the process, the students practice their language skills and presentation skills a great deal. At the conclusion of the class, Ana asks the students to share, with the other members of their groups, one way that they think their groups' work improved as they repeated their performances.

Marilyn's tenth-grade class is studying Arthur Miller's *The Crucible*. She wants her students to explore the dilemma that John Proctor faces in Act IV and decides to have her students engage in an *Academic Controversy*. "Should Proctor, following Reverend Hale's theory, give a false confession to witchcraft and live, or should Proctor refuse to confess and be hanged?" Marilyn begins by dividing her class into groups of four. "Within these groups, students are divided into pairs. One pair will build a case to support the validity of Proctor's position to die rather than make a false confession; the other pair will support Hale's view that it is better to give a false confession and live. At home, students use the text to gather evidence to support their positions and the following day work in their pairs to integrate ideas and evidence into a coherent position. Next, Marilyn asks each pair to separate and consult with members of different pairs who have prepared the same position. Students then return to their partners and work to assimilate the new ideas that they have gleaned from classmates."[1] Before her students leave for the day, Marilyn asks them: "On a scale from one to five, how well did today's discussion help you understand Proctor's motive?" After she gives her students a moment to think individually, she asks them to signal their personal numbers by holding up fingers.

"The following day, in their groups of four, students present their positions. Each pair, in turn, presents its position while the other pair takes notes. Following this initial exposition, pairs ask clarifying questions, point out weaknesses, ask for justification and further evidence, and openly challenge 'opponents.' . . . Following this intense discussion, each pair withdraws to prepare for what might be the most interesting and challenging phase of this controversy—perspective reversal. Pairs who supported Proctor's decision must now support Hale's view; those who supported Hale must now support Proctor. Notes taken in the original exposition of positions serve as the base for discussion, but now each pair adds at least two new pieces of evidence to its argument. The next day, both teams present these new positions. Then, determining the relative merits of each side, they drop advocacy and strive to reach a consensus that supports the view of either Proctor or Hale. Each foursome reports its decision to the class. Groups use oral presentations, written statements, and visual displays. They have been asked to show both the relative weakness of the position rejected as well as the strengths of their own position"[2] While they are still in their groups, Marilyn asks her students each to complete the sentence: "One thing I did today that I think helped my group move towards consensus was ___." The next day, Marilyn asks her students to describe their experience discussing Proctor's dilemma in *The Crucible*. Among other things, students say: "Being in a group helps because there are facts which one person could never think of, and by working together and switching opinions, more understanding can be achieved." "I thought the activity was good because we could discuss with our friends how we felt about moral issues" (p. 44).

[1,2]From "Fishbowls, Creative Controversy, Talking Chips: Exploring Literature Cooperatively," by L. Baloche, M. Lee Mauger, T. Willis, J. Filinuk, and B. Michalsky, 1993, *English Journal, 82* (6), pp. 43-44. Copyright 1993 by the National Council of Teachers of English. Reprinted with permission.

❦ WORKING WITH PEERS ❦

Using Base Groups to Review Chapter Content and Personalize Learning

QUESTION: *Which barrier to high-quality cooperation are you most concerned about? Why?*

1. Students use same basic format described in Chapter 5 for base group discussion and chapter review. (Students should use a different structure to organize their discussion than the one they chose in Chapter 5.)
2. Reflection and Planning:
   Individual:
   • On a scale of 1 to 5 how confident am I that I can explain why the other members in my group chose the barrier they did?
   • How confident am I that they can each explain why I chose the barrier I did?
   Group:
   • Was the structure we chose for our own discussion useful for our purpose?
   • How could that structure be used to help overcome one of the barriers to cooperation?

Using *Simultaneous Roundtable* (Kagan, 1992) to Review the Nine Types of Positive Interdependence

1. Students are in groups of approximately four (base groups are good for this). Students each need their own clean pieces of loose paper. At the top of their papers, students write: "The nine types of positive interdependence are". Without discussion, students write one type on their own papers.
2. Students now rotate their papers one person around their group. Students read what was written on the papers by the last people. If they think one of the nine types of positive interdependence has been listed, they write "yes." If not, they write "?" Each student adds a second type on the second piece of paper.
3. Students rotate papers again, reading both items that have been written on the papers, commenting with "yes" or "?" on each one, and adding a third type.
4. Students continue to rotate papers a few more times until they think they have recorded all nine types.

5. Students put papers and heads together and use information from Chapter 6 to review their work, adding any types of positive interdependence that have been forgotten. Each student keeps one list.
6. Reflection and Planning:
   Group:
   • What are the essential characteristics of *Roundtable?*
   • What other structure might we have used to review the nine types of positive interdependence?

Using Pairs and *Mad Hatter's Tea Party* for Analysis and Application of Chapter Content

1. Students use the same basic format described in Chapter 5. The scenarios are Patrick, Linda, Molly, Dana, Arlene, Ana, and Marilyn. Each pair analyzes a scenario, responding to the following questions:
   a. What were the learning goals?
   b. How were students grouped?
   c. What kinds of positive interdependence did the teacher use?
   d. Did the teacher use any specific structure(s)? If so, which one(s)?
   e. What kinds of problems might the teacher anticipate in this lesson? How has the teacher designed the lesson to help address potential problems?
   f. What additional kind of positive interdependence might the teacher add to the lesson that might make sense?
2. Students then work with their partners to describe how to add one additional kind of positive interdependence to the scenario.
3. Students' first scenarios were assigned. Each pair of students together chooses a second scenario to analyze. Students use the same questions to focus their discussion.
4. Pairs stay together and, using *Mad Hatter's Tea Party,* share their analyses with other pairs.
5. Reflection and Planning:
   Individual:
   • How has this activity helped me understand the subtleties of positive interdependence?
   • How confident am I that I can identify all nine types of positive interdependence in a lesson?
   • How confident am I that I could appropriately structure each of the nine types of positive interdependence into lessons?

Pair:
- One way you helped me understand positive interdependence was ____.
- One thing about positive interdependence I want to learn more about is ____.

Class:
- Was the *Mad Hatter* structure useful for our purpose?
- What else might we have used?
- What kind(s) of positive interdependence were structured into this activity?

Using Pairs and *Trade a Problem* (Kagan, 1992) to Review the Nine Types of Positive Interdependence

1. Students group in randomly chosen pairs. Members of each pair work together to identify the type of positive interdependence represented by each example in Figure 6.2.
2. Each pair links with another pair and compares answers, focusing discussion on examples that are unclear and attempting to reach consensus.

POSITIVE INTERDEPENDENCE: WHAT THE TEACHER MIGHT SAY

- "Ann, your job is to make sure each person contributes an idea."
- "As a group, see if you can better your score from last week."
- "Each group will need a time monitor."
- "Each group will receive one set of markers."
- "Each group will work at a lab table."
- "Each member of your group will receive one paragraph from the story."
- "Everyone has to agree and everyone has to be able to solve the problem."
- "Give yourselves a group handshake!"
- "Great job, group!"
- "If all the groups reach the criteria, we'll have a Mystery Guest on Friday."
- "You are all in a Conestoga wagon traveling west together."
- "You will be the recorder and your partner will be the accuracy seeker."
- "You will look up the word, then your partner will paraphrase the definition."
- "You will slice the seed, then your partner will prepare the slide."
- "Last month it took us 17 days to collect 100 points. Let's see if we can do it in 16 days this month."

- "Last year's class earned 127 points. See if you can earn 130."
- "Let's hear from the Barracudas first."
- "The first person will find the picture, the second person will cut it out, the third person will glue it to the collage."
- "The Marvelous Multipliers"
- "You and your partner are to sit eye-to-eye and knee-to-knee."
- "You and your partner are to sit inside your hula hoop."
- "You and your partner will share one microscope."
- "You are a team of scientists. Your job is to determine the likelihood that this volcano will erupt and decide whether the city should be evacuated."
- "Your group has just discovered a map that will allow you to locate the lost civilization."
- "Your group needs one answer that everyone can explain."
- "Your group will create a team logo based on the commonalties you have discovered."
- "Your group will write one report."

Figure 6.2
Positive interdependence: what the teacher might say.

3. Each pair now writes a new example of "teacher talk" for each of the nine types of positive interdependence.
4. Each pair "trades its problem" with another pair, and each pair now tries to identify the nine types of positive interdependence in the nine examples that were created by the other pair.
5. Pairs link and discuss, noting examples that are particularly clear or novel and clarifying examples that are unclear.
6. Reflection and Planning:
   Individual:
   - How confident am I that I could use all nine types of positive interdependence appropriately?
   Pair:
   - Were pairs appropriate group sizes to examine the examples in Figure 6.2?

- Did we each contribute equally to the work?
- Did we need roles?
Group:
- Was the *Trade a Problem* structure useful for our purpose?
- What kind(s) of positive interdependence were structured into this activity?

Using a *One-Minute Paper* and Base Groups to Reflect on Positive Interdependence

TASK: *In one sentence, describe the essence of positive interdependence.*

1. Each student writes a response.
2. Students share responses in their base groups.

CHAPTER **7**

Interpersonal and Small-Group Learning Skills: Teaching the Basics

🐞 *As you read, you might want to ask yourself:*

What are the essential skills of cooperation?

Why is it important to see the direct teaching of interpersonal and small-group learning skills as part of the discipline of using cooperative learning?

How might teachers structure the direct teaching of interpersonal and small-group learning skills?

Why do teachers need to observe students when they work together?

What are the different kinds of monitoring? Why are they used?

When is it useful for a teacher to intervene in the work of a group?

How does the direct teaching of interpersonal and small-group learning skills help to develop and sustain a learning community?

What might the direct teaching of interpersonal and small-group learning skills look and sound and feel like in a classroom that empowers students as learners?

The discipline of using cooperative learning effectively includes teaching the interpersonal and small-group learning skills that students need to use to be successful in their work with peers. Students are not born with well-developed interpersonal and small-group learning skills; these skills must be identified and taught. Students must be motivated to use good skills and must have many opportunities to use them in authentic learning contexts with peers. *When students have not been taught how to work with others, teachers should not expect to be able to put them together in groups and have them work together effectively.* Teaching students *how* to work together, teaching them the skills of cooperation, is basic—basic not just to the success of cooperative learning but, as we learned in Chapter 1, basic to real-life success as well. In this chapter we will examine how to teach the skills of cooperation.

Why might the barriers to cooperation be likely to increase when students are not taught how to work together?

THE ESSENTIAL SKILLS OF COOPERATION

Because students need many skills in order to work together effectively, teachers sometimes find it difficult to know where to start when teaching students the skills they need in order to cooperative successfully; just telling students to "cooperate" is not sufficient. In fact, when asked "What does it mean to cooperate?" students are as likely to say "do what the teacher wants" as they are to provide a definition of cooperation that relates to substantive interaction with peers. In this chapter we will describe four basic categories of skills (adapted from D. Johnson, R. Johnson, & Holubec, 1992, 1993): (a) skills that help students get into groups, (b) skills that help groups stay together and get the job done, (c) skills that help students build an understanding of academic material, and (d) skills that encourage students to become empowered thinkers. We will also discuss how to teach these skills to students within a cooperative classroom context. When learning how to teach the skills of cooperation, it is important to remember that interpersonal and small-group learning skills are not another curriculum to be "covered." Empowering teachers begin by choosing a few skills on which to focus with their students—skills that they determine are particularly important for their students and relevant to their academic-learning tasks.

"Getting Together"—What Are the Skills?

> We don't use put-downs. So the other person doesn't want to be crummy on purpose to get the other people angry. (Fourth-grade student)

The best place to start learning how to cooperate is at the beginning—with the skills that students need in order to get into groups successfully.

Students with good "Getting-Together Skills" can:

- Move to the group in an orderly fashion
- Stay with the group
- Use quiet voices
- Show interest and participate
- Be positive towards other members (no killer statements)
- Acknowledge the quiet signal

As you read each of these four categories of skills, ask yourself: "What other skill might I want to add in each category?" "What skill do I think is particularly important?"

Sometimes teachers assume that students have these basic skills and then get frustrated when the simple direction to "move into your groups" unleashes unsatisfactory levels of noise and disorganization. Teachers tend to become discouraged when students use put-downs, display an obvious lack of interest in working with others, leave their groups and wander around the room, or run to the teacher with tales of "he said" and "she won't." Careful attention to "Getting-Together Skills" early in the life of a class—and regular reinforcement thereafter—prevent frustration for both the students and the teacher and eliminate behavior that is potentially damaging to the building of an inclusive learning community.

A quiet signal is part of a routine that supports students working together. It is important for teachers to be able to focus student attention—to ask questions, give directions, or make an observation—when students are in groups. A common quiet signal is a raised arm; some teachers develop short chants or routines such as "If you can hear my voice, clap once" to alert young children that their attention is needed. Whatever the signal, the intent is the same: "Finish your sentence (but not your paragraph), turn your focus towards me, and make sure the other members of your group shift focus as well." Students need to practice responding to a quiet signal; once they know from repeated experience that they will soon be able to resume their work together, this becomes a comfortable routine. Along with a quiet signal, some teachers like to establish the idea of "unfinished business." There are times in the life of a classroom when teachers do want students to shift to a new phase of discussion and work. At these times students can decide that they have unfinished business, state this in their group, and make sure they continue their conversations later—during free time, at lunch, on the bus. Unfinished business helps teachers manage group work, helps students build feelings of influence, and helps break down the barriers between "school time" and "free time."

"Getting the Job Done and Staying Together"—What Are the Skills?

If you encourage, people in your group will work better.
We encouraged each other and we let everyone in our group give an idea. (Fourth-grade students)

Once students are able to move into groups in an orderly fashion, stay with their groups, and talk one at a time in a positive manner, students are ready to complete academic *tasks* and to build and *maintain* their relationships with peers. Task (getting-the-job-done) skills and maintenance (staying-together) skills were discussed in Chapter 2 and again in Chapter 6.

Students with good "Getting-the-Job-Done Skills" can

- Ask for information or suggestions
- Give information or suggestions
- Help to organize materials
- Keep the group working; watch the time
- Listen to (and be able to clarify) directions

Those with "Staying-Together Skills" can

- Preserve confidentiality
- Encourage others to participate
- Paraphrase the ideas of others
- Share feelings when appropriate
- Show appreciation for others
- Take turns
- Talk one at a time
- Use appropriate humor

As peers learn to build and maintain their relationships, one important skill that perhaps needs special explanation is confidentiality. Students must feel confident that what they say in their group (or class) will remain there; that they—not their group or classmates—are able to determine who else hears their ideas, thoughts, and feelings. This is to some extent a matter of trust, but it is also a matter of skill, and it is a skill that can be taught. For instance, students can be taught to ask about what is public and what is confidential in their work together, and when reporting what has happened during group work, students can be taught to say "our group discussed" rather than "Jesse said."

"Getting It"—What Are the Skills?

When I work with somebody else, then I really get it.

You have to take the time and split it up so all of you can do or be a part of something instead of just one person.

We did it all together first. We all did it by ourselves to see who had a problem. Then if someone had a problem, we would help them.

We listened to each other carefully and told them nicely if they made a mistake. (Fourth-grade students)

Getting the job done and staying together are not the only goals of cooperative learning—although they are worthy accomplishments for many students when they begin to work together. As we learned in Chapter 1 when we examined briefly the developmental theories of Vygotsky and Piaget and concepts from information processing theory, cooperative learning has the potential to promote high levels of achievement—to help students "get it." But for this to happen, students must learn and practice memory and planning strategies, and they must learn the skills necessary for the kinds of discussions that encourage the sharing of explanations, elaborations, world knowledge, and varied perspectives.

Students with good "Getting-It Skills" can

- Make a plan
- Repeat and summarize
- Seek accuracy by checking or correcting
- Seek clever ways to remember facts and ideas
- Think out loud and ask others to think out loud

"Getting It^2"—What Are the Skills?

> I realize that if someone gives an idea that you don't like, you should tell them about the idea but not put them down, because next time they may have an idea and not say it. (Fourth-grade student)

Skills such as seeking accuracy, planning, and summarizing are all important skills if students are going to build understanding of academic material. For students to become genuinely empowered learners however, they need some additional skills—skills that encourage them to view things from multiple perspectives, ask penetrating questions, and learn to disagree in ways that stimulate thinking. Without these skills, there is a risk that students will define *cooperation* as simply "getting along," "behaving with other people," or "getting a lot done" (Holloway, 1992).

Students with good "Getting-It^2 Skills" can

- Ask in-depth critical and creative questions
- Ask for rationales
- Criticize ideas, not people
- Differentiate opinions
- Extend ideas
- Integrate different ideas and perspectives

❁ TEACHING THE SKILLS OF COOPERATION ❁

Understanding that students need to be taught interpersonal and small-group learning skills and identifying the skills that need to be taught are important to the discipline of using cooperative learning effectively. Learning how to teach these skills—and making the commitment to do so—

are essential as well. In this section we will examine six steps (adapted from D. Johnson, R. Johnson, & Holubec, 1992, 1993) that can be used as a guide when planning and teaching students the interpersonal and small-group learning skills they need to work successfully in cooperative groups and real life. These steps include

1. Developing the context so that students understand the importance of cooperation and of the specific interpersonal skills you want them to learn.
2. Developing an understanding of what a specific skill is and when to use it.
3. Providing opportunities for students to practice the use of the skill: These opportunities include both obvious "practice" situations and opportunities within the context of group work that focus on academic learning.
4. Monitoring group work and observing and collecting data about student use of the skill.
5. Providing feedback to students and facilitating their own reflection about their use of the skill.
6. Providing *more* opportunities for students to use the skill so that they become comfortable with it.

Developing the Context—Understanding the Need for Interpersonal Skills

What might happen if students do not understand the need to develop good interpersonal skills?

Students need to understand that cooperation and specific interpersonal skills are important. The kinds of activities described in Chapter 4, activities that are designed to build a classroom learning community, are a good place to begin and can be used effectively in conjunction with activities that focus specifically on the importance of cooperation. Bulletin boards that emphasize the theme of cooperation can be quite useful. Cartoons and pictures of animal groups, sports teams, music groups, and the like can be used effectively to illustrate the importance of being able to work in a team. Quotes from famous people about the importance of working together are effective, and older students benefit from a planned study about how teamwork is essential in different occupations. Never underestimate the power of examples, and never underestimate the power of the visual context within the classroom. Picture books and other literature selections are wonderful tools to build discussions about the importance of being able to work together.

What age-appropriate books might help students understand the need for good interpersonal skills? How about movies? How about . . . ?

Developing an Understanding of What the Specific Skill Is and When It Should Be Used

Students need to understand what a specific skill is and how and when to use it. Telling students to listen, paraphrase, or ask clarifying questions is not helpful if students do not understand what those skills are. Skills must be defined, explained, and contextualized in ways that students understand. "Happy talk," "encouragement," "no put-downs," "showing appreciation," and "specific positive feedback" serve similar purposes in classrooms that range from kindergarten through middle school, high school, and beyond. "Repeat an idea," "paraphrase," "summarize," and "integrate different ideas" are skills on a continuum that begins with "speak one at a time" and "listen." Questioning strategies that are designed to stimulate multiple levels of thinking, such as those in Figure 7.1 (adapted from Kagan, 1988) and Figure 7.2 (Baloche & Platt, 1993a, 1993b), can be used effectively with students of all ages once students understand the importance of "ask." T-charts (Figure 7.3) are effective ways to provide students with examples of how a specific skill might look or sound. A T-chart is most effective when the teacher and students create it together and use real kid words; a T-chart is less effective when the teacher creates the T-chart *for* the students and includes just teacher words. It is always important to define a skill within the context of students working together and to use observations from students working together to decide what skill to target and teach.

In addition to discussions, role plays, T-charts, and picture books, what else might teachers use to help students understand what a skill is and how it is used? How about puppets? How about short segments of video? How about . . . ?

QUESTIONS A LA BLOOM

Knowledge	*Comprehension*	*Application*
Where did	Tell	What might happen if
What was	What does it mean	How might you
Who was	Give an example	If you were ____, would you
When did	Describe	Where else could you
How many	Illustrate	Would you have done the same as
Find where	Make a map	Adapt
Identify	Summarize	Adopt
Analysis	*Synthesis*	*Evaluation*
What might you use	What might it be like	Would you recommend
What other ways might	Pretend	Select the most interesting
What part was most	Design	What do you think
What is similar (different)	Add something new	What did you like
Outline	Combine	Could this have happened
Separate	Write a different ending	What character might you be

Figure 7.1
Strategy to facilitate in-depth questioning, based on principles of Bloom's taxonomy.

TRANSFORMING QUESTIONS

Listing

List all the potential _____

What are all the possible _____?

In what ways might we _____?

How might we _____?

Imagining

Suppose

Imagine

What might happen if _____?

What could _____?

What if _____?

Perspective-Taking

How might these events look
   to _____?

Tell the story from _____
   perspective.

What other perspective might _____?

Being

If you were _____ how might you
feel?

Relating

How is a _____ like a _____?

Transforming

How might you . . .

Substitute?

Combine?

Adapt?

Modify/Magnify/Minimize?

Put to Other Uses?

Elaborate/Eliminate?

Rearrange/Reverse/Recycle?

How might _____ change if _____?

How might _____ be transformed
   if _____?

Figure 7.2
Strategy to facilitate in-depth questioning, based on principles of divergent thinking.

Figure 7.3
T-chart for "Listening."

LISTENING

Looks Like	Sounds Like
Face focused on the talker	"Un huh"
Leaning toward the speaker	"Really"
Appropriate nods of the head	Paraphrasing
Taking notes if necessary	Silence
Appropriate emotions for what Is being discussed	"Oh WOW!"
	Asking for more details

Providing Opportunities for Students to Practice the Use of Skills

Students need many authentic opportunities to practice interpersonal and small-group learning skills if they are going to learn to use them effectively. Oftentimes, practice is best done within the context of learning groups, but sometimes whole-class practice, games, role plays, and simulations are useful. It is sometimes helpful to provide skill practice by assigning roles to students in their small groups. When roles are used, students might be assigned, for example, the roles of time or materials manager, voice monitor, encourager, or summarizer. Roles tend to sound and feel somewhat artificial, but they do encourage students to practice particular skills and are, therefore, useful tools. On occasion, paper and pencil practice can be used to provide students with opportunities to think about how they might use a particular skill in a difficult situation.

There is a reciprocal relationship between the skills students need to learn to work successfully in small groups and the kinds of learning experiences teachers design so that students have opportunities to practice the skills they need to learn. In other words, when teachers identify an interpersonal skill that students need to practice, they then design learning activities that will emphasize the identified skill. And when teachers identify academic knowledge and skills that they want students to learn and decide how best to teach this knowledge, they then decide what interpersonal skills students will need to use. This perspective on skills and learning is quite different from the one implied by the teacher who said: "I can't let my students work together because they can't cooperate."

Using Structures to Provide Opportunities for Skill Practice   Structures can be used quite effectively to design lessons that emphasize the learning and practice of specific interpersonal and learning skills. For instance, when students need to practice "move in an orderly fashion," *Corners, Graffiti, Mix-Freeze-Pair, Gallery Tour,* and *Stirring Up the Class* are among the structures that might be used to provide practice in these skills. The need to "use a quiet voice" is particularly obvious when many students are talking simultaneously—as in *Inside-Outside Circle* and *Treasure Hunt.* "Paraphrasing" is essential to the success of *Three-Step Interviews, Stirring Up the Class,* and *One-Stay Three-Stray.* "Taking turns" is facilitated by *Talking Chips* and *Pens in the Middle.* The ability to "ask for information" is key to *Find Someone Who Knows, Group Interview,* and *Blind Hand. Trade A Problem* encourages students to "seek accuracy by checking." Students are often motivated to "seek clever ways to remember facts and ideas" when using *Jigsaw* or working in *STAD* teams. When students are asked to create *Team Statements,* they must "integrate different

What other structures might be useful for learning specific interpersonal skills? What is the structure? What is the skill?

ideas and perspectives"; they must "differentiate opinions" to create *Value Lines,* and the essence of *Academic Controversy* is to both "differentiate opinions" and "integrate different ideas and perspectives."

Observing Students Working Together and Monitoring the Appropriate Use of Skills

Identifying, teaching, and practicing skills are important but not sufficient to insure that students develop high levels of interpersonal and small-group learning skills. Students must be given feedback about their use of important skills and they must be given time to reflect on their use of skills; this feedback and reflection should be based on carefully gathered information about how students use their skills when they are working with others. Therefore, when students are working together in their cooperative groups, it is important for teachers to observe students' use of interpersonal and small-group learning skills. Skillful observation is essential to the discipline of using cooperative learning effectively.

As we have seen already, there are many interpersonal skills to choose from when helping students learn to be more successful in their work with peers, and the skills that are targeted and taught depend on the students and the purpose of their work together. Similarly, there are many ways for teachers to observe students, and the specific techniques that are used depend on the students, their skills, and the purpose of their work together. For simplicity's sake, we will describe a basic three-step monitoring procedure that can be used to gather information about how students work together (adapted from D. Johnson, R. Johnson, & Holubec, 1992, 1993).

Monitoring—Round One: Where Is Everybody?   No matter what the goals for a lesson or what the ages of the students are, it is usually a good idea for teachers to walk quickly around the classroom when students first move into their groups. Basic "Getting-Together Skills" are often the focus of this first round of monitoring. In addition, useful questions to keep in mind include

Are there other questions you might want to keep in mind? What are they?

- Is the physical space well arranged?
- Do the students have all the materials they need—including homework?
- Are all group members present, and have any returning members been brought up to date?
- Does everyone understand what needs to be done?

This type of monitoring prevents problems, frustration, and loss of time.

Intervening   When things are going well, there is little need to intervene at this stage of group work. Sometimes teachers make short general comments such as "I see that everyone has brought all their materials to their groups and that all six groups have gotten to work quickly" to reinforce basic skills. If things are not going well, it is best to avoid veiled "you statements" such as "Quiet down!" or "People are wandering around because they are not prepared" and focus on a positive restatement of expectations, such as "I need everyone to practice using twelve-inch voices." or "Check to make sure you have everything you need before moving into your groups."

At this first stage of monitoring, it is not uncommon for confused, dependent, or attention-seeking students to ask the teacher procedural questions. Often this happens even when another group member is able to describe the assignment quite well. Whenever possible, turn problems like these back to the group to solve by asking a question such as "Can the group take a moment to explain the assignment and make sure everyone understands?" When teachers ask questions like this, it is often helpful to take a step back and allow group members time to respond to each other rather than to the teacher. If the group is able to describe what needs to be done, the teacher then moves on. If not, the teacher needs to reexplain—either to the particular small group or, if other groups are also confused, to the whole class. Figure 7.4 contains examples of how minimal teacher intervention might be used to help students learn to become interdependent with peers rather than dependent on the teacher.

Monitoring—Round Two: How Is Everybody Doing?   Once the teacher has done an initial walkabout and students have begun their work, a second, slower round of monitoring is necessary to insure that students are seriously engaged in the work of the group and are interacting in ways that are likely to build and maintain their relationships. This is also a good time to observe for the kinds of status differentials that were described in Chapter 3. Useful questions to keep in mind include

- How is the work going?
- Do groups seem to have the necessary academic skills?
- Are individual members struggling academically?
- Does the group or an individual member need a greater challenge?
- Are all students involved? If not, what needs to happen?
- Do all students have access to the materials? If not, what needs to happen?
- Who is explaining?
- Who is asking questions?

Are there other questions you might want to keep in mind? What are they?

Intervening   Interventions are common during this stage of monitoring. Interventions should be short, and teachers should strive to intervene in ways that keep group members focused on the group and their work together. Although interventions may be common, teachers should always ask themselves

- Why do I want to intervene?
- Should I say something now or can it wait until later?
- Is what I want to say likely to make a positive difference?
- Is it likely that the group can solve this problem without my comment?

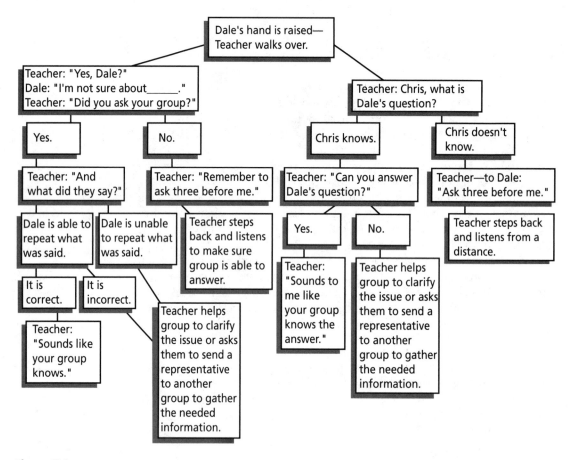

Figure 7.4
What the teacher might say during monitoring—round one.

When the academic task is going well, an intervention might (a) help the students focus on the choices they have made that have facilitated their good work; (b) help them understand what task skills they are using appropriately; (c) provide opportunities to assign competence (see Chapter 3) to students who are seen by peers as less able; and (d) challenge the group to extend its thinking. Examples of simple task interventions include

- "Nice choice of graphic organizer."
- "Good plan."
- "Pat, good explanation."
- "Chris, good question."
- "Why do you think this is true?"
- "How else might you solve this problem?"

When a group is having difficulty with the academic task, an intervention might help students (a) focus on the requirements of the task, (b) focus on the choices they have made—or haven't made—that have affected how their work is going, (c) determine what they do not know, and (d) understand what skills they need to use to be more successful. Examples of simple interventions include

- "Who can explain what the task is?"
- "You might want to go back and check for accuracy."
- "Perhaps you could spend a few moments reviewing your plan."
- "What do you need to know to make this work?"
- "This group seems to be having difficulty with _____." What are three things you might do to make it work?"

What else might you say when things are going well in a group? How about if things are not going well?

When a particular student needs a differentiated academic goal, the teacher will need to help the student and the rest of the group learn how to accomplish this goal. This can often be accomplished with simple interventions such as

- "Remember, Erin, I want you to be able to _____"
- "I'll be back in five minutes and, Erin, I'm going to ask you to _____"
- "Erin, the group needs you to contribute an idea. I'll be back in a few minutes, and I will ask you to tell me the idea you have contributed."

Interventions of this type are helpful to both the targeted student and the rest of the group; they prevent anxiety and frustration and increase feelings of goal interdependence.

When members of the group are using good interpersonal skills, it is sometimes helpful to point these out immediately so that (a) skilled students get the reinforcement they need to continue to use the skill, and (b) other students understand how the skill is used in context. Simple ways to do this include interventions such as

- "Good idea-sharing from all the members of the group."
- "Good eye contact."
- "Pat, it was helpful that you took the time to clarify what Chris said before you went on with your own idea."

When members of the group are not using good interpersonal skills, the teacher may want to intervene to (a) help them understand what skill they need to be using, (b) help them plan how to use the skill, (c) coach the use of the skill, and (d) model the use of the skill. When things are not going well, a simple intervention is likely to be more helpful than an extended monologue. A skillful teacher might say

- "Has everyone shared an idea?"
- "Pat, what was Chris's idea?"

- "What might this group do to ensure that everyone has a chance to speak and everyone listens?"
- "If I were in this group, I might say _____ "
- "This group seems to be having difficulty with _____. What are three ways you might work on that?"

Monitoring—Round Three: What Is Everybody Doing? Once the teacher has done an initial walkabout and has then visited each group to observe the academic work and the general use of interpersonal skills, a third round of monitoring is useful. At this stage of monitoring, teachers (a) choose particular interpersonal and small-group learning skill(s) to look for, (b) tell the students what they will be looking for, and (c) decide how to look—how to collect data. Although teachers do not always collect data of this sort, periodic use of systematic data collection is helpful. In Chapter 3 we examined how teachers' perceptions of students may be influenced by a variety of factors—including race, ethnicity, class, and status—and how these factors may affect their treatment of and expectations for students. Systematic data collection can be a powerful tool for teachers who wish to challenge and expand their perceptions; it helps teachers hone and expand their observation skills. Systematic data collection provides invaluable data to students as they work to develop appropriate interpersonal and small-group learning skills and is fundamental to the building of classrooms were all students have opportunities to become empowered learners. There are many ways for teachers to collect systematic data. An introduction to data collection was provided in Chapter 2. Common methods include anecdotal observation and structured observation sheets.

Have you ever collected systematic data in a classroom? How did you do it? What did you learn?

Anecdotal Observation   When collecting anecdotal data, teachers typically

1. Inform students that the observers will observe one particular skill and will write down each time they see or hear it.
2. Review the skill with the students—perhaps referring to a T-chart or other lessons in which the skill has been emphasized.
3. Plan how they will monitor: In general, it is important for teachers to time their monitoring so that each student and each group is monitored for approximately the same amount of time.
4. Monitor while the students engage in their work—keeping a tally of each time the skill is observed and recording details of good skill use.

Structured Observation Sheets   When using observation sheets, teachers must decide, before constructing the observation sheets

- What skill(s) to observe.
- Whether to collect data about one particular student, one small group, or every small group.
- Who should observe—the teacher, a student(s), or a colleague.

These three decisions are interrelated. For instance, if the teacher or colleague is going to observe one particular student or one small group, the observer can check for many skills; data collection of every group or by students requires simpler observation sheets with fewer skills. As with anecdotal observation, teachers typically inform students that they will be observed and then review the skills that will be observed.

Teachers are most likely to think of themselves or colleagues as observers, and it is important for teachers to engage in structured observations. In addition, students can be used quite effectively as observers; while students are observing behaviors with the help of an observation sheet, the teacher can be engaged in other types of monitoring. All students can learn to be observers and, in general, they enjoy the role. Students can effectively observe selected behaviors of a single peer—this is often done in a fishbowl design—or of a small group. For students to be effective observers, they must (a) understand the skills they are looking for, (b) understand how to tally what they see and hear on an observation sheet, and (c) be willing to be silent observers for a short period of time. The potential benefits of using student observers are high, and social learning theory suggests that it is powerful for students to observe their peers using interpersonal skills in context. Typically, when teachers use student observers, the students observe for only part of the group work time and then join the group as participants. When they join as participants, the group has a natural opportunity to stop and summarize what it has accomplished.

Providing Feedback and Helping Students Reflect on Their Use of Skills

Once important interpersonal and small-group learning skills have been identified and taught, students have had opportunities to practice these skills, and teachers have monitored their work and collected data about their use of skills, students need feedback. Students need to have time to reflect on how they have used their skills; they need to plan how to use and develop their skills in the future. Without time for feedback, reflection, and planning, students tend not to believe that learning these skills is important, they do not have opportunities to plan how to improve their use of skills or plan to focus on new skills, and their use of skills does not improve. In Chapter 8 we will examine the principles of feedback, reflection, and planning in detail.

Providing Continued Opportunities for Students to Work Together and Develop Their Skills

To develop their skills, students need regular opportunities to work together in carefully designed cooperative groups. Once-a-week cooperative learning and occasional fun group activities do not provide the kind of practice that students need to develop their skills. Students need to practice their skills until their use of them becomes automatic. Learning an interpersonal skill is like learning many other skills—at first it feels awkward, clumsy, and difficult. In fact, when teachers first begin to teach and monitor a new skill, students typically make pointed and sometimes silly use of the skill—especially when the teacher is listening—but they neglect to use the skill in appropriate and important contexts. This is natural; with thoughtful, consistent monitoring and continued practice, the use of the skill will become more authentic and integrated. Teachers who are committed to the discipline of using cooperative learning effectively know that regular opportunities for students to work together—in a way that acknowledges the importance of interpersonal and small-group skills—are essential to the integrated, high-level use of interpersonal skills.

🐾   CHALLENGES   🐾

What challenges have you experienced working as a student in a group? What challenges have you had, or can you imagine, as a teacher?

Every teacher knows that—in spite of careful attention to the building of a cooperative learning community, careful planning to ensure opportunities for meaningful learning, careful teaching of the interpersonal and small-group learning skills that students need to use to be successful when working with others, and regular, authentic opportunities to practice these skills—not all students and groups will be highly motivated for learning or will use skills at a level that will insure high-quality cooperation. General lack of appropriate behavior can be a problem, too. Lack of motivation for learning, failure to use good interpersonal skills, and generally poor behavior are not problems related solely to cooperative learning, but the use of cooperative learning does make these problems particularly noticeable. When teachers do not develop strategies to address these problems—strategies that are compatible with the long-term goals of building cooperative classrooms and empowering students—they are likely to compromise their use of cooperation.

Problems caused by lack of motivation, lack of skills, and inappropriate behavior take many forms. Students with chronic absences, students who exhibit frequent disruptive or off-task behaviors, students who dominate, will not contribute, or prefer to work by themselves are all challenges that will likely present themselves. When these challenges arise, teachers may first want to review their own roles in the implementation of the discipline of cooperation. Useful questions include

- Do I regularly incorporate meaningful class and team-building experiences into our work together? Have I focused on the importance of building a learning community?
- Do I carefully structure positive interdependence into cooperative work?

- Is the work meaningful? Do students have choices?
- Am I careful to structure and articulate individual responsibility? (This will be discussed in detail in Chapter 9.)
- Have I been conscientious in my identification, teaching, and monitoring of interpersonal and small-group learning skills? Do students understand the importance of cooperation and the need for these skills?
- Have I collected systematic data about students' behavior and their use of interpersonal skills? Have I shared this data with students and worked with them to set personal and group goals?
- Have I been conscientious in monitoring groups for status problems?
- Do students have time to reflect on their work together—to learn from their successes and difficulties? (Reflection and planning will be discussed in Chapters 8 and 9.)
- Do I use a quiet signal effectively? Do I use the power of proximity?

What other questions might you want to keep in mind?

Once teachers have reflected on these questions and made adjustments in their own planning and behavior, additional action to address specific problems may be necessary.

Using Conferences to Examine Challenging Situations

Oftentimes, a conference with the student or group who is experiencing difficulty is a good place to begin. One reason to conference with students is to try to determine the reasons behind the observed difficulties. Dreikurs (Dreikurs, Grunwald, & Pepper, 1982), for instance, suggests that there are four main reasons students exhibit inappropriate behaviors. These are to (a) get attention, (b) gain power, (c) seek revenge, and (d) cover for feelings of inadequacy. Students frequently do not know the reasons for their difficulties, and a calm, open-ended conversation with the teacher may help both the teacher and the student understand the student's motives more clearly. Conferences between the teacher and a student or group should be inconspicuous and confidential, nonconfrontational, purposeful, short, and action oriented. Conferences, which can be structured similarly to a negotiation session, can be used to

1. Clarify the problem: Students do not always know what the problem is or why the behavior is a problem; teachers do not always know important details related to the problem.
2. Attempt to discover the reason behind the problem.
3. Discuss strategies that will help solve the problem.
4. Evaluate strategies.
5. Choose a strategy that is agreeable to all.
6. Make a commitment to try the strategy.
7. Establish a time frame for implementation and follow up.

Can you identify students who you believe exhibited inappropriate behavior to get attention, to gain power, to seek revenge, or to cover for feelings of inadequacy? How did you know?

Burke (1992) suggests using forms to facilitate and document these problem-solving conferences. Figures 7.5, 7.6, and 7.7 provide examples. When difficulties are related to the poor use of interpersonal and small-group learning skills, conferences can frequently be used to teach, coach, and role play the use of the specific skills that the student lacks.

Common Challenges and Strategies

The Absent Student   Chronically absent students are always a concern but can be particularly troublesome when significant group work is incorporated into the life of the classroom. Absent students are a particular problem

Student's name:

Student's statement of the problem:

Teacher's statement of the problem:

Student's ideas for solutions to the problem:
1.
2.
3.
Which solution will we try? Why?

Action plan:

Follow-up date:

Figure 7.5
Outline of basic problem-solving strategy for teacher/student or group problem-solving conferences.

Student's name:

Teacher's statement of problem:

Student's understanding of, and reaction to, teacher's statement of problem:

Student's ideas for solutions to the problem:

1.

2.

3.

Teacher's ideas for solutions to the problem:

1.

2.

3.

Steps teacher will take to solve problem:

Steps student will take to solve problem:

Positive consequences for student if steps are followed.

Negative consequences for student if steps are not followed.

Follow-up date:

Figure 7.6
Outline of basic problem-solving strategy for teacher/student or group
problem-solving conferences.

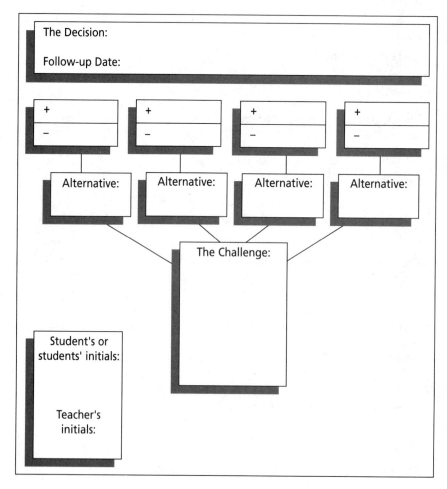

Figure 7.7
Outline of basic decision-making tree for student/teacher or group problem-solving conferences. "Plus" and "minus" boxes represent pros and cons for each alternative.

when formal learning groups last for more than one class period or day and other group members are left trying to decide what to do about "missing pieces" or trying to integrate a returning student into work that is partially completed. Some teachers *like* group work because they believe that placing a chronically absent student in a group not only motivates the student to come to school but, by listening to and working with other students, helps him or her to catch up as well. Despite these benefits, absenteeism is still a problem when students work together. Conferences with students and parents can help determine why students are absent and may help decrease absenteeism. Common strategies that may work with chronically absent students include

- Having base group or formal group members call the students. Phone calls from peers remind students that they have been missed. Phone calls from formal group members can help bring students up to date on group progress.
- Placing chronically absent students in larger groups so that other group members are not as dependent on them and are, therefore, less likely to feel hassled or hostile.
- Asking chronically absent students to work alone.
- Making sure that all groups have designated class space to store their materials. This helps to ensure that crucial information and material remains where it is always accessible.
- Being careful to structure assessment so that other group members are not penalized for work missed by absent students.

What else might you add to this list? Be specific.

The Apathetic Student Who Does Not Contribute Meaningfully   Some students, although present, are apathetic and do not contribute meaningfully to the work of the group. This kind of student is generally not a welcome group member and can, over time, lower the sense of commitment of other group members. Conferences to determine the causes of these behaviors are often useful and will help to determine strategies. Strategies might include

- Assigning roles that build on the strengths of the identified student.
- Placing students in small groups so that it is harder to "hide."
- Breaking large assignments into smaller pieces with clear due dates and criteria.
- Incorporating the use of structures that require each student to contribute.
- Temporarily establishing different criteria for success so that students can incrementally increase their participation and experience interim success.
- Using a K-W-H-L-S (this was described in Chapter 6) or similar strategy to help students establish personal goals that will extend the group work and encourage their personal interest.
- Having apathetic students work alone.

What else might you add to this list? Be specific.

The Dominant Student   Some students dominate. These students are often not welcome group members; other students either actively resent them or simply withdraw their own commitment. Again, conferences can be used to help determine strategies. Strategies might include

- Making a dominant student an observer.
- Assigning roles that do not allow the dominant student to control information, materials, or air time in the group.

- Placing several dominant students in the same group so that each can experience first hand how difficult it is to work with dominant peers.
- Incorporating the use of structures that require each student to contribute.
- Increasing the complexity of learning tasks so that the dominant student has a more difficult time controlling the outcome.

What else might you add to this list? Be specific.

The Student Who Prefers to Work Alone   Some students prefer to work alone, and conferencing is essential to determining why. Typically, students want to work alone when they are experiencing status problems, when they know that they lack good interpersonal skills, or when they feel incompetent. Strategies for working with these problems have been discussed. Some students prefer to work alone because they need more time or a quiet space to process information. To help these students, a teacher might try

- Developing assignments that combine individual and group work and make sure that additional time or quiet is available to the students who need it.
- Including a quiet area in the classroom design.
- Incorporating the use of structures that combine individual think time with group discussion.
- Helping students learn what their needs are so that they can negotiate work plans within a group that meet their individual needs.

What else might you add to this list? Be specific.

Students may prefer to work alone when they are anxious about quality and believe that their work will suffer because others are less driven towards quality. These students may see themselves as smarter than other group members. Strategies for these students include

- Developing assignments that combine individual and group work.
- Emphasizing the cooperative context for learning so that individual work does not assume competitive undertones.
- Being clear that learning to work with others is essential—not optional.
- Using a K-W-H-L-S or similar strategy to help students establish personal goals that will build on and extend the context of the group work.
- Assigning roles that build on the strengths of the student and insure that he or she can positively affect—but not dominate—the quality of the group work.
- Being careful to structure assessment so that group members are not penalized for the poor work of others.
- Stressing individual responsibility.
- Assigning students to work with other students who have a similar drive for quality.
- Articulating clearly that high expectations are the norm for all students.
- Increasing the complexity of learning tasks so that the student *needs* the contributions of other members to achieve the level of success desired.
- Allowing the student to work alone.

What else might you add to this list? Be specific.

Students Working Alone

When discussing cooperative learning and challenging students, many teachers take the position that "working together is a privilege. Working alone is a right and responsibility." This may be true, but what might it mean in a classroom learning community? How is this congruent with the concept that learning is positively influenced by meaningful peer interaction and that meaningful interpersonal relationships can positively influence physical and psychological health? Is it necessary or desirable for students to work alone when the majority of students are working together? If so, when?

Often a student and teacher decide together when working alone is a good choice; this decision is usually made in conjunction with a problem-solving conference. In general, ground rules for working alone include

- The student is responsible for completing the work that would normally be completed in the group. It is important that working alone is not seen as an opportunity to avoid work, and it may not be reasonable for the teacher to spend time to differentiate a task and make it manageable for a student who is working alone rather than in a small group.
- The student describes, and the teacher agrees to, the actions the student will try after returning to the group. A written description is often necessary.
- A time line, or procedure, is established for the student to rejoin a group. The student needs to know that rejoining a group is possible; working alone should not be seen as either semipermanent isolation or a permanent solution to interpersonal difficulties.

In some classrooms students have the right to decide by themselves if they want to work alone (Bellanca & Fogarty, 1991). Students typically choose this option when they feel emotionally volatile or preoccupied with issues they have brought to class with them or simply need time alone. When students choose time alone, they need to be encouraged to make wise choices; working alone should not be chosen every time working together seems difficult. Often, student-selected work-alones are time limited—a few minutes or one activity for young children and one period for older students; routines need to be established that determine how students will opt out, leave, and return to their groups.

Sometimes teachers decide when an individual needs to work alone. When a teacher makes this decision, it is best if the decision is based on teacher observation and data, rather than student complaints, and careful thought and interaction with the student, not anger or impulse. When the teacher decides that an individual is to work alone, the ground rules are the same as when the student and teacher decide together: (a) the student is responsible for completing work, (b) the student must describe what actions she will attempt when returning to the group, and (c) a time line or procedure is established for rejoining the group. Sometimes the group that the student is moving away from—and returning to—will need to be included in decisions about desired actions, procedures, and timelines.

Teachers Responding to Challenge

There is no perfect lesson, T-chart, role play, monitoring technique, or conference to insure that learning—either individual or cooperative—will always go smoothly. At their best, classrooms are—like all of life—interesting, complex, and challenging. Persistence, planning, and testing and retesting ideas are key. Above all, it is important to keep a sense of perspective and humor. Don't panic. Very few decisions—even bad ones—are fatal.

In this chapter we have continued to learn the discipline of creating cooperation through the application of five basic elements to lesson design; we have focused specifically on the careful teaching of interpersonal and small-group learning skills. Next we turn our attention to several classroom scenarios to help us develop a better understanding of how the teaching of interpersonal and small-group learning skills looks and sounds and feels. In these lessons each teacher has planned a deliberate focus on an important skill. As you read, take the time to ask yourself: "What skill(s) has the teacher targeted?" "How is the skill defined?" "How do students practice this skill?" "How does the teacher monitor?" "Why might the teacher have made these choices?" You might also consider how it might feel to be a student in one of these classrooms. How do you think it might feel to be the teacher?

 A VIEW FROM THE CLASSROOM:
TEACHING INTERPERSONAL AND SMALL-GROUP LEARNING SKILLS

Pedro uses a bulletin board with pictures of animal groups and accompanying collective nouns such as "an exaltation of larks," a "parliament of owls," a "school of fish," and a "pride of lions" to help focus discussion about the essential nature of "working together." Early in the year, this bulletin board also helps his students to develop names for their base groups and to develop a class name.

Janet teaches biology. Throughout the year she and her students keep a list of scientists who have become recognized for collaborative work. This list includes scientists mentioned in their textbook, scientists they see on videos, and scientists in the news. Announcements of Nobel Prizes are of keen interest in this class. Their list is labeled *"Nothing new that is really interesting comes without collaboration."*—James Watson (Nobel Prize winner and co-discoverer of the double helix).

Lynnette knows that it is very difficult for beginning kindergarten students to work together in small groups; she also knows that they tend to be more interested in hearing themselves talk than they are in listening to others. Lynnette begins cooperative learning not by placing her students in small groups but by helping them practice their listening skills as a whole class. She and her students sit together in a circle on the story rug. She reads them a story and then, going around the circle, asks each child in turn to tell something he or she liked. When she calls on the second child, she asks him or her to repeat one thing the first child said before sharing what he or she liked; the third child is asked to share what the second child liked, and so on around the circle. At first Lynnette's class finds this to be very difficult, and often children have to ask the children next to them to repeat what they said before they can repeat the idea. After a few days of practice, they become much more skilled at listening and repeating an idea; when Lynnette begins to have her children work in pairs, they will continue practicing this skill.

Laurie notices that her first graders have a difficult time using quiet voices when they work together. As she watches, she also notices that their loud voices seem related to the fact that they tend not to talk one at a time; she decides to target this skill. First, she talks with her students about the importance of listening; she then places them in groups of three. In each group she assigns one person to be the listening monitor. When a listening monitor notices more than one person talking at a time, the monitor's job is to use thumb and index finger to make the letter L to remind everyone to listen. When the groups have finished their task, Laurie asks each individual student to reflect: "Show me with your fingers: On a scale of one to five, how well did you remember to talk one at a time?" Then Laurie asks each group to discuss: "On a scale of one to five, how well were you able to use quiet voices?" After a moment of discussion, reporters in each group raise fingers to share their numbers. Laurie takes a moment to call on a few groups that she thinks have been successful in their use of quiet voices. She asks questions such as "What did you do together that helped you be a four?" and encourages her students to describe specific behaviors that

helped them use quiet voices. She writes these behaviors on the board; tomorrow her students will use this list to establish behavioral goals for themselves, and Laurie will use this list to build an observation sheet so that she can record behaviors that indicate good listening.

Marsha's fifth graders are noisy when they work together, and Marsha has found herself using a loud voice to tell them to quiet down. She is frustrated and begins to think that she just will not have her students work together. Then it occurs to her that her students do not understand what quiet voices are, so she decides to teach "using a quiet voice." She begins by organizing her classroom furniture so that her students can sit closer together when they work; next, she spends time with her students talking about the importance of "using a twelve-inch voice" and "putting your heads together." Marsha develops a plan that she shares with her students. Each day for a week they will work together in the same small groups for twenty minutes; each day she will monitor each group and listen for quiet voices. Every five minutes she goes around the room and gives each group a small circle of colored paper—a green circle means "keep going, your voice level is good;" a yellow circle means "pay attention, your voice level is a little too loud;" a red circle means "your voice level is too loud. Stop for thirty seconds and then try again." At the end of each twenty-minute practice, Marsha collects all the circles she has distributed. Each day she and the class count the total number of green circles and post the total on the blackboard. Before they begin work the next day, they review this number and together set a class goal for how many green circles they will earn in their next practice period. By the end of the week, Marsha's students have become much more aware of when they are using appropriate voices, and Marsha is no longer interrupting their group work to tell them—in a loud voice—that they are too noisy. Marsha does not have to continue this routine each and every time her students work together, but periodically throughout the year she uses her red, yellow, and green circles to reinforce the importance of using quiet voices.

Jane's third-grade students have a difficult time with the skill "stay with the group," and Jane spends a great deal of time monitoring students who seem to be wandering around during group work. Yet when she asks students if they "stay with the group," they almost always say they do. Jane decides to collect systematic data about "staying" and "wandering." Jane designs a group task that students can complete without moving around the room to gather materials. She places her students in groups of four and asks them to work on this task for ten minutes and, during this time, collects data about wandering. At the end of ten minutes, she asks each group to discuss how well members were able to stay with the group. Without using names, she then shares her data with the class; they seem genuinely surprised that sharpening pencils, looking in book bags, and leaning away from their work group to talk with another group is not staying with the group.

The next day, Jane begins by reading *Swimmy* to her class. In this charming book by Leo Lionni, the little fish learn to swim close together in the shape of a giant fish so that they can safely enjoy the wonders of the ocean. Jane and her students discuss how the little fish learn to stay together, and they develop a T-chart that describes what "stay together" looks and sounds like. Jane again places her students in groups of four and asks them to work on a task for ten minutes; again, she collects data about staying and wandering. At the end of ten minutes, she asks each group to discuss how well members were able to stay with the group, and she shares her data. During the next week, Jane and her students repeat this process each day and compare their data and impressions with previous days. By the end of the week, the students have a much better idea of what staying looks and sounds like and Jane observes much less wandering.

Jim notices that his students do not always pay careful attention when others are talking—in fact, sometimes he notices downright rudeness! Jim decides that his students need to learn more about attentive listening. He begins by constructing a T-chart with his students that focuses on listening. He then divides his students into pairs. He asks one person in each pair to spend a few minutes thinking about something funny that happened recently and to be ready to share this story with a partner. He brings the other members of each pair together; together they reflect on the T-chart and develop another "secret" T-chart that can be used to describe nonlistening. The students have a good time with this! Next, students rejoin their partners, and one member tells a story while the other member looks away, yawns, rolls eyes, talks with another group, and so forth. Jim lets this go on for about a minute and then "freezes" the action—asking students to notice the behaviors in the room. Jim asks the "nonlisteners" to repeat the funny stories from their partners and, not surprisingly, they do a very poor job. Jim asks the storytellers to describe what it was like to try to talk to a peer who is obviously not listening. They typically express frustration—even though they had caught on to what was happening.

Jim posts both the listening and nonlistening T-charts in the classroom. For the rest of the week, Jim tallies incidences of both listening and nonlistening behavior each time his students work together; he shares these tallies with the class. Together they add to their T-chart of good listening behaviors. The following week Jim designs several learning activities that require students to work together and listen to each other carefully; he constructs a simple observation sheet of listening behaviors. During the week, students in the class are each given an opportunity to use this observation sheet to record the positive listening behaviors of their peers; and, with the use of the observation sheet, students receive specific positive feedback about their own listening behavior as well (Bellanca & Fogarty, 1991). (See Figure 8.1 for an example of how Jim uses structured observations to provide students with feedback and help them set new goals.)

Joe wants to ensure that all his students contribute their ideas in their literature study groups. He gives them each three plastic chips and instructs each student to place one chip in front of him- or herself each time he or she talks. Once their chips are gone, students have to remain silent until the other people in the group have contributed their ideas and used their chips. To sensitize students to the need for listening and paraphrasing, Joe occasionally instructs his students that the "ticket" for talking is not a chip but the ability to paraphrase correctly the person who has just spoken (Baloche, Lee Mauger, Willis, Filinuk, & Michalsky, 1993).

Marta wants her students to appreciate the importance of asking questions that are intended to clarify information and seek accuracy. She places her students in pairs and arranges seats so that each pair can sit back to back. She gives person #1 in each pair a drawing of several squares "piled together" and person #2 a plain piece of paper. Person #1 describes the figure while person #2 draws what is being described. After a few moments, Marta gives person #2 a different figure and roles are reversed. This time, however, person #1 can ask questions while drawing. After a few minutes, the pairs turn and face each other and share originals and drawings. Not surprisingly, when students are allowed to ask questions, their representations of the figures tend to be more accurate. Marta asks each student to complete: "One way I could ask a question to clarify information would be ___." She and her students then create a list of phrases and questions that they can use to clarify information and seek accuracy, and they talk about when they might use these phrases. Marta will refer to this list regularly and the students will add more phrases as they become more skilled at working together.

Joyce's fourth-grade students work regularly in their literature study groups. She wants them to be less dependent on her to focus their group discussions; one of the ways she does this is by carefully teaching them how to ask good questions. Each group uses a list of questioning stems that are based on Bloom's taxonomy (see Figure 7.1), and Joyce asks each group to design three questions—one each for knowledge, comprehension, and analysis. In previous lessons Joyce has taught each type of question so her students understand her directions and are able to work together to complete this task. Basic roles of materials manager, recorder, checker, and reporter are rotated weekly within literature study groups, and students assume these roles naturally and skillfully as they construct their questions. Each group writes its knowledge and comprehension questions on a single piece of paper that Joyce distributes; Joyce uses *Trade a Problem* (Kagan, 1992) to have each group answer the questions designed by another group and then to discuss both the answers and the questions themselves. Next, Joyce asks all the reporters to come to the board and write their analysis questions. She gives the groups some time to look at each question—not to answer the question but to decide if it really is an analysis question. Each group chooses one question (other than its own) and uses this question to focus a short small-group discussion; after the discussions, Joyce asks each group to answer the question: "How well did the question you chose help you to analyze and discuss your reading?"

Terry targets skills that will help her students engage in discussions that are stimulating and informed. Now she wants them to reflect on how these skills come together to help build a good discussion. They are studying *Macbeth*. She arranges the classroom chairs in a "fishbowl"—two circles, one inside the other—and she assigns each student to one of these two circles. Terry gives the students in the inner circle about eight minutes to discuss the statement: "Men who have been violent on the battlefield can come home to act like criminals in time of peace" and to relate this statement to both Macbeth and contemporary life. Terry has prepared her students for this discussion by asking them to respond to this statement in their journals the previous evening. Terry reviews the ground rules—"state an idea and support it with evidence," "agree with a speaker and add additional evidence," and "disagree with a speaker and offer evidence"—and conversation is lively and informed.

Terry has given each of the students in the outer circle a worksheet; they spend their time listening to the discussion and noting the interactions of one assigned classmate, or "fish," in the inner circle. Throughout the discussion, students tally each time their fish contribute an idea, describe feelings, paraphrase, express support or acceptance, encourage others to contribute, summarize, relieve tension by joking, or give direction to the group's work. (See Figure 2.1 for a sample observation form.) Because the students in Terry's class have learned the importance of task and maintenance skills in group discussions, they seem quite comfortable saying things like "Sue, would you like to add something else to that idea?" "Matt, what do you think about that?" "David, that's an excellent point." Students exchange seats—those formerly in the inner circle now observe; those in the outer circle now take their turn to discuss a second focus statement. Afterwards, the partners face each other; they exchange observation sheets and share positive observations about the uses of interpersonal skills (Baloche, et al., 1993).

❧ WORKING WITH PEERS ❧

Using Base Groups to Review Chapter Content and Personalize Learning

QUESTION: *Which of the six steps of teaching interpersonal and small-group learning skills do you think might be most important? Why?*

1. Students use same basic format described in Chapters 5 and 6 for base group discussion and chapter review. (Students should use a different structure to organize their discussion than the ones they chose in Chapters 5 and 6.)
2. Reflection and Planning:
   Individual:
   - On a scale of 1 to 5 how confident am I that I can explain why the other members in my group chose the step they did?
   - How confident am I that they can all explain why I chose the step I did?
   Group:
   - Was the structure we chose for our own discussion useful for our purpose?
   - How could that structure be used to help teach an interpersonal skill?

Using Pairs and *Mad Hatter's Tea Party* for Analysis and Application of Chapter Content

1. Students use the same basic format described in Chapter 5 and used again in Chapter 6. The scenarios are found in Chapter 6: Patrick, Linda, Molly, Dana, Arlene, Ana, and Marilyn. (It may be useful for students to work with the same partners and use the same scenarios as in Chapter 6.) Each pair analyzes a scenario, responding to the questions:
   a. What interpersonal and small-group learning skill(s) are being targeted? Is the targeted skill a "Getting Together," "Getting The Job Done and Staying Together," "Getting It," or "Getting It [2]" skill?
   b. How might the teacher develop an understanding of the skill?
   c. How do the students practice the skill?
   d. How might the teacher observe?
2. Using the same scenario, students work with their partners to describe how they might
   a. Develop a context for cooperation for the age (or subject) level of the students in their scenario.
   b. Develop an understanding of what the skill is. (If the scenario includes a description of how the teacher did this, choose a different method such as a role play, simulation, story, or video.)
   c. Develop a T-chart for the skill.
   d. Develop an idea for a practice session that does not use academic content.
   e. Develop a plan and an instrument to collect data about the targeted skill.

f. Decide what might be a logical next step for these students to learn more about this skill.

g. Decide what might be a logical next skill on which these students might focus.

4. Pairs stay together and, using *Mad Hatter's Tea Party,* share their analyses with other pairs.

5. Reflection and Planning:

Individual:

- How confident am I that I can develop strategies for all six steps of teaching interpersonal and small-group learning skills?
- How confident am I that I could identify an appropriate skill to focus on in a classroom setting?"

Pair:

- One way you helped me understand teaching interpersonal skills was _____.
- One thing about teaching interpersonal skills that I want to learn more about is _____.

Class:

- What kind(s) of interpersonal and small-group learning skills were needed in this activity?
- How well were we able to use these skills?

Using Trios, *Questions a la Bloom,* and *Trade a Problem* (Kagan, 1992) to Review Chapter Content

1. Students group in random trios. Students work alone to create six questions—one for each level of Bloom's taxonomy and with the help of Questions a la Bloom—that can be used for review.

2. Students put their problems together and create one list of six questions. The list should include at least one question from each individual's work.

3. Each trio "trades its questions" with another trio and now uses new questions for review.

4. Trios link to tell each other which questions generated particularly interesting discussion.

5. Reflection and planning:

Individual:

- How confident am I that I can use all six types of questioning effectively?

Group:

- What interpersonal and small-group learning skills did we need for this activity?
- What skills would we need to teach students?

Using Groups of Four, *Gallery Tour* (Kagan, 1992), and Self-Stick Notes to Reflect on the Four Basic Categories of Interpersonal and Small-Group Learning Skills

1. Students group in random foursomes. Each group is assigned or chooses one level on which to focus their work. Levels are K–2, 3–5, 6–8, 9–12, and university. Students are to examine the four basic categories of skills and create a list of skills in each category using language appropriate for the levels they have been assigned.

2. Students work alone to create individual lists.

3. Students put their lists together and create one list of the four categories. The list should include at least one idea from each individual's work. Once lists have been formulated, they can be written on large paper or blackboards.

4. Students then go on a *Gallery Tour,* visiting the lists of all the different groups (different groups have focused on different levels). They stop and discuss each group's work and, using self-stick notes, leave specific positive comments about the work. (It is useful to fold the notes over so that groups are not influenced by the comments of previous groups.)

5. Groups return to their own work, review the notes, and make any revisions in their lists that seem appropriate.

6. Reflection and planning:

Group:

- What are some of the things teachers might need to think about when adapting skills to different grade levels?

Using a *One-Minute Paper* and Base Groups to Reflect on Challenges

Question: *What one challenge are you most concerned about? Why?*

1. Each student writes a response.

2. In their base groups, students share challenges.

3. Groups discuss each choice and decide what interpersonal and small-group learning skill might be particularly useful to focus on when working with the challenge.

4. Each student adds a skill to his or her paper and describes why the skill might be important.

CHAPTER 8

Reflection and Planning: Examining Interpersonal and Small-Group Learning Skills By Looking Back and Planning Ahead

 **As you read, you might want to ask yourself:**

Why are reflection and planning essential to the discipline of using co-operative learning?

How do reflection and planning help students learn interpersonal and small-group learning skills?

How might teachers design reflection and planning for formal learning groups?

How might teachers design reflection and planning for base groups? For informal groups?

How might the information that is collected during monitoring be used for reflection and planning?

What makes feedback helpful?

How do reflection and planning help to develop and sustain a learning community?

What might reflection and planning look and sound and feel like in an empowering classroom?

The discipline of using cooperative learning effectively includes carefully planned opportunities for students to reflect on the work they have done together and to plan for future collaborative work. Reflection and planning by students are crucial—crucial to the successful use of cooperative learning, crucial to empowering students as learners, and crucial to the development of good interpersonal skills that are important for real-life success. For maximum impact, reflection and planning must be focused on both interpersonal and academic domains; students need to reflect on and plan both for *how* they work together and for *what* they learn when they work together. Because reflection and planning are critically important in both of these domains, they will be discussed in two separate chapters. In this chapter we will learn ways to design opportunities for students (a) to look back—to reflect on how they have worked together and (b) to look forward—to plan and set goals for how they will work together in the future and to plan how to apply the skills they are learning to new situations. In Chapter 9 we will learn ways to design opportunities for students to reflect on (a) what they have learned together and (b) what they can learn together in the future. In Chapter 9, we will also focus on assessment issues and discuss individual responsibility.

Why might the barriers to cooperation be likely to increase if students are not provided with regular opportunities to reflect on how they work together?

❀ THE ESSENTIAL ASPECTS OF ❀ REFLECTION AND PLANNING

A Focus on the Positive—Helpful Feedback

Learning to give and receive feedback is an essential skill in a classroom learning community and is central to reflection and planning. For feedback to be helpful it should, first of all, be positive. Negative feedback builds resistance, not trust, and is therefore of limited use when students and teachers are working together to build a learning community. Your kindergarten teacher, who undoubtedly said, "If you can't say something nice, don't say anything at all," was right—but only partially.

There are other feedback principles that should also be considered if reflection and planning are to be used to their fullest potential. These include the principles that feedback should

Think of a time when you were given feedback that was positive, descriptive, specific, brief, and focused on behavior. What was the feedback?

- Be descriptive and specific: Words like "good" and "excellent" are positive, but they are evaluative and general and should be avoided in favor of more precise language. For example, "The way you varied your tone of voice and the speed of your reading really kept my attention and helped me to picture what you were reading about" is more useful than "You are good at reading aloud."
- Focus on behavior not personality: Words that suggest "you did" are preferable to words that suggest "you are." For example: "I saw you two use good eye contact, share materials, and check each problem when you

worked together during math today" is more useful than "You two are good at working together."
- Be brief and unobtrusive: In general, it is better to say less than more.
- Be immediate: In general, it does little good to tell people about what they did a week ago.

A Focus on I, You, and We

When students work together in small groups, feedback, reflection, and planning can be focused and structured in many different ways. For instance (adapted from Dishon & O'Leary, 1994):

- Individual students might focus on
    themselves—"I"
    another specific individual—"you"
    a small group—"we"
- Small groups might focus on
    themselves—"we"
    other small groups—"you"
- The entire class might focus on
    themselves—"we"

When students have been working together, the teacher—who has been monitoring the groups and collecting data about interpersonal and small-group learning skills—might want to provide feedback as well.

- Teachers might focus their feedback on
    individual students
    small groups
    the entire class

All of these forms of feedback and reflection are useful, and highly-skilled teachers learn to use all of them to help students become empowered learners.

🦋 DESIGNING REFLECTION AND PLANNING 🦋

Understanding that students need opportunities to reflect on the work they have done and to plan for their future collaborative work is important. Making the commitment to provide carefully designed opportunities for this reflection and planning is even more important; just telling students to "talk about how it went" is not careful reflection and will not contribute to student success. In this section we will learn many ways to design feedback, reflection, and planning.

Designing Feedback and Reflection about Observational Data

Anecdotal Observations   In Chapter 7 we examined how teachers might collect anecdotal data about student use of specific interpersonal and small-group learning skills. One way teachers use these observations is to provide feedback to students. This feedback can be focused on individuals, small groups, or the whole class. When the teacher is providing feedback based on anecdotal observation, it is important for students to understand that he or she cannot be everywhere and see and hear everything. This can be explained to students, and students understand it better when feedback is prefaced with "I heard" and "I saw." For instance, a teacher might use anecdotal observation and then report

- "Tommy, I heard you remind people in your group that they needed to check their work."
- "John, Samantha, and Jose, I heard each of you ask a groupmate to share his or her ideas. Making sure everyone in a group has a chance to share ideas is very important."
- "I heard five different people remind their groups to talk one at a time."
- "I observed that groups one, two, and four each made a plan when they first started their work."
- "I saw that every group was careful to arrange its chairs and materials so that everyone could touch the equipment."

Structured Observations   In Chapter 7 we examined how structured observation sheets can be used—by the teacher, a colleague, or students—to collect systematic data about student use of specific interpersonal and small-group learning skills. It is tempting for observers to offer interpretations of the feedback they have collected, but it helps students become empowered learners and highly-skilled group workers when they use the data from observation sheets to examine and interpret their own skills, rather than relying on the interpretations of others (Figure 8.1). To facilitate this process, a teacher might say

- "Are you surprised by any of the data on the observation sheet?"
- "What pleases you most about your use of the interpersonal skills that were included on the observation sheet?"
- "What skill did you use most frequently? Circle that skill. Was it helpful? If so, where else—other than in this classroom—could you use that skill?"
- "What skill do you want to focus on most closely when you work together tomorrow? Why? Put a star next to that skill."
- "What new skill do you think we should add to our observation sheet? Why?"

Notice that a teacher could ask each individual student or each group to answer any one of these questions. Notice, too, that some questions ask students to focus on what they have done, some ask them to set goals for

	Raoul	Samantha	Jeanene	Tom
Asks others for details	IIII	II ✩	IIII	I
Paraphrases others	II	I	I ✩	I
Face focused on speaker	III	III	III	I ✩
Taking notes	I ✩		I	III

Figure 8.1
Structured observation sheet for "Listening." The stars indicate the behavior that individual students have chosen to target as personal goals for the next time they work with others.

their future work together, and others ask them to think about how they might apply the skills they use in different settings.

Designing Feedback and Reflection among Students

As we have already learned, feedback and reflection among students can be facilitated when students focus on themselves or when they focus on others. For instance, individual students might be asked to reflect on their own participation:

- "On a scale of 1 to 5, how well did you remember to paraphrase the ideas of other members in your group before you shared your own ideas?"
- "Signal thumbs up or thumbs down: Today I remembered to stay with my group for the entire time we worked together."
- "What is one thing you did today that helped your group complete its task? Share your answer in a *Roundrobin*."

- "On a scale of 1 to 5, how confident are you that you can explain your partner's ideas?"
- "Going around the group, members are each to share one thing they did that they think helped their group today."

Individual students might focus on the participation of others:

- "What is one thing your partner did today that encouraged you to stick with the work? Tell him—be as specific as possible."
- "Start with person #1 in your group. Person #1 is to turn to the person on his left and complete: 'One way you helped me today was ___.' That person will now turn to the person on her left and complete the same sentence. Continue around the circle so that each person receives and gives one piece of feedback. Remember to be as specific as possible."
- "Today the group helped me by ___."

When teachers design opportunities for students to give each other specific positive feedback, observations that have the potential to influence status positively become part of student-to-student feedback as well as teacher-to-student feedback.

Groups are often asked to focus on themselves. "We" responses require that all students have input into what the group decides and ask students to build understanding and agreement. To structure a "we" focus, teachers might ask for responses such as

- "Today our group was good at ___."
- "I want one number from your group: On a scale of 1 to 5, how well did your group remember to use quiet voices?"
- "What skill did your group use most effectively today?"
- "The best thing about your group work today was ___."

Designing Planning among Students

As we have already learned, planning—both goal setting and application of what has been learned to other situations—can be facilitated by both individual "I" statements and group "we" statements. Either groups or individuals might be asked to plan when teachers say

- "What is one skill you want to target for your work tomorrow? What are three things you can do to focus on that skill?"
- "To soar like an eagle in our group we need to ___."
- "What is one skill that you think will help your group work more effectively? What can you do to practice that skill?"
- "In a group it is helpful to ___."
- "Where else can you practice the skill of ___? How and when will you practice it? Make a plan."

"Goal setting" can help students examine and describe what *did not* work in ways that focus on the possibility of future success—not past difficulties. Goal setting is particularly helpful when groups are going to stay together. Application can help students build an understanding that good group work is not "magic" and that the skills they have used successfully in one setting can be transferred and applied to other settings. Application is particularly helpful when students have experienced success in one group and need to be able to move with confidence into new groups. Application statements also help sensitize students to the value of using good interpersonal skills outside of the classroom.

Reflection and planning are, of course, often combined—as are the focuses of "I" and "we." For instance, a teacher might say

- "Each individual is to rank order group members by participation level. Share your individual rankings in your group and try to create one list that you can all agree on. Then list two things your group could do tomorrow to help make participation levels more equal."

🐞 CHALLENGES 🐞

Once upon a time, when farmers planted their crops, if there was a particularly big tree in the middle of their field, they would plow around it and they would leave brush and trees—hedgerows—at the edges of fields. But as time went on, some farmers began to worry about their yield per acre; they looked at their fields and decided that those big trees and hedgerows wasted valuable space, so they cut down the trees, tore up the hedgerows, and planted more crops. This seemed to work fine— for awhile. But windbreaks of hedgerows and trees help keep soil from blowing off of newly plowed fields and help mitigate the temperatures during season changes. The hedgerows and trees also provide refuge for animals—birds that eat harmful insects, bees that pollinate flowers. So eliminating hedgerows and trees did not necessarily help farmers grow more crops per acre, and many people thought that the fields were less beautiful.

The biggest potential challenge of reflection and planning is that teachers do not believe that they are important and, therefore, do not find the time for students to engage in thoughtful reflection and planning and do not take the time to develop procedures for reflection so that it is meaningful. Reflection and planning are, in some ways, like trees and hedgerows. At first glance, spending time on them may seem too costly. But the reality is quite different. Reflection and planning are essential if students are going to grow in their use of good interpersonal skills and become empowered learners.

As you picture yourself using the discipline of cooperative learning to help create a classroom where all students are empowered as learners, what do you think might be your biggest challenge when you plan opportunities for reflection and planning?

Making Time for Reflection and Planning

The time needed for reflection and planning depends on the learning context. Sometimes, leisurely reflection and planning are essential, and at other times quick responses are sufficient. A series of quick responses spaced throughout a period of cooperative work can be invaluable—providing both the teacher and students with immediate feedback about how their work together is progressing. Quick responses—such as 1 to 5 or thumbs-up-thumbs-down hand signals—are useful when time is in short supply; they are clearly preferable to no reflection at all. At the end of work periods, older students benefit from responding to a teacher's question with the use of a One-Minute Paper. Typically, these papers are collected, read, and perhaps responded to, by the teacher. On occasion an "at-home" journal assignment can be used for self-reflection, but the full impact of reflection and planning are lost when they are routinely relegated to homework time.

Making Reflection and Planning Meaningful

Reflection and planning are most fruitful when teachers prepare carefully. Students sense a casual "afterthought" and will respond casually. One way teachers prepare carefully for reflection and provide their students with the clear message that thoughtful reflection and planning are important is to use written formats. These can be completed by either individuals or groups and can be kept and referred to before subsequent cooperative work. Figures 8.2

Name: _____

Place checkmarks in the three boxes that best describe you in your group work today.

Circle one behavior that you want to make sure you use tomorrow.

❑ I stayed with my group.
❑ I made sure my voice did not get TOO LOUD!
❑ I reminded others to stay on task in an agreeable way.
❑ I helped manage the materials and make sure they got put back in "good shape."
❑ I participated.
❑ I asked others to participate.
❑ I helped my group make a plan.
❑ I helped my group stick with the plan.
❑ I helped summarize our work.

Figure 8.2
Written format for individual reflection and goal setting on interpersonal and small-group learning skills.

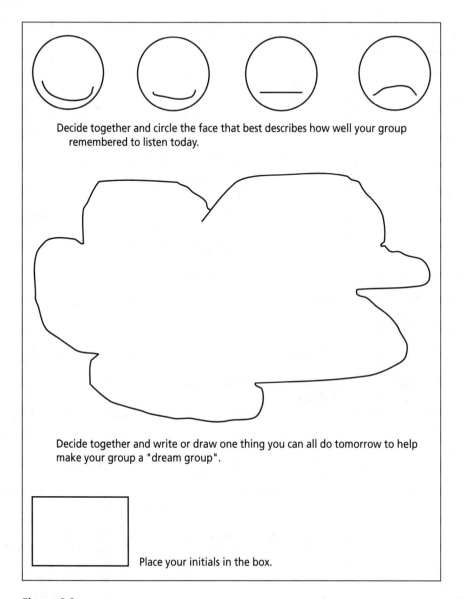

Decide together and circle the face that best describes how well your group remembered to listen today.

Decide together and write or draw one thing you can all do tomorrow to help make your group a "dream group".

Place your initials in the box.

Figure 8.3
Written format for group reflection and goal setting on interpersonal and small-group learning skills.

through 8.4 contain examples of written formats for reflection and planning; Bennett, Rolheiser, and Stevahn (1991) provide many additional examples.

A second way teachers give students the message that thoughtful reflection and planning are important is by using structures during the reflection and

Discuss and reach agreement before coloring each bar on the graph to the level that you all agree best describes your work today.

We remembered most of the time.				
We remembered a lot of the time.				
We remembered some of the time.				
We remembered a little bit.				
We forgot most of the time.				
	We thought about a plan for our work.	We summarized our work.	We asked interesting questions.	We made sure we had more than one idea before we made decisions.

	Place your initials in the box to indicate that you agree with your group's assessment of their effectiveness.

Figure 8.4
Written format for group reflection on "Getting It" and "Getting It²" skills.

planning process. Structures such as *Pens in the Middle, Roundrobin,* and *Paraphrase Passport* help insure that students all participate in the reflection process and listen to their peers. Structures such as *Corners, Value Lines, Mix-Freeze-Pair, Inside-Outside Circle,* and *Stand and Share* facilitate the sharing of individual reflections and plans and build a sense of individual responsibility for the reflection and planning process. *Team Statements,*

Blackboard Shares, and *Numbered Heads Together* facilitate intergroup sharing and a sense of group accountability.

A third way teachers give students the message that reflection and planning are important and relevant is by being flexible in how and when they use processing. When teachers are flexible, they are able to respond to the immediate. If groups have used their interpersonal skills quite effectively, for instance, reflection and planning should respond to and celebrate this success. When a group is having a particularly difficult time, ignoring difficulties until they have finished their work or focusing processing on some generic skill will not convince students that reflection and planning are important and will not help students become more skilled in their work together.

One final key to effective reflection and planning is perseverance. In general, students are not accustomed to thinking about *how* they work together, and teachers are not accustomed to asking students to think in this way. Both teachers and students need to develop skills and procedures for the disciplined use of reflection and planning so that "looking back and planning ahead" becomes a vital element in the disciplined use of cooperative learning.

 WORKING WITH PEERS

Using Base Groups to Review Chapter Content and Personalize Learning

QUESTION: *Which do you think might be most essential to high-quality cooperative learning—reflection, goal setting, or application? Why?*

1. Students use same basic format described in Chapters 5, 6, and 7 for base group discussion and chapter review. (Students should use a different structure to organize their discussion.)
2. Reflection and Planning:
   Individual:
   - On a scale of 1 to 5 how confident am I that I can explain the choices of other members?
   - How confident am I that they can explain my choices?
   Group:
   - Was the structure we chose for our own discussion useful?
   - How could that structure be used during reflection or planning?

Using Pairs and *Mad Hatter's Tea Party* for Analysis and Application of Chapter Content

1. Students use the same basic format described in Chapter 5 and used again in Chapters 6 and 7. The scenarios are found in Chapter 7: Laurie, Marsha, Jane, Jim, Marta, Joyce, and Terry. Each pair analyzes a scenario, responding to the following questions:
   a. Does the scenario describe how the teacher asks students to reflect on their use of interpersonal and small group learning skill(s)? If so, what does the teacher do?
   b. Does the scenario describe how the teacher asks students to plan by setting a goal or describing an application for the use of an interpersonal and small-group learning skill? If so, what does the teacher do?
   c. Does the scenario describe how the teacher observes?
2. Using the same scenario, students work with their partners to plan how they might
   a. Design an opportunity for students to reflect on how they have worked together.
   b. Design an opportunity for students to use either goal setting or application for planning.
   Students should create several options for both reflection and planning; try "I," "you," and "we" statements; try written processing; and create an observation form or plan for anecdotal observation that could be used for feedback and planning. They should make sure the options are appropriate

for the skills the students are using in their lesson and for the age of the students.

3. Pairs stay together and, using *Mad Hatter's Tea Party,* share their analyses with other pairs.

4. Reflection and Planning:
Individual:
   - How has this activity helped you understand the subtleties of reflection and planning?
   - How confident are you that you can develop appropriate strategies to help students reflect on how they have worked together and plan for their future work?

   Pair:
   - One way you helped me understand reflection and planning was ____.
   - One thing about reflection and planning that I want to learn more about is ____.

   Class:
   - What goal do we each need to set so that we will continue to learn about how to use reflection and planning effectively with cooperative learning?

Using Groups of Four, *Gallery Tour* (Kagan, 1992), and Self-Stick Notes to Examine How to Structure Reflection and Planning about Interpersonal and Small-Group Learning Skills

1. Students group in random foursomes. Groups are each assigned or choose one level on which to focus their work. Levels are K–2, 3–5, 6–8, 9–12, and university. Groups are to examine the four basic categories of interpersonal and small-group skills and to develop a way to structure reflection or planning for a skill(s) at each level.

2. Students work alone to create sample strategies for each level.

3. Students put their ideas together and build a set of strategies for the four categories. (For the sake of practice, strategies should include (a) both written and oral ideas; (b) reflection, goal setting, and application; (c) both student and teacher feedback; and (d) I, you, and we foci.) The final plan should include at least one idea from each individual's work. Once the strategies have been formulated, they can be written on large paper or blackboards.

4. Students go on a *Gallery Tour,* visiting the ideas of all the groups (different groups have focused on different levels.) They stop and discuss each group's work and, using self-stick notes, leave specific positive comments about the work. (It is useful to fold the notes over so that groups are not influenced by the comments of previous groups.)

5. Groups return to their own work, review the notes, and make any revisions and additions that seem appropriate.

6. Reflection and Planning:
Group:
   - What are some of the things teachers might need to think about when adapting reflection and planning to different grade levels?

Using a *One-Minute Paper* and Base Groups to Reflect on the Challenges of Reflection and Planning

TASK: *In one sentence, what one thing concerns you personally about your ability to provide careful reflection and planning?*

1. Each student writes a response.
2. Students share responses in their base groups.

CHAPTER 9

Individual Responsibility and Assessment: Checking for Understanding

 ***As you read, you might want to ask yourself:***

Why is individual responsibility essential to the discipline of using cooperative learning?

How are individual responsibility and positive interdependence linked?

How might individual responsibility and assessment be linked?

How might reflection and planning be used to check for understanding?

The discipline of using cooperative learning effectively includes building a sense of individual responsibility; students should never view cooperative learning as an opportunity to "goof off" or contribute less than their best. High expectations are essential. The discipline of using cooperative learning effectively also includes carefully planned reflection about, planning for, and assessment of *what* students learn when they work together. Checking for understanding, like high expectations, is essential.

Traditionally, checking for understanding—assessing what students learn—has been the responsibility of teachers, and assessment has commonly been associated with individual tests and grades. This view has been challenged in recent years by the use of many different assessment and reporting formats. No matter what kinds of assessment are being used, however, when they are linked with cooperative learning, they tend to seem particularly complex, and teachers often express confusion. This confusion sometimes comes from the assumption that "group grades" are either necessary or unavoidable. This assumption has led many teachers, parents, and students to worry about a potential lack of individual responsibility and recognition and to tell stories about "The time I did all the work and 'they' shared my A." Sometimes, perhaps in reaction, teachers choose not to link cooperative learning with assessment at all; this, likewise, causes a variety of concerns. As we continue to develop our understanding of how cooperative learning might be used to help develop empowered learners—learners who are capable of high levels both of meaningful cooperative inquiry and of independent thought—it is important to consider seriously how to build into cooperative group work both a sense of individual responsibility and appropriate opportunities to check for understanding.

Think of a time when you worked in a learning group. Did you feel individually responsible for learning?

When teachers plan assessment, they must first decide *when to check* for understanding. Checking for understanding should be a continuous process and it is essential that teachers and students work together to create a learning community where it is both safe and desirable to assess learning. In Chapter 10 we will examine how checking for understanding can be woven throughout a lesson. In this chapter we will highlight how individual responsibility for learning can be emphasized through the use of monitoring, roles, and structures, and how reflection and planning can be designed to encourage students to check their understanding. Second, teachers must decide *what to check*. When students are working cooperatively, checking for understanding includes a focus on both (a) the interpersonal and small-group learning skills that students need to be successful in their work together and (b) academic knowledge and skills. In Chapter 8 we focused on interpersonal and small-group learning skills; in this chapter we will focus on academic knowledge and skills. Third, teachers must decide *how to check* and assess. In this chapter, we will examine how to use monitoring, reflection and planning, rubrics, tests, journals, and portfolios to assess academic learning. Fourth, teachers must decide *whom to check*. Should checking focus on students as individuals, on groups, or should it include a focus on both individuals and groups? If checking is focused only on the individual, will students be motivated to help each other learn? Will they value the work they do together? Can individual and group assessment be linked? This chapter will explore different ways these concerns might be addressed within a cooperative context. Fifth, teachers must decide *how to share* the responsibilities for checking with students. How might students learn to check their own understanding? How might students check each other? Is it appropriate for students to check each other? We will examine each of these questions in an effort to discover new ways to empower students as learners.

🐞 USING MONITORING, ROLES, AND 🐞 STRUCTURES TO BUILD INDIVIDUAL RESPONSIBILITY AND TO CHECK FOR UNDERSTANDING

One way teachers build a sense of individual responsibility and encourage checking for understanding during cooperative group work is through monitoring. Simple interventions such as

- "Joe, please explain how your group got the answer to number three."
- "Marguerite, what fact from your research did you share with the group?"

help students understand that their individual responsibilities for learning are ongoing.

A second way teachers build a sense of individual responsibility is through the use of assigned roles. For instance, a teacher can heighten a sense of individual responsibility by asking a student to be the group's reporter. When a teacher assigns this role well before the time a group reports its work,

- "Sam, in two minutes, I am going to ask you to report your group's procedures and conclusions."

the expectation of individual responsibility becomes clear for the designated student, and the sense of group interdependence is enhanced as the group works together to ensure that the designated student will be successful in the reporter role. This strategy tends to work well when groups include students with very diverse abilities or motivation. When teachers do not assign this role in advance, expectations for individual responsibility are enhanced for *all* students. Both methods have benefits.

What other roles might be used to help build a sense of individual responsibility?

Structures are a third way that teachers reinforce the message that students are individually responsible for contributing to their groups in meaningful ways.

What other struc-
tures might help
build a sense of indi-
vidual responsibility?

The role of reporter is, for instance, integral to structures such as *Numbered Heads Together, Three-Step Interview, Stirring Up the Class,* and *One-Stay Three-Stray* and these structures are often used to heighten a sense of individual responsibility. A structure such as *Simultaneous Roundtable* can be used to help ensure that all students contribute, and perceptions of individual responsibility for quality contributions are heightened—with *Simultaneous Roundtable,* or with a structure such as *Rotating Review*—when every student in a group uses a different-colored marker or pen. When students use different colors to record their ideas, a teacher can assess at a glance if and what each student contributes.

❧ USING REFLECTION AND PLANNING TO ❧ BUILD INDIVIDUAL RESPONSIBILITY AND TO CHECK FOR UNDERSTANDING

Reflection and planning are critical to building a genuine learning community and are powerful ways to involve students in the process of assessment. There are many ways and many opportunities to structure reflection and planning when students work together; making a commitment to providing opportunities for reflection and planning is crucial in helping students become empowered learners—learners who are intrinsically motivated and individually responsible, learners who are capable of assessing their own work and checking their own understanding, and learners who are able to plan for future work and learning. Just asking students "What did you learn today?" or "What do you want to learn?" will not provide them with carefully structured opportunities for reflection and planning. Typically, asking students to reflect on and plan for learning is a parallel and simultaneous process to asking students to reflect on and plan for how they work together. In the next section we will use a format similar to the one used in Chapter 8. This has been done specifically so that the parallels between these two types of reflection and planning can be examined with ease.

Designing Verbal Reflection and Planning among Students

As we learned in Chapter 8, reflection and planning among students can be facilitated both when students focus on themselves and when students focus on others. Sometimes when teachers ask students to reflect and plan, they ask students to check their own understanding and assess their own learning; at other times, they ask them to assess some product that they have created together as part of their learning. Regardless of how students are asked to reflect, it is important that reflection be designed so that it is positive, specific, and brief.

To check their understanding and develop their sense of individual responsibility, individuals might be asked:

- "On a scale of 1 to 5, how confident are you that you understand the procedures you practiced in your group today well enough to complete a set of problems on your own?"
- "Going around the group, each share one aspect of the procedure that you want to pay careful attention to when you do your homework this evening."
- "What one thing do you think you understood most clearly at the conclusion of your work together today? What is still unclear? Share in a *Roundrobin.*"

To check their understanding and reflect on how working with others has helped them, individuals might be asked:

- "On a scale of 1 to 5, how well did you understand the material after you read it? On a scale of 1 to 5, how well did you understand the material after you discussed it in your group?"
- "What is one thing your partner said today that helped you to understand the material? Be as specific as possible."

To assess the quality of a group product or how each individual's work has contributed to the overall effort, individuals might be asked:

- "On a scale of 1 to 5, how confident are you that your group's answers are accurate and complete?"
- "Starting with person #1 in your group, each person will give each other group member feedback: What is one way that the work each member did for homework enhanced the overall group product?"

To consider how others are learning and emphasize that checking for understanding and individual responsibility are important for every group member, individuals might be asked to state:

- "On a scale of 1 to 5, I am confident to level _____ that each member of my group can complete an individual assignment based on the material we have learned together today."

To reflect on their collective work and check for understanding and assess effectiveness, groups might be asked to decide:

- "Today our most significant 'AHA' was _____."
- "On a scale of 1 to 5, how ready are we for the next phase of our project?"
- "On a scale of 1 to 5, how confident are we that the graphic organizer we chose to explain our ideas will be useful to the other groups in the class?"

To plan, set goals, or consider applications for their skills and learning, groups might be asked:

- "Where do you need to start your work together tomorrow? What does each individual need to bring to the group so that your group can maximize its work time tomorrow?"
- "What part of this lesson still seems difficult? What do you need to learn to feel more confident? How can you learn it?"
- "What questions have you answered? What questions do you still have? How can you gather information to answer your questions?"
- "Where else is it important to check for accuracy? Make a plan to practice this important skill."

The Importance of Feedback about Academic Competencies

In Chapter 3 we investigated the concept of academic status. Teachers who design reflection so that students are asked to consider how other group members have contributed to the group's work and helped them learn create opportunities for students to provide feedback to peers in a way that can positively influence perceptions of academic status. Because perceptions of academic status are important determinants of students' abilities to learn, it is important that students be provided with opportunities to reflect on how the academic strengths of their peers contribute to their own learning and to the success of the group. One of the goals of a learning community is for all students to be acknowledged by peers for their strengths; many of the previous feedback examples are useful for this purpose. Note that these examples never suggest that students should grade each other. It is important to separate feedback from grading and to understand that students should never be asked to grade their peers.

Teacher Feedback about Academic Competencies   As we know, teachers can influence perceptions of academic status. In Chapter 7 we examined how teachers can collect anecdotal data about students' use of specific interpersonal and small-group learning skills. In Chapter 8 we learned how to use this anecdotal data to provide feedback to students. When anecdotal data and feedback focus specifically on the appropriate use of an intellectual skill, it can have a positive effect on academic status and achievement. For instance, after collecting anecdotal data, a teacher might report:

- "Bernadette, I saw you use your visual and spatial abilities to draw a Venn Diagram to help your group understand the similarities and differences between the two characters."

HOW I HELPED MY GROUP

Name _____

Group _____

To prepare for our work together, I

When I came to the group, I contributed

I think my contributions enhanced the overall quality of the group's work by

---

Figure 9.1
Written format to self-assess individual contributions to group work.

Designing Written Reflection and Planning among Students

Written reflection and planning can be used to build a sense of individual responsibility and to help students check for understanding (see Bennett, Rolheiser, and Stevahn [1991]). Like verbal reflection, written reflection is useful when individual students focus on themselves or their group (Figures 9.1 and 9.2), when groups focus on themselves (Figure 9.3), and even when groups focus on each other (Figure 9.4). Written reflection is particularly useful when students have worked together to produce some shared product such as a worksheet, a model, a report, or a presentation. Often, written reflection is presented in the form of a rubric to help students assess what they have done (Figures 9.2, 9.3, and 9.4). Although it is time-consuming, it is helpful for students to participate in the creation of the rubrics since (a) this helps students realize that they know what "good work" is, and (b) it helps teachers share influence with students.

🐜   USING TESTS, JOURNALS, AND PORTFOLIOS   🐜
TO BUILD INDIVIDUAL RESPONSIBILITY
AND POSITIVE INTERDEPENDENCE

Tests, journals, and portfolios are three commonly used assessment formats, and each can be used in the context of cooperative learning to assess the learning of individual students. For instance, students can learn specific

---

MY REFLECTIONS ON OUR GROUP PRESENTATION

Name _____

Assess your contribution to the group presentation using the following scale:

1= my contribution was unsatisfactory
2= my contribution was not so great
3= my contribution was OK
4= my contribution was pretty good—I am pleased
5= my contribution was my personal best—or very close to it

My mastery of the content	1	2	3	4	5
My organization of my work	1	2	3	4	5
Usefulness of my content and organization to the overall group effort	1	2	3	4	5
My enthusiasm	1	2	3	4	5
My professionalism in presentation	1	2	3	4	5

Assess the overall presentation using the following scale:

1= not really ok
2= barely ok
3= ok
4= better than ok
5= YES!

Overall quality of content	1	2	3	4	5
Overall organization of presentation	1	2	3	4	5
Originality and variety in presentation	1	2	3	4	5
Professionalism in presentation	1	2	3	4	5
Usefulness of presentation to audience	1	2	3	4	5

Figure 9.2
Written format to self-assess both individual contributions and group presentation.

knowledge or practice specific skills with the help of a cooperative group and then take individual tests to assess this learning. Likewise, students might keep individual journals or portfolios that reflect learning that they have done cooperatively. Using individual tests, journals, and portfolios with cooperative learning to assess individual achievement is legitimate and, because it is quite straightforward, will not be our focus.

Learning how to use individual tests, journals, and portfolios—to provide both individual assessment and cooperative connections with other students and to enhance both individual responsibility and positive interdependence—

GROUP ASSESSMENT OF OUR REPORT

Decide together and circle the number that best describes your group report.

1= not really ok
2= barely ok
3= ok
4= better than ok
5= YES!

Our report had a main idea.	1	2	3	4	5
Our report had a beginning, middle, and end.	1	2	3	4	5
We included interesting and effective visual organizers.	1	2	3	4	5
We proofread our report.	1	2	3	4	5

Something important that we learned about our topic while doing this report is . . .

What we still want to learn about our topic is . . .

Place your initials in the box to indicate that you agree with your group's assessment of its report.

Figure 9.3
Written format to group-assess a written report.

can add an exciting dimension to the discipline of using cooperative learning. When considering how to link these assessment tools with cooperative learning, the words *enhancement* and *positive* are key. Behind these words are the general principles that

- Students are never penalized for the work of others.
- Students at different levels of learning can help with and comment on the work of others.
- Individuals can be recognized and their contributions and understanding can be assessed, while, simultaneously, peers help each other to learn.

PEER FEEDBACK FOR GROUP PRESENTATIONS

Decide together and circle the number that best describes the presentation you have just seen.

1= not really ok
2= barely ok
3= ok
4= better than ok
5= YES!

They were knowledgeable.	1	2	3	4	5
They showed that they could work together.	1	2	3	4	5
They presented their information logically.	1	2	3	4	5
They thought of ways to make sure the audience was involved.	1	2	3	4	5

What two specific things did the presenters do to capture your interest?

What two specific things did you learn about the topic from the presentation?

What questions do you still have?

Place your initials in the box to indicate that you have discussed the presentation with your group and are comfortable with your group's responses.

Figure 9.4
Written format to group-assess another group's presentation.

Tests

Teachers sometimes find it useful—to enhance both academic learning and feelings of positive interdependence—to link individual tests with peer achievement. One way to do this is through the use of bonus points. Bonus points are a reasonable choice when (a) assessment is frequent and the format of assessment consistent and (b) formal learning groups have been used for input, practice, or review. Eligibility for bonus points is typically calculated based on target scores for individual students, and target scores typically reflect goals set in relation to past performance. When students have opportunities to help establish their own target scores, they share influence in ways that have the potential to affect motivation and achievement. When targets reflect individual goals, opportunities for goal differentiation and differentiation in testing modalities and test content are maximized. (For more discussion of both goal differentiation and the use of bonus points, see Chapter 6.) Bonus points are typically added to each member's individual score when all members reach their personal targets. To increase feelings of positive interdependence throughout the class, bonus points might also be awarded when all students (or groups) reach their personal targets. To increase a focus on learning throughout the class and to de-emphasize a focus on grades, bonus points might also be saved and contributed towards some kind of appropriate class celebration. Examples of these three approaches are

- "If all members of your group reach their personal targets, I will add two points to each member's individual score."
- "For every group in the class that earns bonus points, I will add one extra point to everyone's score."
- "When you reach your personal target, I will add one point towards our celebration target. Remember, when we have 300 points, we will invite the other classes to a math party. Since we have twenty-five students in our class, we have the opportunity to earn twenty-five bonus points with our math tests this week."

A second way teachers link individual tests with peer achievement is by asking students to complete individual assessments and to check the assessments of others and certify that they are of good quality. This is particularly effective (a) with writing samples or complex problem-solving procedures, (b) when students will genuinely benefit from skill practice in proofreading or checking for accuracy and completeness, (c) when students have been taught how to "proof" the work of others, (d) when students believe that proofing is an important skill (sometimes attaching a "grade" to the quality of proofing helps), and (e) when students have had opportunities to work together in substantive ways to learn the skills that are being assessed. When this strategy is used, it is, again, possible to differentiate goals so that students with diverse abilities can benefit from and build a commitment to working with others. For instance:

- "Each person in your math problem-solving group will receive a different problem. Each of you will work your problem individually. When you have all finished, shift your papers—in a *Roundtable* format—to the next person in your group. That person will check to make sure that no steps have been omitted and, in the first blank at the bottom, will sign to indicate confidence that all necessary steps are included. Then shift papers again. The next person will check your calculations to make sure there are no errors and, in the second blank at the bottom, will sign to indicate confidence that the math is correct. Two-thirds of your grade will be determined by your own work on your own problem; the final third will be determined by your ability to check correctly the work of your two group members."

A third way teachers can link individual tests to peer achievement is by having each student complete an individual test and participate in completing a group test. Group tests can precede individual tests and serve as a kind of final review or they can follow individual tests and capitalize on the energy and curiosity that testing tends to create. Combining group and individual tests is most effective when (a) the "stakes" are low for the group test, (b) group tests are used regularly, (c) the test material is complex enough for students to benefit from peer discussion, and (d) students have had opportunities to work together in substantive ways to learn the knowledge and skills that are being assessed.

Sometimes teachers use group tests without linking these tests directly to individual assessment. This option should be used only when (a) groups are functioning well and students have had substantive opportunities to work together, (b) the stakes are very low—sometimes teachers use the points generated by group tests only as bonus points, (c) the procedures and criteria are very clear, and (d) the task is constructed so that students quickly understand that it will be more satisfying to complete in a group than as individuals.

Journals

Like tests, journals can be used to create effective links between individual assessment and substantive work with peers. Keeping individual journals is one way teachers sometimes ask students to prepare for group work. (In the scenarios in Chapters 6 and 7, Terry and Marilyn both use journals this way.) When students are asked to use journals as a preparation tool, it is common for teachers to collect these journals periodically to insure that students are preparing carefully. Sometimes individual journals are collected simultaneously with a group presentation or other "product," and individual grades are given for the quality of journal preparation. This again helps to underscore the importance of individual responsibility. When teachers plan to collect and grade journals, they typically work with students to develop criteria for worthwhile journals. Sometimes they ask students to mark what they believe is their best entry and then read and grade only that entry. This procedure helps build shared influence and provides significant opportunities for students to reflect on and assess their own work.

Sometimes teachers ask students to keep journals, share their journals with partners, and respond to a partner's journal. Sometimes individual notebooks are used for partner journals, at other times students share a single notebook. If loose-leaf paper is used for shared notebooks, these notebooks can later be separated so that students can each keep pieces of their own work. Generally, for partner journals to be successful, students need to be taught how to respond meaningfully to a peer's journal entries. Partner journals can be collected and graded like individual journals, and students benefit from opportunities to self-evaluate and to decide what pieces will be evaluated by the teacher.

Portfolios

In classrooms where students have substantive opportunities for cooperative work with peers, group portfolios can be used to document the work of relatively long-term, formal learning groups. If a group portfolio is created, careful rubrics can be used to assess the portfolio; individual and group reflection and feedback are essential.

Both base groups and formal learning groups can be used as forums for the discussion of individual portfolios. Ideally, the creation of a portfolio is a complex process, requiring students to reflect repeatedly on their work. Peers can be used very effectively in this process; the keys to the successful incorporation of peers into the portfolio process are (a) a shared commitment to learning, (b) good interpersonal and small-group learning skills—especially skills such as confidentiality, listening, asking clarifying and probing questions, and planning, (c) a good understanding of the purpose of the portfolio process, and (d) clear guidelines—preferably ones that the students and teacher have designed together.

🐾 CHALLENGES 🐾

Group Projects, Diverse Abilities, and Group Grades

A concern about group grades is common when teachers use cooperative learning. This concern is common even when teachers use the discipline of cooperative learning carefully—when they build positive interdependence and individual responsibility into learning, insure that students have been carefully taught the interpersonal and small-group learning skills they need to be successful in their work with others, and give students opportunities to reflect on their work together. Does cooperative learning necessarily mean group grades? No. Should group grades be common with cooperative learning? Probably not. Are group grades ever appropriate? Possibly.

Group grades may sometimes be appropriate when students have been working together for significant lengths of time on complex projects. It makes sense at these times to assess work the students have done together,

As you picture yourself using the discipline of cooperative learning to help create a classroom where all students are empowered as learners, what do you think might be your biggest challenge as you build individual responsibility and check for understanding?

and at times this assessment might be connected with a grade. Group grades should, however, not be used just as a matter of course. When group work is to be connected with group assessment, (a) a clear set of criteria—preferably developed with the students—should be established before or during the work, (b) a clear expectation of individual responsibility needs to be articulated, (c) careful monitoring, checking for understanding, and interim checkpoints are essential, (d) students should have ample opportunities for reflection and planning and for assessing their collective work—both as individuals and as a group, and (e) the stakes need to be low—no group grade should seem like a life or death situation.

When groups of students with very diverse abilities work together, positive interdependence and high expectations for all students are essential. (Ways to build positive interdependence with diverse-ability students and more ideas about grades and celebrations were discussed in Chapter 6.) High expectations for all students may require a differentiation in individual responsibilities, assessments, criteria for success, or assessment modalities. Diversity is a challenge; when expectations, responsibilities, assessments, and criteria are both clearly articulated and woven into the collective fabric of work a group does together, diversity can be viewed as an exciting rather than debilitating challenge.

In this chapter we have continued to learn the discipline of creating cooperation through the application of five basic elements to lesson design; we have focused specifically on the careful structuring of reflection about and planning for learning and on building individual responsibility. Next we turn our attention to several classroom scenarios to help us develop a better understanding of how tests, journals, and portfolios can be used to enhance both individual responsibility and positive interdependence. As you read, take the time to ask yourself: "How has the teacher structured assessment to link individual and group responsibility?" "Why has the teacher made these choices?" You might also consider how you think it might feel to be a student in one of these classrooms. How do you think it might feel to be the teacher?

A VIEW FROM THE CLASSROOM: CHECKING FOR UNDERSTANDING

Sherry combines individual and group tests in her chemistry class. Her students work with the same lab partners for an entire testing unit. At the end of a unit, each individual student completes a test that is worth 100 points. The next day, partners work together to complete an equivalent test. This second test is worth 50 points, and both grades are recorded for each student. Sherry started this practice because she noticed that after her students completed a test, they asked important questions and engaged in animated conversations in the hall. She developed this two-test system to encourage the conversations, interest, and collaboration generated by the individual tests. Conversations during the partner test are very animated as students work together to hone their understanding and challenge each other's ideas. Parents report serious phone discussions about chemistry during the evening between tests, and Sherry is pleased with the results of her two-part test. (Berman-Robinson, 1991).

Every two weeks, each of the literature study groups in Phyllis' class completes a brief vocabulary quiz based on a word list students develop from their reading. Students take the quiz individually, and their scores are recorded individually. Before quizzes, each student consults with Phyllis and sets an individual target score. When all students in the group have reached their targets, Phyllis adds a bonus point to each individual score. Her students do an excellent job of helping each other review words, reminding each other to take their word lists home, and encouraging every group member.

Jerry wants his foreign language students to write a paragraph each week in the target language. He wants them to write individually, and he also wants them to help each other with grammar and vocabulary. He has his students work in groups of three. First they write their own paragraphs; next they proofread the paragraphs of their partners; finally they rewrite. They hand in both rough drafts and final copies of their papers in a group folder. Each week Jerry picks one paper to read very carefully; he grades that paper as he would any composition, and the writer receives an individual grade. The other two students receive editing grades for the same paper. When Jerry finds a difficulty that he thinks should have been corrected by the student editors, he checks the rough draft to determine if the problem had been pointed out. Jerry then reads the other two papers through quickly and provides brief written comments but no grade. This system helps Jerry provide his students with considerable writing, reading, and proofreading opportunities while simultaneously helping him to manage his own workload.

Joe bases his literature study on a series of themes and has developed a "movie exam" to accompany each of these themes. The premise behind the movie exam is simple; Joe likes to incorporate more than one medium into his discussions, but because he does not think it is appropriate to show a full-length movie during class time, he asks students to view the movies outside of class. He uses base groups for this process—hoping that it will help them deepen their relationships and help break down the barriers between academic and social talk; he uses bonus points to make these exams optional. Joe assigns the movie; he provides each group with (a) a series of discussion questions, (b) guidelines with interdependent roles, and (c) a signature sheet that all students must sign to indicate they have participated in watching and discussing the movie with their group. Roles include host, procurer of movie, procurer(s) of food, and note taker. Guidelines include that a parent must be present at the host house (he requires a parent signature to indicate this) and that the note taker must provide every participant with a copy of the notes. Students generally have about three weeks to plan the exam, watch the movie, discuss the questions, and then each complete one-page reaction papers. On occasion, Joe has assigned different movies to different groups and has then used a *Jigsaw* to have students share information among groups. These exams are optional, but most groups and most students choose to participate and genuinely seem to enjoy their experiences. Parents report that they are pleased to hear their adolescents watching worthwhile movies and engaging in thoughtful discussion.

Joanne wants to encourage her students to read independently and to think critically; buddy journals help her to structure both. Students have an opportunity to choose from a wide variety of text materials, and Joanne pairs students who choose the same material. Pairs of students share a single notebook, and during the course of their reading, she requests each student to write a total of six times. Most often students choose to initiate three entries each and to respond three times to their partners. Joanne helps her students learn how to journal by modeling the process when they begin. As the year progresses, she has them choose adult journal partners—often parents or older siblings; they have expressed interest in establishing journal partners with younger children. Journal partners know that Joanne will read their entries, and Joanne uses a simple, holistic scoring system to assess each student's thinking (Gillespie, 1993).

Bonita's students use triple-entry logs for math problem solving. On the left-hand pages of their logs, students solve one fairly complex math problem. The right-hand pages are divided in half. While students are using mathematical notation and solving the problems on the left-hand pages, they are "thinking aloud" and writing about their strategies in the left-hand columns of the right pages. Bonita gives the students in each pair different problems, and the next day, they exchange logs with their partners. Their partners read their problems, solutions, and written explanations and, in the right-hand columns, offer corrections, comments, and alternative approaches. While Bonita periodically checks all logs, students also know that anytime they are unsure about their work, they can hand her their logs, and she will respond, in writing or in a short conference, the next day.

Jeff's students work in project groups, often for as long as a month. He uses journals and logs to help build a sense of individual responsibility into the work they do with peers and to help him assess their individual contributions to the groups' work. For instance, his students have been working in groups to create a newspaper-type publication that analyzes events and perspectives immediately after the American Civil War. Within groups, students are researching not just perspectives on events but also such things as fashion, economics, and customs that will be included in their publications. With Jeff's help each group develops its own work plan and assigns tasks to individual members. His students keep both individual journals and group logs, and this helps to insure that they are all contributing to the overall groups. Jeff checks these logs regularly, and they help him both to guide and to assess the individual work. When they complete their final newspapers, each group will assess each newspaper using a class-designed rubric. Jeff will assess both the newspapers and the group logs and individual journals. He also asks each group to use different-colored highlighters for each student and to indicate how contributions from different group members were brought together and used by the group to create the final newspaper. This step generates interesting discussions as groups realize how they weave different ideas together—how "my ideas" become "our ideas."

Mike, Eve, and Kate want their students to keep individual portfolios as part of their year-long theme exploration. They have worked with their students to create guidelines that the students will use to reflect on the quality and meaningfulness of what they include in these portfolios, and Mike, Eve, and Kate work together several times during the year to review individual portfolios. They have incorporated the use of year-long base groups into their linked courses, and each marking period—with the help of guiding questions—base groups interview all members about their portfolios. The teachers find that these interviews help individual members hone their thinking and provide a forum for sharing.

🐾   WORKING WITH PEERS   🐾

Using Base Groups to Review Chapter Content and Personalize Learning

QUESTION: *If you had to choose one way to build a sense of individual responsibility into cooperative work, which do you think might be most important—monitoring, roles, reflection and planning, or tests and grading? Why?*

1. Students individually choose.
2. Using a *Group Interview*, all members are asked to explain their choices.

3. Reflection and Planning:
   Individual:
   - How did your understanding of ways to build individual responsibility deepen by hearing the ideas of others?

Using Pairs and *Mad Hatter's Tea Party* for Analysis and Application of Chapter Content

1. Students use the same basic format described in Chapter 5 and used again in Chapters 6, 7, and 8. The scenarios are found in Chapter 6: Patrick, Linda, Molly, Dana, Arlene, Ana, and Marilyn. Each pair analyzes a scenario, discussing these questions:
   a. Does the scenario describe how the teacher builds a sense of individual responsibility into the lesson? If so, how?
   b. Does the scenario describe how the teacher checks for individual understanding? If so, how?
   c. Does the scenario describe how the teacher asks the students to use reflection and planning to check their understanding of academic learning? The understanding of their peers?
2. Using the same scenario, students work with their partners to plan how they might
   a. Structure a way the teacher might build individual responsibility. Structure a way the teacher might want to check for understanding. What might a teacher check? How?
   b. Structure an opportunity for students to check their own understanding.

Students should create several options: try verbal reflection and planning; try written reflection and planning; and make sure the options are appropriate for the skill level and ages of students.
3. Pairs stay together and, using *Mad Hatter's Tea Party,* share their analyses with other pairs.
4. Reflection and Planning:
   Individual:
   - How has this helped me understand the basic principles of individual responsibility and checking for understanding?
   - How confident am I that I can plan high-quality cooperative learning lessons to include a sense of individual responsibility?
   - Do I feel individually responsible now? What could be done to enhance my own sense of individual responsibility?

Using a *One-Minute Paper* and Base Groups to Reflect on the Potential Challenges of Assessment and Individual Responsibility

TASK: *In one sentence, what is one thing that concerns you personally about your ability to structure individual responsibility and meaningful assessment into cooperative learning?*

1. Each student writes a response.
2. Students share responses in their base groups.

CHAPTER **10**

The Role of the Teacher: Guiding Learning in the Cooperative Classroom

🌺 *As you read, you might want to ask yourself:*

Why is careful planning essential to the discipline of using cooperative learning?

How might careful planning help overcome the barriers to cooperation?

How might planning help to empower students as learners?

How are lesson planning and unit planning similar?

Why is it important to "start simple" with cooperative learning?

How might a cooperative classroom look and sound and feel?

The best of leaders
know how to lead without dominating—
by word or by deed.
And, when they do
the people say,
"Our goal, our plan, our achievement."
*Lao Tzu—*Tao Te Ching

As we have seen in the last several chapters, there is a discipline to creating cooperation, and a large part of that discipline is careful planning by teachers. In this chapter we will examine planning and how careful planning can help to maximize opportunities for simultaneous interaction. We will begin by examining ways to organize the physical environment in the classroom and by discussing issues related to group size, composition, and formation. We will then examine lesson planning, unit planning, and ways teachers can conceptualize an entire day, week, or unit as essentially cooperative. We will discuss practical ways to get started with cooperative learning. We will also examine the role of planning in the larger context of the role of the teacher as a guide in the classroom—a role that has the potential to empower students to say: "our achievement, our ideas, our classroom."

🐝   ARRANGING THE PHYSICAL   🐝
ENVIRONMENT FOR COOPERATION

Careful attention to and arranging of the physical environment is an important ingredient in the successful use of cooperative learning. In Chapters 4 and 7 we examined how pictures, T-charts, bulletin boards, and quotes might be used in classrooms to emphasize the essential nature of cooperation. In this section we will focus on seating arrangements. Seating can be planned to emphasize environmental interdependence and to help facilitate good use of basic "Getting-Together Skills" such as "move to the group in an orderly fashion," "stay with the group," and "use a quiet voice." Special furniture is not needed for cooperative learning. In high schools, when teachers work in classrooms where desks and chairs are attached in a single unit and a room is shared by several teachers, the challenge is to build efficient routines so that desks can be moved into varied configurations that allow students to sit in close proximity. Careful teacher planning and the establishment of routines are important in all classrooms and help build feelings of safety and belongingness. Reasonable routines also enhance feelings of student empowerment as the daily business of the classroom progresses without constant teacher direction and intervention.

When arranging the physical environment to encourage cooperation, teachers might want to consider how the use of informal learning groups, formal learning groups, and base groups will be facilitated in these environments. It is to this consideration that we turn next.

Planning the Physical Environment for Base Groups

As we learned in Chapter 5, base groups ideally remain together for an entire academic year; teachers typically determine membership in base groups quite carefully and with the help of sociometric data, interest surveys, and the like. If classroom seating is arranged so that base groups sit together, seating remains relatively static for long periods of time; when base groups are used in conjunction with homerooms and students move to different rooms throughout the day, this is a useful way to organize seating. However, this is not optimal when students spend the majority of their time in the same classroom; therefore, different options need to be explored. Many teachers find it useful to create and designate "areas" of the room rather than seating to accommodate base-group meetings. The "science corner," "story rug," and "in front of the book shelves" are all places where students might gather for their morning and afternoon base-group meetings. As described in Chapter 5, group-made posters, mottoes, and shields can be used to designate these meeting spots and help groups build a sense of group identity.

Planning the Physical Environment for Informal Groups

As we learned in Chapter 5, informal learning groups are used primarily during direct-teaching episodes and for movement and change of pace. To facilitate the use of informal learning groups for movement and change of pace, teachers organize the physical space so that movement is easy and so that there are places in which to move. Several small pockets of space—ones that can also be used for base groups—or a relatively large space—one that might be created by keeping seating areas compact—make it easier for students to move frequently for informal learning groups.

To facilitate the use of informal learning groups during episodes of direct instruction, teachers typically design seating arrangements so that students sit in pairs or foursomes. This allows them to use a variety of informal structures without constantly moving furniture or students. When these kinds of seating arrangements are combined with frequent use of informal groups and direct instruction, teachers generally have students change seats at regular intervals to give them opportunities over time to interact with many classmates. In self-contained classrooms where teachers use informal structures a great deal, students might change seats every week; in departmentalized settings, each month or marking period might be sufficient.

Planning the Physical Environment for Formal Groups

As we learned in Chapter 6, formal learning groups are carefully formed, heterogeneous groups with carefully articulated work, learning, and interactional goals. Depending on their goals, formal learning groups might stay together for a single class period or for an entire unit. Arranging the physical environment for the use of formal learning groups requires that students sit eye-to-eye in ways to insure that (a) they can all see and have physical

What kinds of physical environments have you seen that were well-suited to the disciplined use of cooperative learning? Why did they work well?

access to materials, (b) they can use quiet voices, and (c) the teacher can move easily among groups to monitor and intervene. The use of formal learning groups for relatively long periods of time also means that groups need a place to keep their supplies and work. In self-contained classrooms, students might work in several different formal learning groups throughout the day or week and, therefore, may sit in more than one location in the classroom. When desks are used and students keep personal belongings in their desks, students need to learn to be respectful of the property of others for this kind of movement and sharing to be successful. Figures 10.1, 10.2,

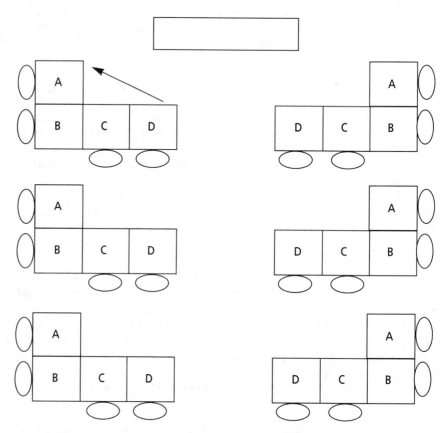

Figure 10.1
Seating arrangement that facilitates the use of both informal and formal cooperative learning groups, #1. In this arrangement, informal pairs are created when *A* joins *B* and *C* joins *D*. Foursomes are formed by having the *D*s move their desks. All students can see the front of the classroom; there are several small pockets of space for student movement and teacher monitoring. Sets of four desks can be used for work in long-term formal learning groups.

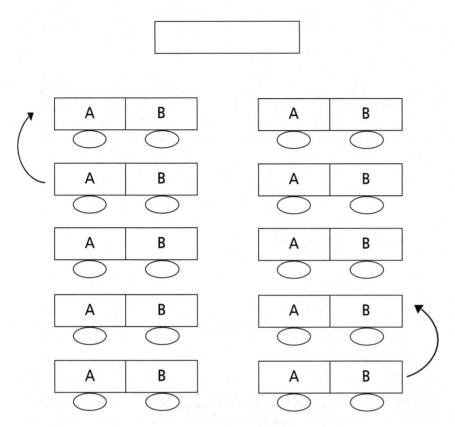

Figure 10.2
Seating arrangement that facilitates the use of both informal and formal cooperative learning groups, #2. In this arrangement, *As* and *Bs* work
together in informal pairs. Foursomes are formed when every other row of
students turns and faces the pair behind them and uses two desks to create
a table for four or, for longer-term formal groups, when they move their
desks and chairs. One teacher developed a system where every Monday
either the *A* students moved clockwise to the next *A* desks or the *B* students moved counterclockwise to the next *B* desks. By doing this each
week, new informal pairs were formed and foursomes changed as well.
This insured that, over time, students had opportunities to learn with
everyone in the class.

10.3, and 10.4 show examples of seating arrangements that several
teachers have developed to accommodate the use of both informal and
formal groups. These figures are provided only as examples. Every teacher,
class, and classroom is unique, and teachers and students need to work together to create physical environments that fit their needs.

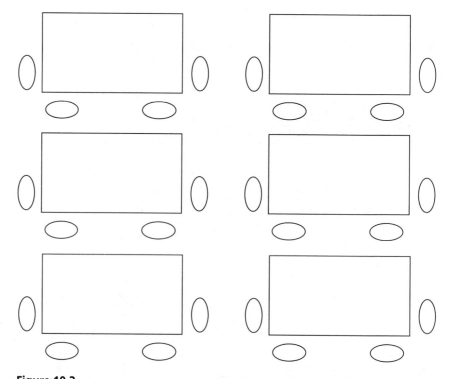

Figure 10.3
Seating arrangement that facilitates the use of both informal and formal co-operative learning groups, #3. When tables are used, it is often best for students to sit at corners—rather than across from each other—for pair work. This facilitates the use of quiet voices and equal access to materials.

🦋 PLANNING GROUP SIZE AND 🦋 COMPOSITION FOR COOPERATION

Group size is critical to the success of learning groups. The size of groups will vary depending on the age of students and circumstances and objectives of the lesson. In general, however, *it is best to keep group size small.* For large groups to be successful, members need very well developed interpersonal and small-group learning skills. Insuring that everyone has a chance to speak, stays on task, understands the material, and agrees with the group's decisions becomes increasingly difficult as group size increases. Pairs are frequently ideal for group work. When a greater variety of ideas, opinions, and work styles is important, threes and fours are helpful. When students first begin to work in fours, it is often useful to form fours by linking pairs that have already shared some ideas or information. (Structures such as

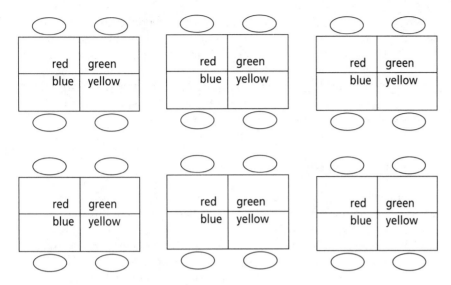

Figure 10.4
Seating arrangement that facilitates the use of both informal and formal co-operative learning groups, #4. A primary teacher who wanted her students to sit at "tables" of four and wanted to use a variety of groupings developed this system with colors. She placed a colored dot on each desk and also numbered each group. She placed students carefully at their tables, changed seating about once a month, and used these groups for many language activities. Within tables she could then regroup by giving simple directions such as "I want blues and yellows to be partners." She could ask students to move around the room with directions such as "I would like all the reds to move to the story corner," "I want all the greens to rotate one group," or "I want all the reds at even-numbered tables to come together."

Three-Step Interview are ideal for this.) Groups larger than four tend to become cumbersome, so when class size does not divide evenly, it is usually best to opt for one or two groups that are smaller—rather than larger—than ideal. Because the primary purposes of base groups differ from those of formal or informal learning groups, base groups are typically larger—four or five members.

As we have seen repeatedly throughout this book, group composition is important to the success of learning groups. In general, the longer a group stays together and the more complex the task, the more important it is that students be placed carefully in groups. There is no one right way for teachers to form groups, and there is no one right or "magic" combination in any given classroom. Sometimes a group that seems difficult can provide an ideal opportunity to learn important interpersonal skills. When the going gets rough in a group, it is often best to keep the group together and monitor carefully to help the members achieve some success; when students understand that they have used important skills to achieve this success, they can then move into new groups with both greater skill and greater confidence.

The many ways to determine group composition tend to fall into three main categories: teacher-selected, random, and seating-related. Seating-related grouping was described in the previous section.

Teacher-Selected Groups

In Chapter 3 we learned how teachers might use sociometric data to learn about the academic and social status of students and how this information can be used to help teachers form groups. Interest inventories and base-line academic data can also be used to help inform teacher decision making about group composition. In Chapter 3 we also learned about the importance of heterogeneity and how to form groups so that individuals cross categories and share different characteristics with different group members.

Random Group Selection

Sometimes random selection of groups is a good idea. Informal groups are often chosen randomly; when students have been working in a variety of groups over time and have built a strong sense of community, random grouping is quick and fun and can even be used successfully for more formal learning groups. Random groups can be formed by simple counting procedures; they can be formed in ways that incorporate academic content; they can be formed using simple nonacademic activities. Following is a list of just a few possibilities.

1. Counting off:
   • Students can learn to count in many different languages
2. Learning cards:
   Students are given pieces of paper and have to find their partners—the students who have pieces of paper with matching or related words, names, concepts, or symbols. It is fun for students to move about the room sharing ideas and answers and helping each other find their groups; and since students typically receive different cards each time, the same set of cards can be used more than once—as an anticipatory set, for practice, or for review. Cards might include
   • Shapes, colors, numbers
   • States and capitols
   • Inventors and inventions
   • Parts of chemical compounds

- The same words in different languages
- Different math problems with the same answer
- Different characters from the same novel, time period, country, etc.

3. Nonacademic ideas:

   Sometimes it is useful for students to get into groups with the help of nonacademic "games." Like learning cards, games give students an opportunity to move around, practice their use of quiet voices, practice their observation and problem-solving skills in nonthreatening situations, and celebrate being together. Nonacademic ideas include

   - Humdinger (Weinstein & Goodman, 1980): Students are given simple melodies to hum—"London Bridge," "Bingo," "Row Your Boat," and so forth. They move around the room humming until they find all the people humming the same melodies.
   - The Zoo: Students are assigned animals—birds, chimps, snakes, and so forth. They move around the room like their animals and form groups; groups might include all like animals or one of each animal type.

What ways can you think of to form groups that incorporate academic content? How about nonacademic ideas?

🐝 PLANNING LESSONS FOR COOPERATION 🐝

Basic Principles of Lesson Design

Careful planning is, as we have seen, essential to the successful use of cooperative learning. This should not be surprising, since careful planning is, in general, key to classrooms that center on learning. To discuss the specifics of planning that emphasize *positive interdependence, simultaneous interaction, individual responsibility, interpersonal and small-group learning skills, and reflection and planning*—the basic elements of cooperative learning—we will examine some general principles of lesson design. These principles are adapted from but not unique to Madeleine Hunter (1982). When considering these principles, it is important to remember that (a) not each and every learning experience in a classroom is easily classified as a "lesson," (b) these principles do not need to be used in order, and (c) not every lesson must contain all of these principles to be successful.

- Anticipatory Set: The purpose of an anticipatory set is to focus the students' attention on what is to be learned. An anticipatory set serves as a kind of "warm-up" or motivator for learning. It can be used to activate prior knowledge. A set can help a teacher determine what students already know about a topic; it can be a powerful tool to help students understand what they and their peers bring to the learning situation. A set that includes physical activity may be particularly helpful for young children (Nash, 1975).
- Understanding of the Objectives: It is helpful if students understand the short-term objectives for *what* they will be doing—what they are learning

or will be able to do as the result of the time spent on the lesson. Whenever possible, it is helpful for students to understand *how* the specific objectives of the lesson fit into larger learning goals and *why* these goals are important.

- Input and Modeling: Information and skills are essential for learning. Students need to learn basic information and skills so that they can organize, reorganize, and extend them into more complex concepts and processes. Students also need models of how this information and these skills might be used successfully.

- Practice: Students need opportunities to practice using the information, concepts, and skills they are learning. Sometimes practice is guided, sometimes independent. In general, independent practice follows some sort of guided practice so that both the teacher and students are reasonably confident that independent practice will help students to move towards fluency rather than reinforce mistakes.

- Checking for Understanding: Teachers need to check to insure that students are learning the information and/or skills that they need to learn to accomplish the objectives. Checking for understanding is an ongoing process. Formal assessment is one form of checking; less-formal checking is essential as well. Checking for understanding does not necessarily mean something teachers "do" to students; students can learn to check their own understanding and the understanding of their peers.

- Closure: The purpose of closure is to help the students reflect on what has been learned and how it has been learned. Closure can also help focus the student on what needs to be learned and how it might be learned.

Planning for Cooperative Learning Using Basic Principles of Lesson Design

When designing cooperative learning lessons—lessons that emphasize positive interdependence, simultaneous interaction, individual responsibility, interpersonal and small-group learning skills, and reflection and planning—it is useful to consider the general principles of lesson design. In this section we will examine each one of these principles—anticipatory set, understanding the objectives, input and modeling, checking for understanding, practice, and closure—and consider how they might inform lesson planning that focuses on the five basic elements of cooperative learning. Figures 10.5 and 10.6 contain planning guides.

Anticipatory Set   When planning a lesson, it is useful to ask:

- How and why might the students become interested?
- What do the students already know?

Academic Objectives:
Interpersonal Objectives:
How the lesson fits into larger learning objectives:

Anticipatory Set:

How can students share what they know and be motivated to learn more?

Types of groups that can be used:

1. Base groups
2. Informal groups

   Created by:
   seating arrangements
   random grouping strategy

   (If informal groups are to be used later, this is a natural choice. If formal groups are to be used later, the use of informal groups for set helps to build the learning community.)

3. Formal groups

   Created by:
   teacher assignment
   random grouping strategy

   (If formal groups are to be used later, the use of this formal group for set helps to build positive interdependence.)

Will the structure help build positive simultaneous interaction?

Understanding (Stating) the Objectives:

Academic objectives: The students will work together . . .

**Goal interdependence is essential
Positive interdependence can be strengthened with:**

resource interdependence
role interdependence
identity interdependence
sequence interdependence
fantasy/simulation interdependence
outside-force interdependence
environmental interdependence
celebration interdependence

Interpersonal and small-group learning skills objectives: The skills we will need to use to work together include . . .

"Getting Together" Skills
"Getting the Job Done and Staying Together" Skills
"Getting It" Skills
"Getting It²" Skills

Checking for Understanding:

How might an anticipatory set help the teacher and students check what they already know?

How might the teacher and students check that the students understand the academic and interpersonal objectives and how the lesson fits into the larger learning objectives?

Figure 10.5
Planning guide for cooperative learning.

(continued on next page)

Input and Modeling: **What information and skills do students need in order to achieve the objectives of the lesson and the larger learning goals?**

Academic information and skills:
How will students learn the information and skills?
1. Informal groups
   Will a structure help insure positive simultaneous interaction?
2. Formal groups
   Will a structure help insure positive simultaneous interaction?
How about resource and role interdependence?

Interpersonal skills:
How will students learn the skills?
T-charts
role plays
simulations
discussions
books, movies
displays
structures, roles

Checking for Understanding:
How might the teacher and/or students check that students understand the information and skills?

How might the teacher and/or students check the use of what they are learning?
monitoring
the use of roles
observations
tests, quizzes, journals
presentations
homework
Will a structure help organize careful checking?

Practice: **How will students practice using the information and skills they are learning?**

Academic information and skills:
Group practice: Informal or formal groups
Will a structure help insure equal access and high quality practice?
How about roles and resources?
Individual practice: In class or at home
How might individual and group practice be linked?

Interpersonal skills:
How will students practice the skills?
structures
roles
anecdotal and structured observations

Closure: **How will students reflect and plan?**

Academic information and skills:
a focus on the positive
I, you, we statements
reflection, application, goal setting
Will a structure help ensure careful reflection and planning?

Interpersonal skills:
a focus on the positive
I, you, we statements
reflection, application, goal setting
anecdotal and structured observations
Will a structure help?

How might reflection and planning help focus the teacher and students on understanding?
How might it be used as an anticipatory set for future work?

Figure 10.5
(continued)

Anticipatory Set:
How will students share what they know and be motivated to learn more?

Understanding (Stating) the Objectives:
Academic objectives:
Interpersonal and small-group learning skills objectives:
The larger context:

Checking for Understanding:
Academic understanding:

Interpersonal skill understanding:

How will I know my students are learning?
How will my students know they are learning?
How can I check student understanding?
How can students check their own understanding and the understanding of their peers?

How can we build a community that focuses on learning together in ways where checking for understanding is ongoing and welcome?

Input and Modeling: What information and skills do students need in order to achieve the objectives of the lessons and the larger learning goals? How might they best learn this information?
Academic information and skills:

Interpersonal and small-group learning skills:

Practice: How will students practice the information and skills they are learning?
Academic information and skills:

Interpersonal and small-group learning skills:

Closure: How will students reflect and plan?
Academic information and skills:

Interpersonal and small-group learning skills:

Figure 10.6
Abridged planning guide for cooperative learning.

When planning a lesson that will incorporate meaningful cooperative interaction, it is also useful to ask:

- How can the principle of simultaneous interaction be used so that students can share what they know, learn what others know, and become motivated to work together to learn more?

When anticipatory sets are cooperative in design, they help students activate and share their world knowledge, they help individuals maximize their academic learning, they help classes learn about and appreciate what all class members bring to the learning situation, and they help build a sense of community that focuses on learning. Anticipatory sets with these characteristics can be incorporated into lessons in many different ways. A grouping strategy that focuses on academic content (such as those described earlier in this chapter) can be used to create an active anticipatory set. Anticipatory sets can be incorporated into base-group routines; they might link to homework. Informal groups can be used with direct instruction or linked with formal groups to create anticipatory sets that provide opportunities for movement and sharing throughout a class.

How might an anticipatory set help to empower students as learners?

The following scenarios show how Brenda, Mary, Joe, and Janet all incorporate anticipatory sets into their lessons. They use a variety of groups—base groups, formal groups, and informal groups—and their anticipatory sets are active, interactive, and cooperative.

Brenda's Kindergarten class has begun its study of money. She has scheduled her math lesson for right after snack, and she asks her students to sit with their story buddies for snack. Brenda has placed pretzels, raisins, graham crackers, and popcorn in small bags and she "advertises" what the children can buy. Pretzels cost 3 cents, popcorn and raisins cost 2 cents each, and a graham cracker is 1 cent. She gives each pair 5 pennies. Each pair must decide what they will buy with their 5 cents; by linking and raising their hands, they signal when they have decided. The children have a good time purchasing—and eating—their snacks, and Brenda has used snack time both to check their understanding of counting pennies and as an anticipatory set for the math lesson which will "begin" after snack. In this lesson she will introduce the nickel.

The next day Brenda again combines checking for understanding with an anticipatory set. While the children are on the story rug, she gives them each a slip of paper with a photocopied picture of pennies. Each paper has a picture of one, two, three, or four pennies. She asks the children to walk around and find someone who has the number of pennies that, if added to their own pennies, will equal one nickel. She tells the children that, when they find their nickel partners, they are to come to her; she gives each pair a real nickel to use in the math lesson. The children enjoy this—they count each others' pennies, they hold their papers together, and soon, with very little help from Brenda, the students are in pairs, with their nickels, ready to continue their math lesson.

Mary asks her students to list, in their morning base groups, words they associate with winter. She has the groups post their lists; during the day and again during their study of climate zones, she and her students refer to this list to find examples of descriptive adjectives.

At the beginning of a lesson where he will focus on how Conroy develops his characters, Joe uses a *Three-Step Interview* to have his students share favorite passages that describe one of the powerful characters from *Prince of Tides*.

Janet begins her biology lab by having students discuss at their lab tables what was most unclear about their reading from the night before.

Understanding the Objectives   When planning a lesson, it is useful to begin by asking:

- What should the students be learning and how might they best learn it?
- What are the objectives of the lesson, and how does this lesson fit into larger learning objectives?

When planning a lesson that incorporates meaningful cooperative interaction, it is also useful to ask:

- How can positive goal interdependence be structured so that students both understand the objective and understand that they are to work together collaboratively to achieve their objective?
- What interpersonal and small-group skills will students need to use to achieve these learning objectives?

When students are to work cooperatively, a clear statement of the objective of the lesson and a statement that students are to work together to achieve the objective are essential to the creation of positive goal interdependence and to high-quality cooperation. A statement of the specific interpersonal and small-group learning skills that will help students achieve their goal—what the skills are and how they will be observed—is also important. As we learned in Chapter 2 when we explored Bales' ideas of task and maintenance, attention to the academic (task) objective without attention to the interpersonal (maintenance) objective does not lead to either high-quality cooperation or a high-quality product. In the following example we see how one teacher, Joyce, begins a math lesson by writing both objectives on the board.

Why might it be important for students to understand the objectives of the lesson? How might it help to empower them as learners?

Learning objective: To work together in your math groups to practice solving word problems that ask you to calculate area. Remember, we need to be able to calculate area when we create our blueprints for the playground renovations.

Cooperative objective: "Checking for accuracy." (Refer to the T-chart.) Remember, too, that each person should participate and every person should be able to explain how the group got the answer to each problem.

Input and Modeling   When planning a lesson, it is useful to ask:

- What information and what skills do students need in order to achieve the objectives of the lesson and the larger learning goals?
- How will they understand how to use this information and these skills?
- How might they best learn this information and these skills?

When a teacher is committed to planning that emphasizes simultaneous interaction, it is also useful to ask:

- How can students work together and use memory strategies such as oral rehearsal, semantic organization, and elaboration?
- How much responsibility can students assume for planning how to gather and/or sift information?
- What academic skills do students need?
- What interpersonal and small-group learning skills do students need?
- How can the use of important information and academic and interpersonal skills be modeled so that students understand how to use them in appropriate contexts?

When teachers are committed to using cooperation for learning, they will need to decide how information might be best taught. When direct instruction seems appropriate, informal learning groups can be used to help provide students with opportunities for discussion; these were discussed extensively in Chapter 5. When it seems appropriate for students to assume more responsibility to organize and explain information—when it will benefit them cognitively to engage in considerable oral rehearsal and peer discussion—formal groups with carefully structured positive interdependence are a good choice. When the teacher provides students with a clear body of information, structures like *Jigsaw, STAD,* and *Blind Hand* can be useful to help students organize their work together. When the body of information is less straightforward and requires extensive investigation, research, and reconceptualization—and when students will benefit from opportunities to develop strategies for the gathering and sifting of information—*Academic Controversy* and *Group Investigation* are useful and exciting tools.

When planning, it is useful to ask:

- What information do students need to know about appropriate interpersonal and small-group skills?
- Have the requisite skills been clearly defined and explained with the help of T-charts, discussions, and the like?
- Has the appropriate use of these skills been modeled?

For instance, do students understand how to ask questions and paraphrase in a *Three-Step Interview?* How to find the main idea or three important facts to teach their peers in a *Jigsaw?* The answers to these kinds of questions help teachers decide how input and modeling are used in lessons that emphasize students' learning together.

Practice   When planning a lesson, it is useful to ask:

- How will students practice using the information and skills they are learning?

When planning a lesson for cooperation, it is also useful to ask:

- How might working together help students practice the information and skills they are learning?
- When should students work together and when is independent practice appropriate?

Vygotsky believed that what children learned in collaboration with peers they would be able to use independently later. Exploring and appreciating the links between cooperative work and independent work are critical.

How might teachers help students understand the importance of practice and perseverance?

When planning practice in small groups, teachers need to think carefully about how to structure positive interdependence; shared resources and roles are often useful to help insure that all students have opportunities for meaningful practice within a supportive peer context. Practice also means practicing the interpersonal and small-group learning skills that students have been learning. As we have stressed, monitoring is essential and must include both the academic and interpersonal aspects of cooperative work.

Checking for Understanding   When planning a lesson, it is useful to ask:

- How will I know that my students are learning?
- When should I check?

When planning a cooperative lesson that is designed to empower students as learners, it is also useful to ask:

- How will my students know they are learning?
- How can students check their own understanding and the understanding of their peers?

Checking for understanding is an ongoing process. In the example above, for instance, Brenda's anticipatory set also helps to check the students' understanding of money. During direct teaching, informal groups can be used regularly to check for understanding. Simple directions and routines help:

- "Turn to your partner and make sure they can explain the three steps you will need to follow once you get into your groups."
- "Make sure both you and your partner can list four events that influenced the decision."

Signals are helpful when students are asked to check and respond individually:

- "Use your hand to signal—one to five: How confident are you that you can explain your homework?"

Structures such as *Three-Step Interview, Mad Hatter's Tea Party,* and *Inside-Outside Circle* help students check that they understand the ideas of others; structures such as *Group Interview* help groups probe the understanding of individual members; structures such as *Send A Problem* help groups challenge the understanding of other groups. Structures such as *Gallery Tour* and *One-Stay Three-Stray* are useful ways for formal learning groups to report their work and check their own understanding; they also help the teacher and other groups check.

Why is it important for students to learn to check their own understanding?

Monitoring is essential—for checking both understanding of academic content and understanding of important interpersonal and small-group learning skills. Data from structured observations help students check their use of skills. Monitoring was described in detail in Chapter 7; structured observations were discussed in Chapters 2, 7, and 8. Checking for understanding of academic content is also accomplished through tests, quizzes, portfolios, journal entries, homework, and *One-Minute Papers*. Essential to the concept of checking for understanding is that the classroom climate must encourage the kinds of inquiry where checking for understanding is ongoing and welcome.

Closure   When planning a lesson it is useful to ask:

- How will students reflect on what they have learned and how they have learned it?
- How will students plan what needs to be learned and how it might be learned?

Why is it important to ensure that closure is incorporated as a meaningful part of learning?

Reflection and planning are basic to cooperative learning and have been discussed extensively in Chapters 8 and 9. It cannot be stated too strongly that carefully planned closure is essential—to insure high levels of academic learning and to facilitate the building of learning communities where all students can become empowered learners.

PLANNING UNITS FOR COOPERATION

> There is a simple reason why some students resist thinking: they live in a world where relationships are often quite fragile. They are desperate for more community, not less, so when thinking is presented to them as a way of disconnecting themselves from each other and from the world, they want nothing of it. (Palmer, 1983/1993, p. xvi)

Unit—or thematic—planning is in many ways a "big picture" form of lesson planning. Units can be used to integrate curriculum across subject matter, to focus on essential questions, to teach to multiple intelligences, to create a community centered on learning, and to connect learning to the world. Rich themes provide virtually endless possibilities for students to work in a variety of groups and authentic ways to integrate individual and group work within a cooperative context. As in all lesson planning and all teaching, there is no one right way to plan or teach a unit but, as in lesson planning, there are some basic principles that can be used as guidelines. It is beyond the scope of this book to launch into an exhaustive explanation of unit planning, themes, and theme immersion but, because units are "a natural" for planning learning opportunities that have the potential to empower students as learners, we will examine some basic principles of thematic design.

Basic Principles of Thematic Design

Choosing a Theme   Choosing an appropriate theme is critical to the success of unit planning. Worthwhile themes (based on Kovalik, 1994) have application to the world of the students; they

- Have a "here and now" quality that allows opportunities for touching, visiting, interviewing, doing
- Help students understand how the learning might be applied and valued outside the classroom
- Impact how students relate to the world around them

Worthwhile themes are complex; they

- Integrate a variety of disciplines
- Can be investigated using different intelligences
- Can be engaged at different levels of complexity
- Require the use of a variety of resources that can be made available to students

Worthwhile themes are worth the time spent on them.

Incorporating Basic Principles of Lesson Design into Unit Planning
The basic principles of lesson design—anticipatory set, understanding the objective, input and modeling, practice, checking for understanding, and closure—are as relevant to unit planning as they are to lesson planning. While these principles might be used within individual lessons, it is also useful to consider how they fit into the overall unit. For example, what kinds of experiences—anticipatory sets—might be needed at the beginning of a unit to motivate students, to help students activate their prior knowledge, to help them share what they know with each other? What information—input—do students need? How will it be gathered? What kinds of checking for understanding need to be incorporated throughout? How will closure be used to help students reflect on specific learnings and on aspects of the overall theme? What kinds of culminating experiences might help students "tie it all together"?

Incorporating Cooperative Learning into Unit Planning   All three types of groups—base groups, informal groups, and formal groups—can be used effectively within the context of unit planning. Typically, teachers find that they use informal groups extensively at the beginning of units, more formal groupings for in-depth investigations and projects as units progress, and perhaps base groups to help weave the unit theme throughout the day and week. *Cooperative groups are fundamental to the success of learning that centers on complex themes.* Among other things, cooperative groups facilitate the investigation of themes from a variety of perspectives and modalities and help structure ways for students to learn from the investigations of others.

Well-chosen themes help build a sense of positive interdependence throughout a classroom and can help build an authentic learning community. A complex theme often helps students understand that it is worth working together—that they cannot do it all themselves and need the talents of others to learn (J. Egan & C. Egan, 1996; Fogarty & Stoehr, 1995, 1996; Slavin, Madden, Dolan, & Wasik, 1994). When planning units for cooperation, teachers ask themselves—and their students—questions such as

- How might we share resources?
- What is a logical sequence to aspects of our work together and how might we coordinate this sequence?
- How might we best use the talents of each and every class member?
- How might we learn from each other's talents?
- How will we each be responsible for our own work and learning?
- How will we encourage the work and learning of others?
- How will we reflect on our progress, our goals, and how we work together?
- How might we use the skills we are learning in other settings?
- How might we build a commitment to a spirit of cooperation for life-long learning?

Next we will visit three settings where teachers use a variety of thematic approaches successfully. Although each follows the same basic principles, there are differences that are worth mentioning. Linda has planned most of the activities in her unit before she begins; she chooses themes that help to integrate subject areas, information, and skills that she has decided her students should learn. Karen, Eva, and Howard all plan their own discipline-specific units of study to center around novels, critical events, and the like, and to cover the district core curricula. Their use of an essential question helps them build a year-long theme that gives added depth to their work and helps them to integrate units and disciplines that students have sometimes seen as both isolated from each other and irrelevant to themselves. Sharon's unit is, in many ways, more complex. Although many different subject areas and specific skills are incorporated into her unit, that is not the central focus of her planning and she does not plan a "unit" before she introduces the theme, "Kids Around Town," to her students. (See Figure 10.7 for an overview of different subject areas that are integrated into Sharon's theme.) The approach Sharon uses is sometimes called theme immersion (Manning, Manning, & Long, 1994); this approach, and the theme she

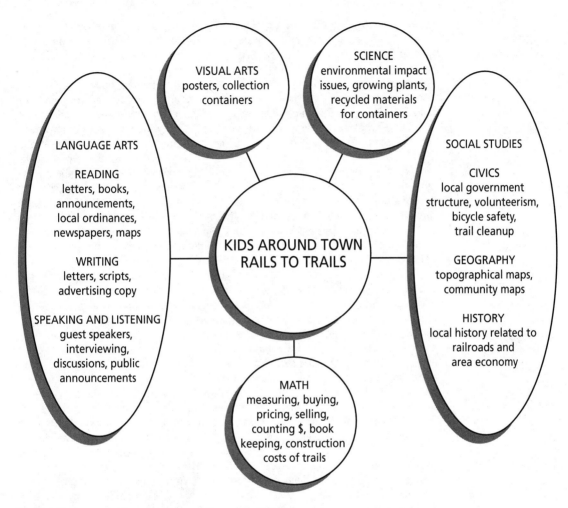

Figure 10.7
Integrating subject areas into "Kids Around Town."

chooses, has great potential to help her students learn to empower themselves as learners and as active citizens in a democracy. As you read these scenarios, ask yourself: "How might each of these units help empower students as learners?" You might also want to consider how it might feel to be a student in these classrooms. How might it feel to be a teacher?

Remember Linda, the teacher we read about in Chapter 6 who used "Jack and the Beanstalk" to provide her first-grade students with practice using their sequencing skills? That lesson was part of "Seeds"—a month-long thematic unit. During the month of April, Linda's students read and are read a variety of fictional and nonfictional books about flowers, vegetables, gardens, and growing. They sing songs about gardening; they use imagery and dramatic play to discover what it might be like to be a seed planted in the earth; they plan vegetable gardens to include their favorite vegetables and draw pictures of their garden plans. They plant flower seeds for Mother's Day. They plant bean seeds, place them in a variety of growing conditions, make daily observations, and keep logs of how they care for their plants and what happens. They place unhulled sunflower seeds in bird feeders they have made themselves; they sprout and eat sunflower sprouts and several other sprout varieties; they toast and eat sunflower and pumpkin seeds. They keep food diaries and learn to categorize the things they eat that come from seeds. They visit a local farm and talk with the farmer to learn what the farmer plants at different seasons. Throughout the month, Linda and her students explore their theme through many active learning experiences. Linda has collected much print material and much other "stuff" to help her students explore their theme. She carefully plans many lessons around the theme that will integrate many subject areas and many age-appropriate skills. She is also responsive to the interests of her students; many of the areas that she and her class explore during their unit are the result of questions or materials her students bring to the classroom.

Sharon wants her sixth-grade students to learn more about local government; she also wants them to become active participants in discussions about local issues. Her students come from five small communities; she begins her unit about local government—"Kids Around Town"—by asking the township manager of one of these communities to come speak to her class about local issues. The manager talks about several local issues and describes a piece of land that has recently been designated for development as an area recreation site. Sharon's students ask a lot of questions about the proposed recreation site and, by the time the manager leaves, Sharon feels confident that her students have identified an issue they would like to know more about. She divides her class into groups of four, and, with the help of large paper and colored markers, asks her students to list: "What are all the things we might want to know about the proposed recreation site?" Conversations are quite animated. When Sharon senses her students have had sufficient time to record their ideas, and when she is confident—because in each group each student uses a different-colored marker—that each student has contributed at least one idea, she has students hang their papers around the room. The groups next embark on a *Gallery Tour;* as groups visit each list, Sharon asks them to discuss what they read and to notice similarities and differences among the lists. When they return to their own lists, Sharon asks them to circle two or three items that they think are particularly important issues to pursue.

A pattern begins to emerge, and it is one that surprises Sharon. Her students are less concerned about the recreation center than they are about getting to it and about getting around their five-community area in general. The roads through their communities are hilly, narrow, and crowded. The children cannot visit each other or get to a recreation center without being driven. They see this as the most important "issue" in their communities and one that they want to learn more about. And so it begins—an exploration of a local issue that has been identified, by the students, as a problem to investigate. Throughout the next several weeks the students not only learn a great deal about their communities, they enter into a project that will help change their communities as well. Through a series of large- and small-group problem-identification and problem-solving activities, the students decide that they need some bicycle trails in their communities. At first, they think they should build these trails themselves; next, that they should ask the local governments to build them. Sharon guides them gently in their inquiry; they write letters, she makes phone calls, and they gather information. They are quite excited to find that there is a local rails-to-trails group that is in the process of building trails in their area. They invite speakers from this group; they learn to read community maps and topographical maps to find out where the trails will be located; they find out how much it costs to convert old rail lines to hiking and biking trails.

They decide that their biggest impact might be to help the group that has already been established; they decide to raise money for the project and discuss ways to do this. Over a period of several months, they grow and sell plants, hold bake sales in their school, and place posters and collection containers around their communities. These projects require a great deal of letter writing—to ask permission to place posters and containers in stores, to organize bake and plant sales, and to build their relationship with the local rails-to-trails group. They conduct a survey to find out what baked goods the other students in the school want to buy and then they buy the ingredients and bake, price, and sell their goodies. They learn about planting mediums and identify annuals that will grow in their area before they begin their work with plants. They develop bookkeeping skills. They learn that the realities of pricing include making a product affordable, paying expenses, and making a profit. They study the history of the local railroads and learn a great deal about the history, economy, geology, and geography of their region. They visit a section of the trail project that has been completed and a section that has not. They organize a Saturday cleanup for one section of rails. Once they have begun their money-making campaign, they involve the entire school by regularly reporting their progress over the public-address system. In these announcements they include safety tips for bicycle riding. They learn that one of the communities has an annual bicycle inspection program, and they volunteer to help at this event. Sharon gently guides her class throughout this whole project. She arranges field trips, she helps her students gather resources, she invites speakers. Her students work in a variety of formal and informal groups. Sometimes these groups form around particular interests; sometimes Sharon structures the membership to ensure a variety of needed talents.

Sharon's students contribute several hundred dollars to the rails-to-trails group and are excited about their work. They also realize, however, that this project will not solve all their transportation problems, and they decide that they need to propose a system of linking trails. Sharon is able to identify a local planner who is willing to work with the students to plan possible locations for these links; through this segment of their work, they learn even more about map reading—as well as about the practical realities of rights-of-way and local governments. They become aware that getting things done is difficult because they live in not one, but five, small communities. They decide that their communities need to establish a single board that would investigate issues that concern citizens across communities; they write letters to the local township committees outlining their suggestion (Kletzien, 1995, 1996; Rappoport & Kletzien, 1996).

Karen and Eva teach tenth-grade English, Howard teaches tenth-grade American history, and the three work together in a suburban comprehensive high school that is organized around traditional departments, curricula, and schedules. They teach the same groups of students. All three teachers use the discipline of cooperative learning quite well in their lesson planning and all three conceptualize their yearly curricula as a series of units. They have decided to work more closely together—within the constraints of their curricula—to help students make connections between the two subjects. They decide to use a single essential question: "What does this [novel, poem, treaty, or other work] tell us about what it means to be an American?" as a kind of metafocus for the year. They agree to plan so that students will work together in the same formal cooperative groups for entire units in both disciplines. They also agree to read what each is assigning students and to eat lunch together once a week to share ideas, connections, and questions.

❧ GETTING STARTED WITH COOPERATIVE ❧ LEARNING IN THE CLASSROOM

Sometimes teachers find it difficult to get started with cooperative learning. Why might that be?

From the beginning the purpose of this book has been to build an understanding of the classroom context for cooperative learning, an understanding of a conceptual framework for the planned use of cooperative learning, and an understanding of the potential for cooperative learning to help students become empowered learners. Understanding is, however, not enough; understanding must translate into doing.

Getting started with cooperative learning may depend, primarily, on three basic principles:

- Start simple
- Start small
- Keep going

For the remainder of this chapter we will explore what it might mean to start simple and start small, and we will examine what it might look like if we keep going. In the final chapter, Chapter 11, we will examine briefly personal, interpersonal, and structural forces that impact on teachers—forces that can help teachers keep going with cooperative learning and work continually towards building an exciting profession.

Start Simple, Start Small

Once upon a time, a first-grade teacher decided her students were ready to begin to work together—they were ready for cooperative learning. It was the end of October. For her first project, she placed her students in groups of four and had each group cut up a fresh pumpkin and make a pumpkin pie for the upcoming Halloween Party. They shared resources and each student had a role. She even talked with her students about what "taking turns" would look and sound like. But, as one might suspect, things turned out a little bit messy; the teacher was quite disappointed. This teacher forgot to start simple; she forgot to start small; and, in her frustration and disappointment, she decided her students could not work together—in fact, she decided that cooperative learning just did not work. Therefore, this teacher did not keep going!

Starting simple and starting small will mean different things in different classrooms and will depend, among other things, on the ages of the students and their previous experiences working together. Starting simple and starting small always means extending an invitation to all students to work with you and each other to build a sense of inclusion, respect, and appreciation. Starting simple and starting small always means attending to the physical environment in the classroom and working with students to help them understand the importance of cooperation—both in learning and in other contexts.

Starting simple and starting small may mean collecting sociometric data; it may mean initiating base groups so that students begin and end each day in a supportive, small-group environment. It may mean using a few simple informal structures to help students begin to share their ideas with other students in an organized fashion. It may mean beginning with some simple whole-class activities that are designed to help students practice basic cooperative skills before group work even begins.

Where do you think you might want to start with cooperative learning? Where have you started?

Starting simple and starting small sometimes means working to allay students' anxiety about working together. Many students arrive in classrooms with experiences in "group work." Often, however, these experiences were not carefully designed to emphasize positive interdependence and did not incorporate individual responsibility. Sometimes students were not given opportunities to learn the skills they needed to work together successfully, a few students dominated, and the only reflection was unofficial but widespread complaining or blaming. When this has been the case, it is easy to understand why students might not be eager to work together and may not even believe that cooperation is possible or desirable.

Starting simple and starting small may mean building an understanding that working together can be meaningful. If students have previously worked together only to complete simple worksheets that they could have done alone or to learn content that they have no interest in, then they are likely to resist the effort that genuine cooperation demands. Palmer (1983/1993) provides additional insights into why students sometimes react negatively when asked to engage in learning that centers around cooperative inquiry.

> [Students] cling to the conventional pedagogy because it gives them security . . . a fact well known by teachers who have tried more participatory modes of teaching. When a teacher tries to share the power, to give students more responsibility for their own education, students get skittish and cynical. They complain that the teacher is not earning his or her pay, and they subvert the experiment by noncooperation. Many students prefer to have their learning boxed and tied, and when they are invited into a more creative role they flee in fear. Conventional pedagogy persists because it conveys a view of reality that simplifies our lives. . . [It] pretends to give us mastery over the world, relieving us of the need for mutual vulnerability. (p. 39)

When teachers choose what to teach cooperatively, they sometimes start simple and start small by choosing a single subject, unit, lesson, or class period that they are so comfortable teaching that they are confident they can try something different and still be successful. At other times, however, teachers start with something they are unsure of—figuring they have nothing to lose! Often, something that has a routine to it is a good place to start because, once the routine has been planned to incorporate meaningful cooperation, it builds in a sense of security and the kind of practice both the teacher and students need in order to increase their skills. Whatever it is that teachers choose to teach, starting simple and starting small always means careful planning, implementation, reflection, and then more planning.

In the following scenarios, we visit two teachers to help us further understand how to start simple and start small.

 Carol, a third-grade teacher, decides that her students are ready to begin working together on the first day of school. She knows her students are not accustomed to a great deal of cooperative work so she knows she needs to start simple. She plans her seating so that she can use partner activities. During the first week, she uses seating partners often and teaches her students the steps in *Think-Pair-Share*. By the end of the week, she introduces the skills of paraphrasing and begins to ask her students to share what their partners have said. She starts a bulletin board entitled "All About Us" and has all students bring in something about themselves to contribute. She brings something to share about herself as well. During the first week of school, she and her students work together to develop an "Interest Survey," and she uses information from this survey and her observations to assign students to base groups. Once students are in base groups, she begins to establish careful routines for both morning and afternoon base-group meetings.

Each day for several weeks, Carol reads a story or poem that emphasizes cooperation, and she and her students build a word list of behaviors that "help" when people or animals work together. On the playground they learn noncompetitive games. To prepare her students to move among a variety of groups, Carol begins, by the second week, to work on "Getting-Together Skills." After defining and modeling these skills, she uses the structure *Corners* so that her students can practice their use of these skills. Whenever Carol introduces a new structure to her students, she plans to use the structure several times so that her students can get used to it. (Carol also makes a commitment to herself. She decides to introduce structures that are new for her, too; repeated use of these structures helps her to understand how to use them effectively in a variety of contexts.)

Eva, a tenth-grade English teacher, knows that her students have had considerable experience working cooperatively in previous years; she wants to begin to build a sense of a serious learning community from the very first day of class. She begins the year's study of literature with several short stories; she is confident that these stories will stimulate considerable discussion and will help her launch the theme "What It Means to Be an American" that she and the history teacher have planned to focus a year-long, cross-disciplinary collaboration. Eva has planned short, varied, written responses to accompany each reading assignment. She uses this written work to start conversation among students; she uses simple structures such as *Corners*, *Inside-Outside Circle*, and *Mix-Freeze-Pair* to organize these conversations and insure that students have many opportunities to move around and share ideas. Each day she has students reflect on how the day's work—and their peers—have helped them extend their understanding of the readings and the larger theme. Each day she collects their writing and she returns it the next day with brief comments. This helps her learn about her individual students and helps her establish the expectation of individual responsibility. She observes the student-to-student conversations carefully; after about three weeks, she will use this information, along with the knowledge she has gained from reading her students' writing, to form formal work groups. These groups will work together for about a month. During this time she will continue to use some simple informal structures so that her students will have opportunities to "connect" with everyone in the class.

Keep Going

At its best, learning cooperatively is not simple and it is not straightforward; students and teachers alike need to be both patient and persistent as they explore ways to use the power of cooperation. At first, using cooperation for learning might seem phony or "weird." This is natural. It is only through persistence that these feelings change and cooperation feels like a natural way to do things. Persistence does not mean using cooperative learning once every week or two; neither teachers nor students will gain in expertise with such infrequent use.

What is your vision of cooperation in the classroom?

Building a Cooperative Classroom—A Vision

Teachers frequently ask: "How much cooperative learning should I use?" Not surprisingly, this is a difficult question to answer, but if we are to get started and keep going with cooperative learning, it is an important question. Remember: the context of the classroom must be cooperative. There is little evidence to suggest that when students compete against each other or work in isolation they achieve more, feel better about school or themselves, or are more prepared for life. But does that mean that students will always be eye-to-eye and knee-to-knee in small-group discussion and work? Not necessarily. Once again, we will visit a classroom to help us clarify these issues.

Joyce's students are in their four-person literature-study groups. It is Thursday and Susie has just returned to school after being sick for two days. Her group had originally planned to finish independent reading by Friday, but group members know that Susie has been unable to read for the last two days. They have about thirty minutes together and they begin by planning how to adjust their time schedule. It is clear that they are both anxious to talk about their reading and sensitive to Susie's needs; it takes them about five minutes to examine their options. Susie decides she can take the book home and finish reading over the weekend, and the group decides to wait until Monday to begin its discussions. For the next twenty minutes, the group is silent. Matthew and Marguerite have finished reading; Matthew writes in his journal, and Marguerite begins to develop discussion questions for the group. (In Chapter 7 we saw how Joyce uses Bloom's taxonomy to help her students develop their own discussion questions.) Both Jon and Susie continue reading. Joyce listens, from a distance, while the group makes its plans; then she leaves them alone for the rest of their work time.

To a casual observer, it may seem that, after the initial discussion, the students in Joyce's class are working independently—and they are. This independent work is, however, imbedded in the context of a literature study group that is quite cooperative, and the literature study group is part of a cooperative classroom learning community. It is the *context* which makes this seemingly independent work quite different than it would be if these students were sitting quietly and working individually on teacher-directed assignments.

Joyce has worked for several years to learn how to build a cooperative context with her students, to become disciplined and sophisticated in her use of cooperative learning, and to learn how to integrate meaningful cooperative work throughout the school day and year. Her students work in several different partner and group configurations throughout the day, but these configurations do not change each day. She has incorporated both variety and routine into the rhythm of her classroom. Her daily plan looks something like this:

- Base groups: These groups stay the same for the entire year.
- Literature Study Groups or Language: Literature Study Groups change periodically—usually about every six weeks; other language work is done using direct instruction, independent work, and informal groups that are typically formed by seating arrangements.
- Math: Math is sometimes a combination of direct instruction, independent work, and informal groups that are typically formed by seating assignments; at other times students work in problem-solving groups that change each marking period.
- Lunch
- "Specials" (music, art, physical education)
- Social Studies or Science: Joyce uses a unit approach to the teaching of social studies and science, and she typically connects some aspect of her theme to literature in the literature study groups or to additional literature that students explore as part of this afternoon block. Joyce uses a combination of flexible project groups and formal and informal learning groups.
- Base groups: Afternoon base groups review key points from the day's work and complete classroom jobs.

Joyce teaches in a self-contained elementary classroom. But whether in a self-contained classroom, in a departmentalized setting, or in a "pod" or "house" where a team of teachers works intensely with a group of students throughout the day and week, the principles are the same. To "keep going," there must be

- A commitment to building a cooperative context for learning
- A commitment to the discipline of cooperative learning
- Flexibility

In Chapter 11 we will examine commitment, not just to cooperative learning but to becoming an excited—and exciting—professional.

WORKING WITH PEERS

Using Base Groups to Review Chapter Content and Personalize Learning

QUESTION: *How might careful planning be used to empower students to say "our goal, our plan, our achievement"?*

1. Students discuss question in their base groups.
2. Reflection and Planning:
   Individual:
   - On a scale of 1 to 5 how confident am I that I can explain the ideas of other group members?
   - How confident am I that they can explain my ideas?
   Group:
   - Did we use a structure? Did we need one?
   - Were we careful to include every group member in the discussion?

Using Pairs and *Mad Hatter's Tea Party* for Analysis and Application of Chapter Content

1. Students use the same basic format described in Chapter 5 and used again in subsequent chapters. The scenarios are found in Chapter 6: Patrick, Linda, Molly, Dana, Arlene, Ana, and Marilyn. (It may be particularly useful for students to work with the same partners and use the same scenarios.) Each pair analyzes a scenario, using Figures 10.5 and 10.6 as a guide and answering these questions:
   a. Using basic principles of lesson design as a guide, analyze your scenario. What are the main objectives of the lesson? What basic principles of lesson design are most evident? Least evident?
   b. Is there anything you might add?
2. Pairs stay together and, using *Mad Hatter's Tea Party,* share their analyses with other pairs.
3. Reflection and Planning:
   Individual:
   - How has this activity helped me understand the basic principles of lesson design and how they fit with cooperative learning?
   - How confident am I that I can use the basic principles of lesson design to plan high-quality cooperative learning lessons?
   Pairs:
   - One way you helped me understand basic principles of lesson design was ___.

- One thing about lesson design that I want to learn more about is ___.

Using *Corners, Gallery Tour,* Self-Stick Notes, and *Group Interview* (Kagan, 1992) to Examine How to Structure Classrooms for Cooperation

1. Students group in corners that are designated K–2, 3–5, 6–8, and 9–12. In each corner students discuss specific grade-level or subject interests; they may subgroup. (Groups should generally contain two or three people.) Each group examines physical environments, grouping strategies, and lesson design.
2. Students work alone to develop their ideas.
3. Students put their ideas together, making sure to include ideas from each person's work, and together begin to build a "picture" of a cooperative classroom.
   Included in this picture are
   a. A seating arrangement that might work for the grade-level or subject.
   b. An example of a random grouping strategy that incorporates appropriate academic content and could be used as an anticipatory set.
   c. An example of an age-appropriate, random-grouping strategy that is not based on academic content.
   d. Ideas for how and where to get started that are simple and grade or subject appropriate.
   e. An outline of what a cooperative day or week might look like for the chosen grade or subject.
   f. An idea for an age- or subject-appropriate theme that has the potential to be worthwhile.
4. Students prepare any materials that are needed to implement the grouping strategy, and they try their strategy with the class.
5. Seating plans and outlines of days or weeks can be written on large paper or blackboards.
6. Students then go on a *Gallery Tour,* visiting the ideas of the different groups. (Different groups have focused on different levels.) They stop and discuss each group's work and, using self-stick notes, leave specific positive comments about the work. (It is useful to fold the notes over so that groups are not influenced by the comments of previous groups.)
7. Groups return to their own work, review the notes, and make any revisions and additions that seem appropriate.

8. Students now regroup in fours so that each group includes, insofar as possible, one student from each corner. Using a *Group Interview,* students are each asked to clarify and extend the ideas that were presented in the *Gallery Tour.*

9. Reflection and Planning:

Group reflection in *Group Interview* group:
- What are some of the things teachers might need to think about when getting started at different grade levels?

Group reflection in *Corners:*
- How successful were our grouping strategies?
- What are some things teachers need to think about when planning random grouping strategies?

Individual:
- I want to learn more about ____ to help me understand the role of the teacher in a classroom that empowers students as learners.

Using a *One-Minute Paper* and Base Groups to Reflect on the Potential Challenges of "Keeping Going" with Cooperative Learning

TASK: *In one sentence, what is one thing that concerns you personally about your ability to "keep going" with cooperative learning?*

1. Each student writes a response.
2. Students share responses in their base groups.

PART

III

Developing Commitment to an Exciting Profession

CHAPTER 11
*Becoming an Excited—and
Exciting—Professional*

CHAPTER *11*

Becoming an Excited—and Exciting—Professional

🐾 *As you read, you might want to ask yourself:*

Why is it as important for teachers to collaborate with other teachers as it is for students to cooperate with peers?

Why are change and uncertainty natural?

How do collegiality and inquiry help to build an exciting profession?

Why is vision essential? How are vision and values related?

How might it feel to be an excited—and exciting—professional?

What I think is important in this school is that the adults have created a world here that is first of all attractive to themselves, that's an interesting place, where they are powerful and interesting people. . . . And there's a possibility then for them to recruit kids . . . into the world of powerful and interesting adults, to make it seem feasible to kids that growing up might be a wonderful thing to do. You can't recruit kids to your club if you have made your club seem very unattractive. . . . This is a faculty that thinks they belong to an exciting profession.

Debra Maier, High School Principal, Central Park East, New York (Smith, 1995, p. 161)

As we have seen in this book, there is a discipline to becoming an empowering teacher—a teacher who encourages students to become learners capable of high levels of meaningful cooperative inquiry and independent thought. This discipline begins with understanding the power of cooperation in school, in the workplace, and in society. This discipline includes an appreciation and understanding of the class as a group, an understanding of the power and potential of diversity, and an understanding of the essential nature of community. This discipline requires careful teacher planning for regular and rich instructional opportunities that emphasize positive interdependence, simultaneous interaction, individual responsibility, reflection and planning, and a specific focus on the interpersonal and small-group learning skills that students need to learn to use to be successful group participants and learners. But there is more to this discipline. Becoming a empowering teacher also means committing oneself to the exciting and very personal process of becoming a life-long learner. One cannot become a good teacher—a Ms. A—without becoming an excited and exciting professional. Being a good teacher is not an end point; it is a continuous process—a process of action, a process of reflection and planning, and a process of collaboration. In essence, this process is much the same as the process we have been learning throughout this book—and in this final chapter, we apply the process to ourselves.

 ## MEANINGFUL LEARNING IN AN EXCITING PROFESSION

Think of two situations that you have been in that were quite challenging— one situation where you felt confident and one where you felt less confident. How were they different?

"Things hardly ever go easily during change efforts" (Fullan & Miles, 1992, p. 746), and meaningful learning always involves change and uncertainty. In this book we have learned how and why to build cooperative classrooms; a commitment to building cooperative classrooms is a commitment to meaningful change. Kohn (1992b) has described four changes that are linked with cooperative learning and the uncertainty that tends to accompany these changes.

1. COOPERATIVE LEARNING REDUCES CONTROL AND PREDICTABILITY. . . . Traditional . . . teaching amounts to a rehearsed solo performance by the instructor (with students relegated to the role of audience), whereas cooperative learning not only offers instruments to everyone in the room but invites a jazz improvisation. . . . [It introduces] uncertainty in place of a predictable progression through a prepared lesson plan.

2. COOPERATIVE LEARNING DEMANDS ATTENTION TO SOCIAL GOALS. . . . Many educators assume their charge is limited to providing instruction in the traditional academic subjects. Even when attention is given to the development of children's social skills and prosocial orientation, this enterprise is "frequently viewed through an instrumental prism of how [these

skills] affect academic achievement rather than as schooling goals with inherent legitimacy" (Rich, 1990, p. 83). . . . Models that call for the creation of a caring classroom community, and not merely the teaching of discrete social skills such as listening carefully or making eye contact, would be even more disconcerting to teachers who see such objectives as inappropriate.

3.   COOPERATIVE LEARNING CHALLENGES OUR COMMITMENT TO INDIVIDUALISM. It would not be an exaggeration to say that the watchword of the American classroom is: "Keep your eyes on your own paper! I want to see what you can do, not what your neighbor can do." This orientation, typically taken for granted, is entirely compatible with—indeed, a reflection of—the wholesale individualism of American culture. . . . [But] individualism has its costs . . . and in the classroom, . . . our exclusive focus on individual accomplishment holds us back. . . . [On the other hand our exaggerated fears about collectivism need to be allayed.] Children do not sacrifice their own psychological or academic development when they work with others; they do not lose their individual selves in an amorphous blob of a group. . . . Cooperative learning is not tantamount to unanimity, conformity, or the subjugation of the individual.

4.   COOPERATIVE LEARNING CHALLENGES OUR COMMITMENT TO THE VALUE OF COMPETITION. Students in American schools . . . are [often] set against each other, told in effect that their success comes at the price of someone else's failure. Grading on a curve, . . . choosing only the best papers to be displayed, . . . playing games such as spelling bees, . . .—all of these explicit contests, along with the subtler competition for recognition and approval in the classroom, teach children one enduring, fundamental message: *Other people are potential obstacles to my own success.* This message continues to be learned in classrooms around the nation despite literally hundreds of studies confirming that competition in the classroom not only sabotages relationships and undermines self-confidence but also impedes achievement and long-term interest in learning.[1]

There are many things teachers can do to help them negotiate these and other changes and to see change as continuous and as integral to personal and professional learning. For the remainder of this brief closing chapter, we will explore several possibilities.

Building Collegiality

Never doubt that a small group of thoughtful, committed people can change the world; indeed it's the only thing that ever has.

Margaret Mead—as quoted on a poster in an elementary classroom

[1]From "Resistance to Cooperative Learning: Making Sense of Its Deletion and Dilution," by A. Kohn. Reprinted from *Journal of Education,* Boston University School of Education (1992), 174 (2), pp. 42–45, with permission from The Trustees of Boston University (copyright holder) and the author.

Reaching out to colleagues is one of the best ways to keep going with cooperative learning. Just as students need to work with other students, there are many reasons teachers need to work with each other to maximize their professional learning. The first is to learn and help others learn about teaching. The second is to learn about learning cooperatively by engaging with peers in a serious cooperative endeavor. The third is to provide a model of cooperation and excitement for students. The fourth is to build a sense of belongingness and to move towards the sense of empowerment that comes when one identifies oneself as a member of an exciting profession.

Collegial Support Groups—Teacher as Colleague   Building feelings of power and excitement takes commitment; collegial support groups are one way to build that commitment. Not *every* group of teaching professionals that "get together" is a collegial support group. Successful collegial support groups share certain basic norms; they meet regularly and provide (based on D. Johnson, R. Johnson, & Holubec, 1992)

- A safe place; a place where people are trusting and trustworthy
- A place where there is support, concern, and celebration; a place where people want to be
- A place where the primary goal is to improve the professional teaching expertise of members; a place where people gather who are willing to take risks in their commitment to professional learning

When schools are designed as learning communities that empower teachers and students alike, collegial support groups become part of the structure of school life, and teachers meet regularly in these groups to discuss students and curriculum and to coplan. When collegial support groups are well integrated into the structure of a school, teachers are able to use them to build a practice of coteaching and regular peer observations. Unfortunately, many schools are not conceptualized as learning communities, and collegial support groups are not part of the structure of the schools. In these schools, teachers may feel fragmented, isolated, and even in competition with each other. When teachers feel fragmented and isolated, collegial support groups are both more difficult to form and sustain and are, paradoxically, more needed. In these situations the development of a support group may depend on a single individual reaching out to a colleague or two.

If significant collegial support has not been integrated into the structure of the school where you work, begin by looking around and identifying one or two people with whom you feel comfortable. Ideally, your partner(s) "should be a 'nourishing person' for you . . . [someone] who has few, if any, plans for your improvement. Partners may have a vision of your potential, but they thoroughly accept you as you are now" (Senge, Roberts, Ross, Smith, & Kleiner, 1994, p. 75). You may have to extend your looking past the walls of the building in which you work; many committed professionals have developed collegial support with the help of long-distance telephone calls. Proximity is nice; trust and commitment are essential. Begin an informal process to discover if this person, or people, might want to commit to regular professional discussions. Be up front about your needs and goals and be as committed to being a good colleague as you are to finding one.

A collegial support group or partnership is most likely to be successful if it develops a simple yet flexible routine to help organize the time members spend together. In many ways this routine is similar to the routines established in student base groups. A typical routine might include

Whom do you know who might fit Senge's definition of a "nurturing person" and could be a collegial partner?

1. Finding out how members have been since the last meeting: Remember that all groups serve both task and maintenance functions. Pay attention to the feeling tone that members bring to the meeting—what they say and do not say.
2. Sharing a teaching success: Be as descriptive as possible so that other people can learn from and adapt good ideas. In a well-developed collegial support group, talking about success is not considered bragging, and using the good ideas of others is not considered stealing!
3. Sharing a difficulty and asking for help with problem-solving: Since, in a well-developed collegial support group, everyone is committed to confidentiality and the improvement of professional expertise, it is safe—and essential—to talk about problems. Nothing drains professional energy more quickly than a need to pretend that everything is going well when it is not. When this happens, a support group becomes part of the problem—not part of the solution.
4. Discussing a new resource, reading, or idea: All groups need new ideas; inquiry is essential. The sharing of new ideas can be casual or organized—from "Next time everyone will read __ so that we can discuss it" to "Next time it is Dale's turn to bring something new to the group."
5. Making a commitment to try something new or to work on a problem before the next meeting: This is essential to keeping going.
6. Committing to the next meeting: This, too, is essential to keeping going. In some schools, where collegial support groups are integral to the fabric of school life, groups meet every day. Every two weeks or once a month may be more realistic in other circumstances. Agendas will, of course, vary depending on the frequency of meetings, but the essential principles—trust, a balance of task and maintenance, sharing of good and bad times, inquiry, and goal setting—remain fairly constant.

Asking Questions

The degree to which I can create relationships which facilitate the growth of others as separate persons is a measure of the growth I have achieved in myself. In some respects this is a disturbing thought, but it is also a promising or challenging one. It would indicate that if I am interested in creating helping relationships I have a fascinating lifetime job ahead of me, stretching and developing my potentialities in the direction of growth.[2]

Continuous inquiry is essential to the life-long learning of an exciting professional. At its best, inquiry helps teachers to empower themselves by encouraging them to ask questions and to answer—at least partially—the questions they have asked. Inquiry can be undertaken alone or in collaboration with others; familiar forms of inquiry include reading, course work, and staff development. Another, perhaps less familiar, form of inquiry is action research, a form of research that was developed by Kurt Lewin and others in their work to advance democratic processes. What is this kind of research, and how might it help a teacher move towards being an excited professional? Thomas Newkirk, who uses the term "teacher research," suggests:

> Teacher research is not a small-scale version of traditional academic research. It is something distinct. . . . The authority of the teacher-researcher comes primarily from experience in the classroom, from questioning, observation, and reflection. Whereas the academic researcher describes questions arising out of prior research, the teacher-researcher describes questions arising out of prior experience. . . . The relationship of the teacher-research to his or her material also differs. Traditionally, the academic researcher maintains a detachment. . . . [But] the emotional life of teaching cannot—and should not—be excised from teacher research; in fact, questions often arise out of a sense of something not going right in the classroom. . . . There is [also] a sense of incompleteness. It's the belief that we [teachers] will never outgrow our ignorance, that we are blessed with problems we cannot solve. To me, this sense of ignorance is *the* primary motivation of personal development, and is far more potent than "inspirational" talks or writing. . . . When we ask new questions about our classroom (and ourselves), we admit the possibility of real self-transformation. To ask if things might be done differently is to loosen the hold of routine and habit. (Newkirk, 1992, pp.7–8)

What questions do you have about classrooms that might help you to discover the power of teacher research?

It is beyond the scope of this book to launch into a full description of teacher research, but it is important to say that (a) inquiry includes research; (b) each and every teacher is capable of conducting research that is informed by, and will inform, practice; (c) research is fueled by questions, attachment, uncertainty, and even failure; and (d) when teachers see themselves as researchers they empower themselves and their profession.

[2]From *On Becoming a Person* (p. 56). Copyright © by Carl R. Rogers. Reprinted by permission of Houghton Mifflin Company. All rights reserved.

Developing Purpose and Vision

Teaching is a moral profession (Goodlad, Soder, & Sirotnik, 1990)—a profession which, at its heart, is about making a difference in the lives of students and helping to improve society. While this may at first sound lofty, Sarason (1993) recommends that "teaching is not and should not be for those unwilling or unable to be active agents of educational-institutional change" (p. 19). Fullan (1993) believes that it is this very sense of vision and purpose that gives meaning to the work of teaching. All teachers need continually to develop their sense of vision and purpose, to keep vision alive, and to act in accordance with that vision—anything less robs both personal satisfaction and professional integrity. In *Walden,* Thoreau described his own lack of genuine purpose and vision and his failed attempt at being a teacher. He wrote, "As I did not teach for the good of my fellow-man, but simply for a livelihood, this was a failure."

Think of a teacher you have had who seemed to have a genuine sense of purpose and vision. Who was the teacher? How did you know?

Vision and purpose can be both personal and shared; shared purpose emerges from an ongoing process of reflection and conversation. It is beyond the scope of this book to launch into detail about the processes an organization might use to engage in this challenging work, but it is important to remember that purpose and vision are essential.

Establishing Goals and Learning to Celebrate

Burnout, although the word itself may sound simplistic and trite, is an all too familiar feeling for many teachers. Classrooms and schools are extremely complex places, the responsibilities of teaching are enormous, and teachers sometimes lose sight of the purpose and vision that attracted them to the profession. Many individuals do, however, learn to transform potential adversity into enjoyable challenges, and there are basic principles that can guide us as we move to empower ourselves and to make our profession an exciting one. Like Maslow, whose work we learned about in Chapter 1, Csikszentmihalyi (1990) studied people who were successful, enjoyed challenge, achieved a sense of perspective and balance, and seemed to be able to work at an optimal level of engagement—a level which he called "flow." From these people he learned that goal setting is fundamental to their success and satisfaction. He also identified several principles of goal setting that we can use as we continue to develop ourselves as excited and exciting professionals.

Think of a time when you felt "optimally engaged." What were you doing? How did it feel?

Goals are most empowering when

- People set their own goals. They are intrinsic to and congruent with the needs, interests, and sense of purpose and vision of the individual or group and are not imposed by others. They represent a good match between the goal setter and the environment.

- People learn to identify and develop the skills necessary to achieve their goals.
- People take action to achieve aspects of their goals and are able to "lose themselves"—become immersed and absorbed in the actions undertaken to achieve their goals. Goals that are "too hard" or "too easy" are not likely to offer optimal involvement.
- People learn to pay attention to feedback about, and reflect on, the results of actions taken to achieve their goals: They are flexible and able to modify both their actions and their goals without necessarily abandoning the vision that helped to focus their goals.
- People learn to enjoy and celebrate their immediate experience—the process—as much as the goal itself.

We will close with this notion of enjoyment and celebration. It is key to empowerment—for students, for teachers, for students and teachers working together.

🌿 WORKING WITH PEERS 🌿

Using Base Groups to Reflect on Challenges

QUESTION: *Which of the changes that Kohn suggests are linked with cooperative learning do you think will be most challenging to you personally? Why?*

1. Each student thinks individually.
2. Students discuss their individual responses in their base groups.
3. Reflection and Planning:
   Group:
   - How might we, as a group, offer support to each other as we consider these challenges?

Building a Personal Vision of the Ideal Classroom

1. As individuals: Students respond individually to the following questions—using journals, mindmaps, pictures, lists, or any other medium that seems appropriate for their personal styles of reflection.
   - What would you like your ideal classroom to be? How would it look? How would it sound? How would it feel? What would focus the curriculum?
   - What would your reputation be as a teacher—among students, among parents, among colleagues, among administrators?
   - How would your students describe you?
   - What would your students look and act like?

What would you hope your students would be like when they leave your classroom?
   - How would you sustain excitement about your chosen profession?
   - How would you feel when you left your classroom at the end of the day?
   - How would you build balance into your life? What might your interests be?

Reflecting on Personal Values and on the Relationship of Values to Vision (adapted from Senge, et al., 1994)

As we learned in Chapter 2, values are beliefs that are considered important; they tend to elicit an emotional response. Values are an essential part of us, and we bring them to our classrooms—both as teachers and as students.

1. As individuals:
   - Circle the ten values from Figure 11.1 you consider most important to you personally, adding any core values that you think the list lacks.
   - Examine these ten core values. Which five are most central to you? Which five could you give up? Cross off those five.
   - How did it feel to give up a value that you had identified as important? Have you ever had this feeling before? When and where?

affection	excellence	intellectual abilities	self-respect
challenge	excitement	interdependence	solitude
change	family	knowledge	sophistication
close relationships	fine arts	leadership	stability
collaboration	freedom	loyalty	status
collegiality	friendship	meaningful work	success
commitment	harmony with	physical fitness	time management
community	nature	pleasure	tranquillity
competence	helping others	power	truth
competition	honesty	privacy	_____
creativity	independence	problem solving	_____
democracy	influence	recognition	_____
eco awareness	inner harmony	responsibility	
ethics	integrity	self actualization	

Figure 11.1
Core values.

- How well does the personal vision of a classroom you described in the previous exercise reflect these five core values? If there is not a good match, is it possible your vision needs to be reexamined? Or is it possible to reconsider your core values?
- What might it be like to live a life where your core values and your daily work are in synchrony?

Moving Towards the Personal Vision of the Ideal Classroom: Force-Field Analysis (adapted from D. Johnson & F. Johnson, 1994)

A problem is sometimes defined as the difference between reality and the ideal—between "what is" and the vision of "what should be." An important aspect of solving a problem is identifying forces that influence the problem—forces that help move "what is" towards "what should be" and forces that hinder this movement. Force-field analysis, developed by Kurt Lewin is a useful tool for this purpose.

1. Look at the force field analysis diagram in Figure 11.2. "What should be" is in the right-hand side of the figure and is represented by a plus sign. What should be is the ideal classroom—the classroom that reflects personal vision and values. On the left-hand side of the figure is a particularly negative classroom situation—one that is quite the opposite of the classroom that represents the personal vision and values. This is represented by a minus sign. Take a minute to create—in pictures, graphics, or words—a "picture" of this least desirable classroom. "What is"—the status quo—is in the middle. Notice that this middle is not a single line but a space that allows some movement. Often, when change occurs in classrooms, it is within the boundaries of "what is." When change happens within these boundaries, the change does not upset or activate the balance of forces in the force field; neither does it move "what is" significantly closer to the ideal. Within the force field, many forces are at work. Some forces help to pull the classroom towards the ideal while other forces restrain this change.

2. As individuals:
   a. Take a moment to clarify the pictures you have created of the ideal and negative classrooms.
   b. List all the forces that might be helping forces—forces that might help you build a classroom that is close to your ideal. List all the forces that might be restraining forces—forces that might keep you from building a classroom that is close to your ideal.

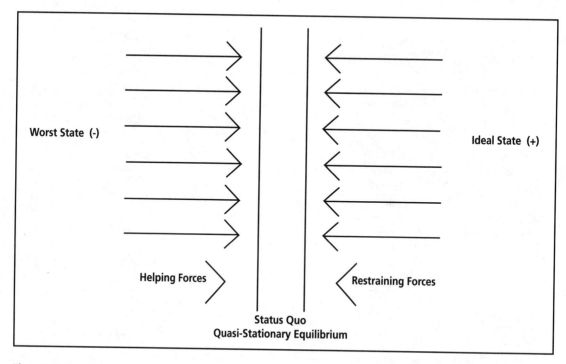

Figure 11.2
Force-field analysis.

c. Rank both of these lists of forces according to their importance for affecting the status quo—the quasi stationary equilibrium.

d. Select a few of the most important helping and restraining forces to include in your list. For now, avoid listing those forces which you are sure that you—with the help of colleagues and classmates—cannot influence with your available resources and status.

e. Identify one restraining force that you are willing to share with members of your base group.

There are two basic ways to use the information generated by a force-field analysis; both are based on the premise that changes in the status quo—the present situation—will happen only when the helping and restraining forces are changed so that the area of balance in between changes too. One method is to focus on and strengthen the helping forces; the other is to focus on and reduce the restraining forces. Reducing restraining forces is usually a prefer-able first step; it tends to cause less tension, fear, and uncertainty. Therefore:

3. As a base group:
   a. Have each group member share one restraining force. Ask questions to help clarify the nature of the force. (A *Group Interview* might be useful for this purpose.)
   b. Help individuals identify something they might do to reduce the power of this restraining force and to establish a personal goal related to this force. Discuss how group members might help each individual reach this goal.

4. Reflection and Planning:
   Individual:
   • How committed am I to pursuing my goal to reduce the power of this restraining force?
   • How committed am I to helping other members of my group pursue their goals?
   Group:
   • Were there areas of common concern identified in the restraining forces? In goals and plans?

Using Base Groups for Celebration and Closure

1. As individuals:

   Take a moment to think about the other members of your base group. What are their goals? What are they looking forward to? What do they enjoy? If you could give members of your base group symbolic gifts—gifts that would help them reach a goal or deepen their enjoyment of a meaningful aspect of their lives—what might they be?

2. As a group:

   Have each member of the base group give every other member a symbolic gift. The recipient responds, simply, "Thank you."

BOOKS WITH MORE INFORMATION

INTRODUCTION
Kohn, *No Contest: The Case Against Competition.*
Katzenbach and Smith, *The Wisdom of Teams.*
Goleman, *Emotional Intelligence.*

PART I:

Group Development
D. Johnson and F. Johnson, *Joining Together.*
R. Schmuck and P. Schmuck, *Group Processes in the Classroom.*
Diversity
J. Banks, *Multiethnic Education: Theory and Practice.*
J. Banks and C. McGee Banks, *Multicultural Education: Issues and Perspectives.*
Cohen, *Designing Groupwork.*
Gardner, *Frames of Mind.*
hooks, *Teaching to Transgress: Education as the Practice of Freedom.*
Kozol, *Savage Inequalities.*
Levine, Lowe, Peterson, and Tenorio, *Rethinking Schools: An Agenda for Change.*
Nieto, *Affirming Diversity.*
Oakes, *Keeping Track: How Schools Structure Inequality.*
Sternberg, *The Triarchic Mind.*

Community Building
Gibbs, *Tribes: A New Way of Learning Together.*
Kohn, *Beyond Discipline: From Compliance to Community.*
Lickona, *Educating for Character.*
McCaleb, *Building Communities of Learners.*
Moorman and Dishon, *Our Classroom: We Can Learn Together.*
Newkirk with McLure, *Listening In: Children Talk About Books (and other things).*
Peterson, *Life in a Crowded Place.*
Rohnke, *Silver Bullets: A Guide to Initiative Problems, Adventure Games, Stunts and Trust Activities.*
Spolin, *Theatre Games for the Classroom: A Teacher's Handbook.*
Weistein and Goodman, *Playfair: Everybody's Guide to Non-Competitive Play.*

Conflict Resolution
D. Johnson and R. Johnson, *Teaching Children to be Peacemakers.*
Kriedler, *Creative Conflict Resolution: More than 200 Activities for Keeping Peace in the Classroom.*
Prutzman, *The Friendly Classroom for a Small Planet.*
Sadalla, Henriquez, and Holmberg, *Conflict Resolution: A Secondary School Curriculum.*
Sadalla, Holmberg, and Halligan, *Conflict Resolution: An Elementary School Curriculum.*

PART II:

The Five Basic Elements
Bennett, Rolheiser, and Stevahn, *Cooperative Learning: Where Heart Meets Mind.*
Dishon and O'Leary, *A Guidebook for Cooperative Learning.*
D. Johnson and R. Johnson, *Learning Together and Alone.*
D. Johnson, R. Johnson, and Holubec, *Circles of Learning.*

The Structural Approach
Kagan, *Cooperative Learning.*

Teaching Interpersonal and Small-Group Learning Skills
Davidson and Worsham, *Enhancing Thinking Through Cooperative Learning.*

250

Dalton, *Adventures in Thinking: Creative Thinking and Cooperative Groups.*

Cooperative Learning In The Content Areas

Curran, *Lessons for Little Ones: Language Arts and Cooperative Learning.*

Curran, *Lessons for Little Ones: Mathematics and Cooperative Learning.*

Daniels, *Literature Circles: Voice and Choice in the Student-Centered Classroom.*

Davidson, *Cooperative Learning in Mathematics: A Handbook for Teachers.*

Stahl, *Cooperative Learning in the Social Studies: A Handbook for Teachers.*

Stahl, *Cooperative Learning in Language Arts: A Handbook for Teachers.*

Stone, *Cooperative Learning and Language Arts: A Multi-Structural Approach.*

Thematic Instruction

Fogarty and Stoehr, *Integrating Curricula with Multiple Intelligences: Teams, Themes, and Threads.*

Gardner, *Frames of Mind.*

Lazear, *Seven Ways of Teaching.*

Manning, Manning, and Long, *Theme Immersion: Inquiry-Based Curriculum in Elementary and Middle Schools.*

Checking for Understanding

White and Gunstone, *Probing for Understanding.*

Darling-Hammond, Ancess, and Falk, *Authentic Assessment in Action: Studies of Schools and Students at Work.*

PART III

Friend and Cook, *Interactions: Collaboration Skills for School Professionals.*

Fullan, *Change Forces: Probing the Depths of Educational Reform.*

D. Johnson, *Reaching Out: Interpersonal Effectiveness and Self-Actualization.*

❧ REFERENCES ❧

Amabile, T. (1983). *The social psychology of creativity*. New York: Springer-Verlag.

Amabile, T., & Gitomer, J. (1984). Children's artistic creativity: Effects of choice in task materials. *Personality and Social Psychology Bulletin, 10,* 209–215.

Amidon, E., & Hough, J. (Eds.). (1967). *Interaction analysis: Theory, research and application*. Reading, MA: Addison-Wesley.

Aronowitz, S., & Giroux, H. (1985). *Education under siege*. South Hadley, MA: Bergin & Garvey.

Aronson, E., Blaney, N., Stephan, C., Sikes, J., & Snapp, M. (1978). *The jigsaw classroom*. Beverly Hills, CA: Sage Publications.

Bales, R. (1950). *Interaction process analysis: A method for the study of small groups*. Cambridge, MA: Addison-Wesley.

Bales, R. (1970). *Personality and interpersonal behavior*. New York: Holt, Rinehart and Winston.

Baloche, L., & Blasko, J. (1992). Learning together—A new twist. *The Journal of Physical Education, Recreation and Dance, 63*(3), 26–28.

Baloche, L., Lee Mauger, M., Willis, T., Filinuk, J., & Michalsky, B. (1993). Fishbowls, creative controversy, talking chips: Exploring literature cooperatively. *English Journal, 82*(6), 43–48.

Baloche, L., & Platt, T. (1993a). Converging to diverge: Creative thinking in the cooperative classroom. *Cooperative Learning, 13*(2), 26–28.

Baloche, L., & Platt, T. (1993b). Sprouting magic beans: Exploring literature through creative questioning and cooperative learning. *Language Arts, 70*(4), 264–271.

Banks, J. (1993). Multicultural education: Progress and prospects. *Phi Delta Kappan, 75*(1), 22–28.

Banks, J. (1994). *Multiethnic education: Theory and practice* (3rd ed.). Boston: Allyn and Bacon.

Banks, J., & Banks, C. McGee (1993). *Multicultural education: Issues and perspectives* (2nd ed.). Boston: Allyn and Bacon.

Bellanca, J., & Fogarty, R. (1991). *Blueprints for thinking in the cooperative classroom*. Palatine, IL: Skylight.

Bennett, B., Rolheiser, C., & Stevahn, L. (1991). *Cooperative learning: Where heart meets mind*. Toronto, Ontario: Educational Connections.

Berger, J., Conner, T., & McKeown, W. (1974). Evaluations and the formation and maintenance of performance expectations. In J. Berger, T. Conner, & H. Fisek (Eds.), *Expectation states theory: A theoretical research program* (pp. 27–51). Cambridge, MA: Winthrop.

Berman-Robinson, S. (1991). Adding heart and soul to the chemistry classroom. *Journal of Chemical Education, 68*(12), 999–1000.

Boggiano, A., Shields, A., Barrett, M., Kellam, T., Thompson, E., Simons, J., & Katz, P. (1992). Helplessness deficits in students: The role of motivational orientation. *Motivation and Emotion, 16*(3), 278–280.

Bowles, S., & Gintis, H. (1976). *Schooling in capitalist America: Educational reform and the contradictions of economic life*. New York: Basic.

Breitborde, M. (1996). Creating community in the classroom: Modeling new basic skills in teacher education. *Journal of Teacher Education, 47*(5), 367–374.

Burke, K. (1992). *What to do with the kid who . . . Developing cooperation, self-discipline, and responsibility in the classroom*. Palatine, IL: Skylight.

Carew, J., & Lightfoot, S. (1979). *Beyond bias: Perspectives on classrooms*. Cambridge, MA: Harvard University Press.

CEO Briefing. (1994, September 13). *Investor's Business Daily*.

Chambliss, W. (1993). The saints and the roughnecks. In W. Feigelman (Ed.), *Sociology full circle* (pp. 450–462). Fort Worth, TX: Harcourt Brace Jovanovich.

Clarke, J., Wideman, R., & Eadie, S. (1990). *Together we learn*. Scarborough, Ontario: Prentice-Hall.

Cobb, P., Wood, T., Yackel, E., Nicholls, J., Wheatley, G., Trigatti, B., & Perlwitz, M. (1991). Assessment of a problem-centered second-grade mathematics project. *Journal for Research in Mathematics Education 22*(1), 3–29.

Cohen, E. (1984). The desegregated school: Problems in status, power and interethnic climate. In N. Miller & M. Brewer (Eds.), *Groups in contact: The psychology of desegregation* (pp. 77–96). New York: Academic Press.

Cohen, E. (1986). *Designing groupwork.* New York: Teachers College Press.

Cohen, E. (1994). *Designing groupwork* (2nd ed.). New York: Teachers College Press.

Coleman, M., Gallagher, J., & Nelson, S. (1993). *Cooperative learning and gifted students: Report on five case studies.* Chapel Hill: The University of North Carolina, Gifted Education Policy Studies Program.

Cook, S. (1984). Cooperative interaction in multiethnic contexts. In N. Miller & M. Brewer (Eds.), *Groups in contact: The psychology of desegregation* (pp. 156–186). New York: Academic Press.

Costa, A., Bellanca, J., & Fogarty, R. (1992). *If minds matter: A foreward to the future* (Vols. 1 & 2). Palantine, IL: Skylight.

Csikszentmihalyi, M. (1990). *Flow: The psychology of optimal experience.* New York: Harper.

Curran, L. (1990). *Lessons for little ones: Language arts and cooperative learning.* San Juan Capistrano, CA: Kagan Cooperative Learning.

Curran, L. (1994). *Lessons for little ones: Mathematics and cooperative learning.* San Juan Capistrano, CA: Kagan Cooperative Learning.

Dacey, J. (1989). Discriminating characteristics of the families of highly creative adolescents. *The Journal of Creative Behavior, 23*(4), 263–271.

Dalton, J. (1992). *Adventures in thinking: Creative thinking and cooperative groups.* Portsmouth, NH: Heinemann.

Daniels, H. (1994). *Literature circles: Voice and choice in the student-centered classroom.* York, ME: Stenhouse.

Darling-Hammond, L., Ancess, J., & Falk, B. (1995). *Authentic assessment in action: Studies of schools and students at work.* New York: Teachers College Press.

Davidson, N. (Ed.). (1990). *Cooperative learning in mathematics: A handbook for teachers.* NY: Addison-Wesley.

Davidson, N., & Worsham, T. (1992). *Enhancing thinking through cooperative learning.* New York: Teacher's College Press.

Dewey, J. (1956). The school and society. In J. Dewey, *The child and the curriculum and The school in society* (pp. 3–157). Chicago: University of Chicago Press. (Original work published 1915)

Dewey, J. (1968). *Problems of men.* Westport, CT: Greenwood Press.

Dishon, D., & O'Leary, P. (1994). *A guidebook for cooperative learning: A technique for creating more effective schools* (2nd. ed.). Holmes Beach, FL: Learning Publications.

Dreikurs, R., Grunwald, B., & Pepper, F. (1982). *Maintaining sanity in the classroom: Classroom management techniques* (2nd ed.). New York: Harper and Row.

Dumaine, B. (1990, May 7). Who needs a boss? *Fortune, 121* (10) pp. 52–60.

Egan, J., & Egan, C. (1996). The integrated curriculum and cooperative learning. *Cooperative Learning, 16*(3), 17–18.

Epstein, J. (1983). Selection of friends in differently organized schools and classrooms. In J. Epstein & N. Karweit (Eds.), *Friends in school.* New York: Academic Press.

Epstein, J. (1995). School/family/community partnerships: Caring for the children we share. *Phi Delta Kappan, 76*(9), 701–712.

Fogarty, R. (1991). *The mindful school: How to integrate the curriculum.* Palatine, IL: Skylight.

Fogarty, R., & Stoehr, J. (1995). *Integrating curricula with multiple intelligences: Teams, themes, and threads.* Palatine, IL: Skylight.

Fogarty, R., & Stoehr, J. (1996). Collaborative teams: A multiple intelligences approach to learning. *Cooperative Learning, 16*(3), 19–24.

Friend, M., & Cook, L. (1996). *Interactions: Collaboration skills for school professionals* (2nd ed.). White Plains, NY: Longman.

Fullan, M. (1993). *Change forces: Probing the depths of educational reform.* Bristol, PA: Falmer.

Fullan, M., & Miles, M. (1992). Getting reform right: What works and what doesn't. *Phi Delta Kappan, 73*(10), 745–752.

Gallagher, J., & Coleman, M. (1994). Cooperative learning and gifted students: Five case studies. *Cooperative Learning, 14*(4), 21–25.

Gardner, H. (1983). *Frames of mind.* New York: Basic.

Gardner, H. (1995). Reflections on multiple intelligences: Myths and messages. *Phi Delta Kappan, 77*(3), 200–209.

Getzels J., & Jackson, P. (1962). *Creativity and intelligence: Explorations with gifted students.* New York: Wiley.

Gibb, J., & Gibb, L. (1978). The group as a growing organism. In L. Bradford (Ed.), *Group Development* (2nd ed., pp. 104–116). La Jolla, CA: University Associates.

Gibbs, J. (1994). *Tribes: A new way of learning together.* Santa Rosa, CA: Center Source.

Gillespie, J. (1993). Buddy book journals: Responding to literature. *English Journal, 82*(6), 64–68.

Glasser, W. (1969). *Schools without failure.* New York: Harper and Row.

Glasser, W. (1986). *Control theory in the classroom.* New York: Harper and Row.

Goldberg, N. (1993). *Long quiet highway: Waking up in America.* New York: Bantam.

Goleman, D. (1995). *Emotional intelligence: Why it can matter more than IQ.* New York: Bantam.

Goodlad, J. (1983). *A place called school.* New York: McGraw-Hill.

Goodlad, J., Soder, R., & Sirotnik, K. (Eds.). (1990). *The moral dimensions of teaching.* San Francisco: Jossey-Bass.

Graves, L. (1992). Cooperative learning communities: Context for a new vision of education and society. *Journal of Education, 174*(2), 57–79.

Graves, N., & Graves, T. (1990). Sue Smith: The child development project in action. *Cooperative Learning, 10*(3), 10–14.

Hertz-Lazarowitz, R., & Shachar, H. (1990). Teachers' verbal behavior in cooperative and whole-class instruction. In S. Sharan (Ed.), *Cooperative learning: Theory and research* (pp. 77–94). New York: Praeger.

Heterington, E., & Parke, R. (1986). *Child Psychology: A contemporary viewpoint* (3rd ed.). New York: McGraw-Hill.

hooks, b. (1994). *Teaching to transgress: Education as the practice of freedom.* New York: Routledge.

Holloway, S. (1992). A potential wolf in sheep's clothing: The ambiguity of "cooperation." *Journal of Education, 174*(2), 80–99.

Hunter, M. (1982). *Mastery teaching.* El Segundo, CA: TIP Publications.

Johnson, D. (1993). *Reaching out: Interpersonal effectiveness and self-actualization* (5th ed.). Boston: Allyn and Bacon.

Johnson, D., & Johnson, F. (1994). *Joining together: Group theory and group skills* (5th ed.). Upper Saddle River, NJ: Prentice Hall.

Johnson, D., & Johnson, R. (1983). Social interdependence and perceived academic and personal support in the classroom. *Journal of Social Psychology, 120*, 77–82.

Johnson, D., & Johnson, R. (1984). *The impact of cooperative, competitive, and individualistic experiences on minority individuals' educational and career success* (Report No. CLC 001). Arlington, VA: Office of Naval Research.

Johnson, D., & Johnson, R. (1989). *Cooperation and competition: Theory and research.* Edina, MN: Interaction Books.

Johnson, D., & Johnson, R. (1991). *Teaching children to be peacemakers.* Edina, MN: Interaction Books.

Johnson, D., & Johnson, R. (1992). *Creative controversy: Intellectual challenge in the classroom.* Edina, MN: Interaction Books.

Johnson, D., & Johnson, R. (1994). *Learning together and alone.* Boston: Allyn and Bacon.

Johnson, D., & Johnson, R. (1995). Why violence prevention programs don't work—and what does. *Educational Leadership, 54*(5), 63–68.

Johnson, D., Johnson, R., Buckman, L., & Richards, P. (1985). The effect of prolonged implementation of cooperative learning on social support within the classroom. *The Journal of Psychology, 119*(5), 405–411.

Johnson, D., Johnson, R., & Holubec, E. (1992). *Advanced cooperative learning.* Edina, MN: Interaction Books.

Johnson, D., Johnson, R., & Holubec, E. (1993). *Circles of learning: Cooperation in the classroom.* Edina, MN: Interaction Books.

Johnson, D., Maruyama, G., Johnson R., Nelson, D., & Skon, L. (1981). Effects of cooperative, competitive, and individualistic goal structures on achievement: A meta-analysis. *Psychological Bulletin, 89*, 47–62.

Johnson, D., & Norem-Hebeisen, A. (1981). Relationships between cooperative, competitive, and individualistic attitudes and differentiated aspects of self-esteem. *Journal of Personality, 49*, 415–426.

Johnson, R., & Thomson, C. (1962). Incidental and intentional learning under three conditions of motivation. *American Journal of Psychology, 75*, 284–288.

Kagan, S. (1980). Cooperation-competition, culture, and structural bias in classrooms. In S. Sharan (Ed.), *Cooperation in education* (pp. 197–211). Provo, Utah: Brigham Young University.

Kagan, S. (1989, 1992). *Cooperative learning.* San Juan Capistrano, CA: Kagan Cooperative Learning.

Kagan, S. & Zahn, G. (1975). Field dependence and the school achievement gap between Anglo-American and Mexican-American children. *Journal of Educational Psychology, 67*, 643–650.

Katzenbach, J., & Smith, D. (1993). *The wisdom of teams.* New York: Harper.

Kelley, R., & Caplan, J. (1993). How Bell Labs creates star performers. *Harvard Business Review, 71* (4), 128–139.

Kerman, S., Kimball, T., & Martin, M. (1980). *Teacher expectations and student achievement.* Bloomington, IN: Phi Delta Kappa.

Kletzien, S. (1996). Kids Around Town: Valuing multiple perspectives. *Cooperative Learning, 16*(3), 45–47.

Kletzien, S., & Baloche, L. (1994). The shifting muffled sound of the pick: Facilitating student to student discussion. *Journal of Reading, 37*(7), 540–545.

Kletzien, S. (with Rappoport, A.) (1995). *Kids Around Town: A local government educational model.* Harrisburg, PA: League of Women Voters.

Kohn, A. (1991). Caring kids: The role of the schools. *Phi Delta Kappan, 72*(7), 496–506.

Kohn, A. (1992a). *No contest: The case against competition.* (rev. ed.). Boston: Houghton Mifflin.

Kohn, A. (1992b). Resistance to cooperative learning: Making sense of its deletion and dilution. *Journal of Education, 174*(2), 38–56.

Kohn, A. (1993). Choices for children: Why and how to let students decide. *Phi Delta Kappan, 75*(1), 8–20.

Kohn, A. (1996). *Beyond discipline: From compliance to community.* Alexandria, VA: Association for Supervision and Curriculum Development.

Kovalik, S. (with Olsen, K.) (1994). *ITI: The model* (3rd ed.). Kent, WA: Books for Educators.

Kozol, J. (1991). *Savage inequalities: Children in America's schools.* New York: HarperCollins.

Krackhardt, D., & Hanson, J. (1993). Informal networks: The company behind the chart. *Harvard Business Review, 71 (4),* 104–111.

Kriedler, W. (1984). *Creative conflict resolution.* Glenview, IL: Scott, Foresman.

Lazear, D. (1991). *Seven ways of teaching: The artistry of teaching with multiple intelligences.* Palantine, IL: Skylight.

Levine, D., Lowe, R., Peterson, B., & Tenorio, R. (1995). *Rethinking schools: an agenda for change.* New York; New Press.

Levi's Lessons. (1992, December 12). *Investor's Business Daily.*

Lewis, C., Schaps, E., & Watson, M. (1995). Beyond the pendulum: Creating challenging and caring schools. *Phi Delta Kappan, 75*(1), 547–554.

Lickona, T. (1990). Cooperative learning and moral development. *Cooperative Learning, 10*(3), 2–5.

Lickona, T. (1991). *Educating for character: How our schools can teach respect and responsibility.* New York: Bantam.

Light, R. (1990–1992). *The Harvard assessment seminars* (Vols. 1–2). Cambridge, MA: Harvard University.

Lyman, F. (1992). Think-pair-share, thinktrix, thinklinks, and weird facts: An interactive system for cooperative learning. In N. Davidson & T. Worsham (Eds.), *Enhancing thinking through cooperative learning* (pp. 169–181). New York: Teacher's College Press.

Manning, M., Manning, G., & Long, R. (1994). *Theme immersion: Inquiry-based curriculum in elementary and middle schools.* Portsmouth, NH: Heinemann.

Marrow, A. (1969). *The practical theorist.* New York: Basic.

Maslow, A. (1962). *Toward a psychology of being.* Princeton, NJ: D. Van Nostrand.

Maslow, A. (1970). *Motivation and Personality* (2nd ed.). New York: Harper and Row.

Maslow, A. (1976). *The farther reaches of human nature.* New York: Penguin.

McCaleb, S. (1994). *Building communities of learners: A collaboration among teachers, students, families, and community.* New York: St. Martin's.

McNamara, H., & Fisch, R. (1964). Effects of high and low motivation on two aspects of attention. *Perceptual and Motor Skills, 19,* 571–578.

Miller, N., & Harrington, H. (1990). A situational identity perspective on cultural diversity and teamwork in the classroom. In S. Sharan (Ed.), *Cooperative learning: Theory and research* (pp. 39–76). New York: Praeger.

Miller, N., & Harrington, H. (1992). Social categorization and intergroup acceptance: Princi-ples for the design and development of cooperative learning teams. In R. Hertz-Lazarowitz & N. Miller (Eds.), *Interaction in cooperative groups: The theoretical anatomy of group learning* (pp. 203–227). New York: Cambridge University Press.

Mills, T. (1967). *The sociology of small groups.* Upper Saddle River, NJ: Prentice Hall.

Moorman, C., & Dishon, D. (1983). *Our classroom: We can learn together.* Bay City, MI: Personal Power Press.

Nash, W. (1975). The effects of warm-up activities on small group divergent problem-solving with young children. *Journal of Psychology, 89,* 237–241.

Nevin, A. (1993). Curricular and instructional adaptations for including students with disabilities in cooperative groups. In J. Putnam (Ed.), *Cooperative learning and strategies for inclusion* (pp. 41– 56). Baltimore: Paul H. Brookes.

Newkirk, T. (Ed.). (1992). *Workshop 4: The teacher as researcher.* Portsmouth, NH: Heinemann.

Newkirk, T. (with McLure, P.) (1992). *Listening in: Children talk about books (and other things).* Portsmouth, NH: Heinemann.

Nicholls, J. (1989). *The competitive ethos and democratic education.* Cambridge, MA: Harvard University Press.

Nieto, S. (1992). *Affirming diversity: The sociopoliti-cal context of multicultural education.* New York: Longman.

Noblit, G., Rogers, D., & McCadden, B. (1995). In the meantime: The possibilities of caring. *Phi Delta Kappan, 76*(9), 680–685.

Oakes, J. (1985). *Keeping track: How schools structure inequality.* New Haven, CT: Yale University Press.

Oakes, J., & Lipton, M. (1990). *Making the best of school.* New Haven, CT: Yale University Press.

Palmer, P. (1983/1993). *To know as we are known: Education as a spiritual journey.* San Francisco: Harper.

Parker, J., & Asher, S. (1987). Peer relations and later personal adjustment: Are low-accepted children at risk? *Psychological Bulletin, 102,* 357–389.

Pedersen, E., Faucher, T., & Eaton, W. (1978). A new perspective on the effects of first-grade teachers on children's subsequent adult status. *Harvard Educational Review, 48*(1), 1–31.

Peterson, R. (1992). *Life in a crowded place: Making a learning community.* Portsmouth, NH: Heinemann.

Piaget, J. (1965). *The moral judgment of the child* (M. Gabain, Trans.). New York: The Free Press.

Pittman, T., Emery, U., & Boggiano, A. (1982). Intrinsic and extrinsic motivational orientations: Reward-induced changes in preference for complexity. *Journal of Personality and Social Psychology, 42,* 789–797.

Powell, A., Farrar, E., & Cohen, D. (1985). *The shopping mall high school: Winners and losers in the educational marketplace.* Boston: Houghton Mifflin.

Prutzman, P. (1988). *The friendly classroom for a small planet.* Nyack, NY: Children's Creative Response to Conflict.

Qin, Z., Johnson, D., & Johnson, R. (1995). Cooperative versus competitive efforts and problem solving. *Review of Educational Research, 65*(2), 129–143.

Rainey, R. (1965). The effects of directed versus non-directed laboratory work on high school chemistry achievement. *Journal of Research in Science Teaching, 3*, 286–92.

Rappoport, A., & Kletzien, S. (1996). Kids Around Town: Civic lessons leave impressions. *Educational Leadership, 53*(8), 26–29.

Ripple R., & Rockcastle, V. (Eds.). (1964). P*iaget rediscovered.* Ithaca, NY: Cornell University Press.

Rist, R. (1971). Student social class and teacher expectations: The self-fulfilling prophecy in ghetto education. *Harvard Educational Review, 40*, 411–451.

Rogers, C. (1961). *On becoming a person: A therapist's view of psychotherapy.* Boston: Houghton Mifflin.

Rogers, C. (1969). *Freedom to learn.* Columbus, OH: Charles Merrill.

Rohnke, K. (1984). *Silver bullets: A guide to initiative problems, adventure games, stunts and trust activities.* Hamilton, MA: Project Adventure.

Rosenthal, R., & Jacobson, L. (1968). *Pygmalion in the classroom: Teacher expectation and pupils' intellectual development.* New York: Holt, Rinehart and Winston.

Rothbert, M., & John, O. (1985). Social categorization and behavioral episodes: A cognitive analysis of the effects of intergroup contact. *Journal of Social Issues, 41*(3), 81–104.

Rubovitz, P., & Maehr, M. (1973). Pygmalian in black and white. *Journal of Personality and Social Development, 25*(2), 210–218.

Sadalla, G., Henriquez, M., & Holmberg, M. (1987). *Conflict resolution: A secondary school curriculum.* San Francisco: The Community Board.

Sadalla, G., Holmberg, M., & Halligan, J. (1990). *Conflict resolution: An elementary school curriculum.* San Francisco: The Community Board.

Sapon-Shevin, M. (1994). *Playing favorites: Gifted education and the disruption of community.* Albany: State University of New York Press.

Sapon-Shevin, M., Ayres, B., & Duncan, J. (1994). Cooperative learning and inclusion. In J. Thousand, R. Villa, & A. Nevin (Eds.). *Creativity and collaborative learning* (pp. 45–58). Baltimore: Paul H. Brookes.

Sarason, S. (1993). *You are thinking of teaching.* San Francisco: Jossey-Bass.

Schmuck, R. (1963). Some relationships of peer liking patterns in the classroom to pupil attitudes and achievement. *School Review, 71*, 337–359.

Schmuck, R., & Schmuck, P. (1996). *Group processes in the classroom.* (7th ed.). Dubuque, IA: William C. Brown.

Schutz, W. (1966). *The interpersonal underworld.* Palo Alto, CA: Science and Behavior Books.

Senge, P. (1990). *The fifth discipline: The art and practice of the learning organization.* New York: Doubleday.

Senge, P., Roberts, C., Ross, R., Smith, B., & Kleiner, A. (1994). *The fifth discipline fieldbook: Strategies and tools for building a learning organization.* New York: Currency Doubleday.

Shapira, Z. (1976). Expectancy determinants of intrinsically motivated behavior. *Journal of Personality and Social Psychology, 34*, 1235–1244.

Sharan, S., & Shaulov, A. (1990). Cooperative learning, motivation to learn, and academic achievement. In S. Sharan (Ed.), *Cooperative learning: Theory and research* (pp. 173–202). New York: Praeger.

Sharan, Y., & Sharan, S. (1992). *Expanding cooperative learning through group investigation.* NY: Teachers College Press.

Sharan, Y., & Sharan, S. (1994). What do we want to study? How should we go about it? Group investigation in the cooperative social studies classroom. In R. Stahl (Ed.), *Cooperative learning in the social studies: A handbook for teachers* (pp. 257–276). Menlo Park, CA: Addison Wesley.

Slavin, R. (1985). Cooperative learning: Applying contact theory in desegregated schools. *Journal of Social Issues, 41*(3), 45–61.

Slavin, R. (1991). Are cooperative learning and untracking harmful to the gifted? *Educational Leadership, 48*(6), 68–71.

Slavin, R. (1995). *Cooperative learning.* Boston: Allyn and Bacon.

Slavin, R., DeVries, D., & Hulton, B. (1975). *Individual vs. team competition: The interpersonal consequences of academic performance* (Report No. 188). Baltimore: Johns Hopkins University, Center for Social Organization of Schools.

Slavin, R., Madden, N., Dolan, L., & Wasik, B. (1994). Roots and Wings: Universal excellence in elementary education. *Educational Leadership, 52*(3), 10–13.

Smith, H. (1995). *Rethinking America.* New York: Random House.

Spolin, V. (1986). *Theatre games for the classroom: A teacher's handbook.* Evanston, IL: Northwestern University.

Stahl, R. (Ed.). (1994). *Cooperative learning in the social studies: A handbook for teachers.* Menlo Park, CA: Addison-Wesley.

Stahl, R. (Ed.). (1995). *Cooperative learning in language arts: A handbook for teachers.* Menlo Park, CA: Addison-Wesley.

Sternberg, R. (1988). *The triarchic mind: A new theory of human intelligence.* New York: Penguin.

Stevahn, L., Johnson, D., & Johnson, R. (1996). Reading between the lines: Learning to creatively resolve conflict through literature. *Cooperative Learning, 16*(3), 30–37.

Stone, J. (1989). *Cooperative learning and language arts: A multistructural approach.* San Juan Capistrano, CA: Kagan Cooperative Learning.

Thelen, H. (1981). *The classroom society.* New York: Wiley.

Tuckman, B., & Jensen, M. (1977). Stages in small group development revisited. *Group and Organizational Studies, 2,* 419–427.

Vygotsky, L. (1978). *Mind in society: The development of higher psychological processes* (M. Cole, V. John-Steiner, S. Scriber, and E. Souberman, Eds.). Cambridge, MA: Harvard University Press.

Wang, M., & Stiles, B. (1976). An investigation of children's concept of self-responsibility for their school learning. *American Educational Research Journal, 13,* 159–79.

Weinstein, M., & Goodman, J. (1980). *Playfair: Everybody's guide to noncompetitive play.* San Luis Obispo, CA: Impact.

Westby, E., & Dawson, V. (1995). Creativity: Asset or burden in the classroom? *Creativity Research Journal, 8,*(1), 1–10.

Wheelan, S. (1994). *Group processes: A developmental perspective.* Boston: Allyn and Bacon.

Wheelock, A. (1992). *Crossing the tracks: How "untracking" can save America's schools.* New York: New Press.

White, R., & Gunstone, R. (1992). *Probing understanding.* Bristol, PA: Falmer.

Yackel, E., Cobb, P., & Wood, T. (1991). Small-group interactions as a source of learning opportunites in second-grade mathematics. *Journal of Research in Mathematics Education, 22,* 390–408.

Zuckerman, H. (1977). *Scientific elite: Nobel laureates in the US.* New York: Free Press.

❧ Name Index ❧

Amabile, T. 5, 80
Amidon, E. 21
Aronowitz, S. 6
Aronson, E. 19, 63, 121
Asher, S. 7
Ayres, B. 117, 128
Bales, R. 21, 126, 221
Baloche, L. 71, 110, 121, 140, 151, 171–172
Banks, J. 40, 48, 53
Bellanca, J. 68, 167, 170
Bennett, B. 12, 127, 183, 195
Berger, J. 50
Berman-Robinson, S. 83, 203
Blaney, N. 19, 63, 121
Blasko, J. 71
Boggiano, A. 80, 133
Bowles, S. 56
Breitborde, M. 68
Buckman, L. 29
Burke, K. 162
Caplan, J. 9, 35–36
Carew, J. 45
Chambliss, W. 44
Clarke, J. 93
Cobb, P. 80
Cohen, E. 19, 50–53
Cohen, D. 55
Coleman, M. 58
Conner, T. 50
Cook, S. 19
Costa, A. 68
Csikszentmihalyi, M. 245–246
Dacey, J. 74
Daniels, H. 127
Dawson, V. 44
Deutsch, M. 18
DeVries, D. 6
Dewey, J. 6–7, 57, 72, 124
Dishon, D. 82, 177
Dolan, L. 226
Dreikurs, R. 72, 161
Dumaine 8
Duncan, J. 117, 128
Eadie, S. 93
Eaton, W. 46
Egan, J. 226
Egan, C. 226
Emery, U. 133
Epstein, J. 24, 74, 84–85
Farrar, E. 55
Faucher, T. 46
Filinuk, J. 121, 140, 171–172
Fisch, R. 133
Fogarty, R. 68, 167, 170, 226
Fullan, M. 240, 245
Gallagher, J. 58

Gardner, H. 42
Getzels, J. 44
Gibb, L. 25
Gibb, J. 25
Gibbs, J. 11, 23
Gillespie, J. 204
Gintas, H. 56
Giroux, H. 6
Gitomer, J. 80
Glasser, W. 72, 74
Goldberg, N. 39, 53
Goleman, D. 8–9
Goodlad, J. 6, 245
Goodman, J. 215
Graves, N. (L.) 68–69, 73
Graves, T. 73
Grunwald, B 72, 161
Hanson, J. 9
Harrington, H. 40, 48–49, 69
Hertz-Lazarowitz, R. 22
Heterington, E. 4
Holloway, S. 149
Holubec, E. 7, 92–93, 99, 116, 146, 150, 154, 242
Hough, J. 21
Hulton, B. 6
Hunter, M. 215
Jackson, P. 44
Jacobson, L. 43, 50
Jensen, M. 24
John, O. 19
Johnson, F. 18, 29, 92, 247
Johnson, D. 3, 5, 9, 10, 18, 19, 26, 29, 76, 79, 92–93, 99, 116, 122, 146, 150, 154, 242, 247
Johnson, R. 3, 5, 7, 9, 10, 19, 26, 29, 76, 79, 92–93, 99, 116, 122, 133, 146, 150, 154, 242
Kagan, S. 3, 12–13, 35, 41, 64–65, 70, 85, 87, 101–108, 112–113, 120, 124, 130, 141–142, 151, 171–173, 186, 235
Katzenbach, J. 8–9
Kelley, R. 9, 35–36
Kerman, S. 45
Kimball, T. 45
Kleiner, A. 242, 246
Kletzien, S. 110, 229
Kohn, A. 5, 6, 73, 81, 124, 240
Kovalik, S. 225
Krackhardt, D. 9
Lao Tzu 207

Lee Mauger, M. 121, 140, 171–172
Lewin, K. 18, 26, 244, 247
Lewis, C. 72
Lickona, T. 73–75, 80
Light, R. 41
Lightfoot, S. L. 45
Lipton, M. 45
Long, R. 226
Lyman, F. 102
Madden, N. 222
Maehr, M. 44
Maier, D. 47, 239
Manning, M. 226
Manning, G. 226
Marrow, A. 18
Martin, M. 45
Maruyama, G. 3
Maslow, A. 10, 26–27, 96, 215
mastery needs 10, 96
McCadden, B. 47
McCaleb, S. 72
McKeown, W. 50
McNamara, H. 133
Mead, M. 241
Michalsky, B. 121, 140, 171–172
Miles, M. 240
Miller, N. 40, 48–49, 69
Mills, T. 21
Moorman, C. 82
Nash, W. 215
Nelson, D. 3
Nelson, S. 58
Nevin, A. 118
Newkirk, T. 244
Nicholls , J. 5–6
Nieto, S. 40, 56
Noblit, G. 47
Norem-Hebeisen, A. 10
O'Leary, P. 177
Oakes, J. 45, 54–56
Palmer, P. 67, 224, 231
Parke, R. 4
Parker, J. 7
Pedersen, E. 46
Pepper, F. 72, 161
Piaget, J. 3–5, 73
Pittman, T. 133
Platt, T. 151
Powell, A. 55
Qin, Z. 3
Rainey, R. 80
Rappoport, A. 229
Richards, P. 29
Ripple, R. 3
Rist, R. 44

Roberts, C. 242
Robovitz, P. 44
Rockcastle, V. 3
Rogers, D. 47
Rogers, C. 46, 243–244
Rolheiser, C. 12, 127, 183, 195
Rosenthal, R. 43, 50
Ross, R. 242
Rothbert, M. 19
Sapon-Shevin, M. 55, 117, 128
Sarason, S. 245
Schaps, E. 72
Schmuck, P. 23, 25, 29
Schmuck, R. 23, 25, 29, 46
Schutz, W. 23, 96
Senge, P. 6, 242, 246
Shachar, H. 22
Shapira, Z. 133
Sharan, S. 41, 124–125
Sharan, Y. 124–125
Shaulov, A. 41
Sikes, J. 19, 63, 121
Sirotnick, K. 245
Skon, L. 3
Slavin, R. 6, 19, 58, 131, 226
Smith, B. 242, 246
Smith, D. 8–9
Smith, H. 47, 239
Snapp, M. 19, 63, 131
Soder, R. 245
Stephan, C. 63, 121
Sternberg, R. 42–43
Stevahn, L. 12, 76, 127, 183, 195
Stiles, B. 80
Stoehr, J. 226
Thelen, H. 6–7, 124
Thomson, C. 133
Thoreau, H.D. 245
Tuckman B. 24
Vygotsky, L. 3–5, 223
Wang, M. 80
Wasik, B. 226
Watson, M. 72
Weinstein, M. 215
Westby, E. 44
Wheelan , S. 19
Wheelock, A. 45, 57
Wideman, R. 93
Willis, T. 121, 140, 171–172
Wood, T. 80
Yackel, E. 80
Zahn, G. 41
Zuckerman, H. 9

✿ Subject Index ✿

absenteeism/dropouts 7, 57, 95–96, 162–165

achievement, and cooperative learning 3–6, 40, 41, 44–45, 50–53, 57, 93, 149

action research 18, 26–33, 59–63, 243–244

affection 11, 19, 23–24, 50, 81–86, 95–96

assessment 20, 53, 165, 190–205, 217–219

attitudes, towards school and cooperation 7, 10, 32

authentic activity and learning 67, 69, 72, 80–81, 226, 231

balance 26, 245–246

base groups 93–99, 208–209, 220, 225, 231, 234, 243
  in "Working with Peers" 111–113, 141, 143, 172–173, 185–186, 204–205, 237–238, 246–249

behaviorial challenges 23–26, 51, 57, 72, 75, 160–168

belongingness and love needs 10, 20–23, 72, 96–97

bonus points 133–134, 198–199

brainstorming 73, 86–87

burnout 6, 245

caring/compassion 7, 11, 23, 81–85, 96

celebration 67, 70–71, 81–83, 86, 133–134, 199, 242, 245–256, 249

choice, the importance of 6, 80, 92, 161

class meetings 74–76, 84

cognitive style(s) 41–45, 48, 52–53, 62, 64, 68–69, 166

collegiality 242–243

community 11, 23–24, 59, 95–97,
  learning community 68–87, 91, 96, 100, 104–105, 160, 190

conflict 19, 23–26, 73, 76–79, 92, 96

control 6, 23–24, 72–81

constructivism 3–4, 45

cooperation, barriers to 92

cooperative learning, basic elements of 92–93,
  see also "Positive Interdependence," "Simultaneous Interaction," "Individual Responsibility," "Interpersonal and Small-Group Learning Skills," "Reflection and Planning"

creativity 44, 56–57, 74, 80

democracy 6, 40, 57, 72, 124, 227, 244

direct instruction/lecture 100–104, 209, 222, 234

discussion, and cooperative learning 5, 58, 74, 100, 105, 127, 222

empathy 46, 81

esteem and mastery, need for 10, 20, 96

feedback 25, 123–124, 153–160, 176–181, 246

force-field analysis 18, 247–248

formal learning groups 71, 100, 116–143, 209–210, 215–236

gender 48–50, 60, 93

goal structures
  competitive 3, 5–6, 18, 40–41, 50, 69, 241
  cooperative 3, 18–19, 25, 40
  individualistic 3, 18, 25, 41, 241

grades/grading 19, 132–134, 194–202

graphic organizers 64–65, 70

group structure and development 18–37

grouping
  ability (tracking) 19, 40, 44, 53–59
  "gifted" education 44, 55, 58
  heterogeneous grouping 40, 49, 53–59, 93–94, 99, 117–119, 212–214
  physical environment 101, 105, 132–133, 208–212
  size 212–214
  "special" education 56, 58
  strategies for 49, 62, 93, 101, 111, 212–214

inclusion 11, 23–26, 68–72, 86, 95–96, 100, 104, 107, 119

individual responsibility 92, 116, 161, 190–205
  and differentiated goals 117–119
  and positive interdependence 192–202
  and roles 125–129, 191
  and structures 191–192
  designing reflection for 192–198
  monitoring and observing for 191
  tests, journals, portfolios, and grades 195–202

influence/power 6, 10, 23–24, 72–81, 84, 86, 96, 147, 161, 195, 231, 239

informal learning groups 71, 99–113, 209, 220, 222, 225, 231, 234

information processing theory 4–5

intelligence(s) 41–46, 50–53, 69, 224

Interaction-Process Analysis 21–22

interpersonal and small-group learning skills 92, 146–186, 217–219
  and roles 21, 120–128
  and structures 101–108, 120–125, 130–132, 153–154, 183–185
  categories of skills 146–149
  feedback and interventions about 153–160, 176–181
  importance of at work 9, 34, 36, 56–57, 241–243
  importance of in society 9–11

monitoring and observing the use of 28–30, 154–159, 178–179
  reflecting on and planning for 176–186
  teaching and practicing 95, 146, 149–160, 222

journals, the use of 200–201

KWHLS 118, 165–166

lesson and unit design 100–108, 215–236
  anticipatory set 95, 100, 104, 111, 214–221, 225
  checking for understanding 154–159, 190–205, 216–219, 223–225
  closure 24, 95, 100, 104, 107–108, 111, 216–219, 223–225
  input and modeling 121, 216–219, 221–222, 225
  practice—guided and independent 215–219, 221
  understanding the objective 215–216, 219, 222

Likert scale 32–33

literature circles 127, 234

motivation, and cooperative learning 5–7, 103, 133–134, 160–168

motivation, intrinsic 5–6, 10, 25, 80, 133

multicultural education 40–65
  content integration 40
  empowering school culture and social structure 40, 53–59
  equity pedagogy 40, 48–53
  knowledge construction 40–43
  prejudice reduction 40, 43–48

multiple abilities classrooms 43–46, 52–53, 57–59, 117–119, 128–129, 133, 165–166, 197–202, 226

negotiation/mediation 11, 76–79

Nobel Prize 9

norms 19–20, 24–25, 29, 35, 53, 72–76, 79, 242

observation, classroom 27–37, 51, 59–63, 158–160, 178–179, 194

one-minute paper 13, 35, 65, 87, 111, 113, 143, 173, 182, 186, 205, 224, 236

parents 55–56, 71–72, 80–81, 84–85

peer negotiation and mediation 76–79

perspective-taking ability 10–11, 26–27, 122

portfolios, the use of 201

positive interdependence 25, 81, 92, 116–143, 160, 195–200, 217–219
  celebration 117, 133–134
  environmental 117, 132–133, 208–212
  fantasy or simulation 117, 130–131

goal interdependence 3, 25, 68, 117–119
identity 117, 129
outside force 117, 131–132
resource 117, 119–125, 130
role interdependence 117, 125–129, 165, 191
sequence 117, 129–131
problem solving 3, 76
questioning strategies 45, 94–95, 100–101, 103, 106, 151–152, 173
quiet signal 147, 161
race and ethnicity 11, 21, 41, 44–45, 48–51, 56, 60, 80, 85
references to specific racial and ethnic groups 11, 41–44, 56
reflection and planning 93, 116, 159, 176–205, 217–219, 224, 246–249
and closure 24, 224
and observations and monitoring 178–179, 191–192
and structures 183–185, 192
challenges of 181–185
feedback 176–177
incorporated in "Working with Peers" 11, 34–35, 64–65, 86–87, 111–113, 141–143, 172–173, 235–236, 246–249
on academic learning 190–205
on interpersonal and small-group skills 176–186
respect 7, 11, 25, 46–47, 68–69, 74, 80, 84, 95
rewards 133–134
roles 20–35, 45
see also "task and maintenance" and "positive interdependence—role"
routines, importance of 20, 93–97, 111, 208–212, 243
rules 19–20, 67, 72–76, 87
safety needs 10, 20, 49–50, 64, 96–97, 100
seating arrangements 24, 45, 101, 105, 132–133, 208–212

self actualization 10, 96
simultaneous interaction 68, 92, 208
lesson planning for 208–236
social class 44, 48, 56, 60, 69, 80, 85, 93
social identity 48–53, 69
sociometrics 51, 59–63, 64, 93, 111, 214, 231
status 6, 19, 44, 46, 48, 50–65, 68, 74, 80, 93, 102–103, 105, 107, 117, 120, 130, 155, 158, 161–168, 194
stereotypes 19, 43–45, 48–49, 96
structures 101, 105, 111–112, 119–125, 130–132, 153–154, 165–166, 183–185, 191–192, 217–219, 223–224
Academic Controversy 122–123, 154, 222
Blackboard Share 112, 184
Blind Hand 119–120, 153, 222
Carousel 70
Corners 65, 105–106, 153, 184, 232, 235
Find Someone Who Knows 107, 153
Fishbowl 33, 171
Gallery Tour 35, 124, 153, 224, 228, 235
Graffiti 12, 153
Group Interview 35, 64–65, 103, 105, 112 153, 204, 223, 235, 248
Group Investigation 124–125, 222
Inside-Outside Circle 35, 107, 153, 184, 223, 242
Jigsaw 63–64, 121–122, 153, 203, 222
Mad Hatter's Tea Party 107, 112–113, 141–142, 185, 205, 223, 235
Mix-Freeze-Pair 13, 106–107, 153, 184, 232
Numbered Heads Together 102–103, 184
One-Stay Three-Stray 64–65, 87, 123–124, 153, 192, 224
Paraphrase Passport 87, 112, 184
Pens in the Middle 102, 111, 153, 184
Roam the Room 87

Rotating Interviews 86
Rotating Review 107–108, 192
Roundrobin 103, 112, 184, 193
Roundtable with Roundrobin 103
Roving Reporter 87
Send a Problem 224
Simultaneous Roundtable 12, 130, 141, 192, 199
Simultaneous Stirring Up the Class 64, 192
Stand and Share 113, 184
Stirring Up the Class 104, 153
Student Teams-Achievement Divisions 131–132, 153, 222
Talking Chips 153
Team Statements 87, 153, 184
Think-Pair-Share 102, 232
Think-Pair-Square 102, 112
Three-Step Interview 12, 104–105, 112, 153, 192, 213, 221–223
Trade a Problem 142, 153, 171, 173
Treasure Hunt 12–13, 107, 153
Value Lines 87, 106, 154, 184
Yarn Yarn 75
T-chart 151–152, 158, 221
task and maintenance 21, 26, 28, 30, 33–35, 49, 92, 126, 148, 221, 243
teacher behaviors and expectations 19–24, 42–48, 52–59, 64, 68, 103, 158
testing 55–56, 132, 195–200
thinking skills 3, 26, 46, 56, 80, 106, 120, 123, 127
time, importance of 45, 49–50, 73, 92
trust 7, 10, 25, 45–46, 64, 75, 100, 242–243
values 6, 18–19, 29, 35, 68, 73–76, 81, 87, 96, 246–248
Verbal Interaction Category System 21–22, 29, 31
work, satisfaction and success 8–9, 34–36, 240–248